The Pengui...
Cryptic Crosswords

THE PENGUIN GUIDE
TO
CRYPTIC CROSSWORDS

A new guide to solving Cryptic Crosswords
by understanding how they are compiled

Complete with its own Cryptic Glossary

Compiled by

Jack Dunwoody

PENGUIN BOOKS

PENGUIN BOOKS

Published by the Penguin Group
27 Wrights Lane, London W8 5TZ, England
Viking Penguin, a division of Penguin Books USA Inc,
375 Hudson Street, New York, 10014, USA
Penguin Books Australia Ltd, Ringwood, Victoria, Australia
Penguin Books Canada Ltd, 10 Alcorn Avenue, Toronto, Ontario,
Canada M4V 3B2
Penguin Books (NZ) Ltd, 182-190 Wairau Road, Auckland 10, New Zealand
Penguin Books, Amethyst Street, Theta Ext 1, Johannesburg, South Africa

Penguin Books Ltd, Registered Offices: Harmondsworth, Middlesex, England

First published by Penguin Books 1994

Copyright © Jack Dunwoody 1994

All rights reserved

The moral right of the author has been asserted

ISBN 0 140 51305 1

Typeset by Creda Press
Printed and bound by Creda Press
Cover designed by Hadaway Illustration & Design

CONTENTS

CONTENTS

PREFACE

One would fairly expect that the crossword puzzle originated in England and would probably further hazard a guess that the first one appeared in *The Times* of London. Not so. We crossword addicts, now counted in multi-millions, have to look across the Atlantic for its first publication in the *New York World* on 21 December 1913.

The British had to wait until 1925, and readers of *The Times* a further five years, before being introduced to what would become the nation's favourite word power pastime. Despite this later start (or perhaps because of it) my book is directed at the English crossword solver, with a knowledge of spelling English the Queen's way; of British geography, history, literature and institutions. There are perforce some foreign words, but only of a basic schoolboy standard.

My own first crosswords were encountered during schooldays and were invariably of the simple synonym variety, referred to as concise crosswords. Infrequent and private glances at the complicated clues of cryptic cross-words, however, did not offer a reasonable enough prospect of success. To an achievement-orientated youngster such as myself the risk of failure and the resultant blow to the ego could not be contemplated!

My conversion to cryptic crosswords was therefore somewhat of an accident during an Air Training Corps camp in 1958 at Hornchurch in Essex. The accident was missing the last train from London, the place was Trafalgar Square, the reason was trying to pass the time until morning. An English cadet, in the same dilemma, proceeded to do the crossword in a discarded newspaper and had enough time (all night) and interest (we only had one newspaper) to explain the quirks employed by the cryptic compiler to baffle simple Irish students like myself.

Whilst individual compilers have their own characteristics, there are nevertheless basic approaches and rules which are applied generally. The purpose of this book is to give an insight into these basics and, hence, it is aimed at the new cryptic solver. Like my own initiation, he or she may be still at school or as in the case of a colleague of mine, suddenly decide at age forty to brave the vagaries of the compiler.

The would-be solver will find here the techniques used in the compilation of crosswords, with lots of examples of how they are employed. There are, however, no exhaustive references to all possible meanings of a dictionary full of words, but rather which words are commonly used and the special meanings or mnemonics which they generate automatically for a regular solver.

Above all, resolution of a cryptic crossword clue is a process of applying logic or lateral thinking. Certainly, a good general knowledge will help, as will a wide vocabulary, but so will solving the puzzles lead to the development of these attributes. It is my opinion, and indeed experience, that the best thing a parent can do to broaden his child's knowledge and command of the English language is to encourage him or her to devote quality leisure time to solving crossword puzzles, both of the concise and cryptic varieties.

I have long held this view of the educational benefit of crosswords and recently came across a real life example which served to highlight my claims to fellow parents. Through a mutual acquaintance I met a senior director of a listed retail company who had escaped from Hungary to the United Kingdom when he was twenty-one. At that time he knew no English at all and — you've guessed it — he used crosswords as a method of learning the language. He finds it amusing now that he learnt words like **genuflect, agnail, etui** and **ecru** before achieving a working vocabulary!

The use of good reference books is not cheating. As you duly progress to the more difficult puzzles, not so much in logic terms but in their use of obscure words and references, it is advisable to equip yourself to help determine the answers (or subsequently to understand them). It is from this research and understanding that the main educational benefit is derived.

I recommend the following reference books:

Reader's Digest Universal Dictionary

With more than 180 000 definitions and references, the Reader's Digest claims that this book is outstanding among single-volume dictionaries of the English language. I can only agree. Since acquired five years ago, it has replaced all my other standard dictionaries as my first choice reference.

Unlike most other dictionaries, it is a single source of proper names, abbreviations, biblical and mythological characters, historical and geographical names, maps, institutions and organisations, as well as old words and new words, difficult words and everyday words — words, in fact, for all purposes and occasions.

It is a rare occasion, indeed, when I have to take my reading glass to *The Compact Oxford English Dictionary* in search of some obscure word which I have failed to find here.

Reader's Digest Reverse Dictionary

The purpose of this text is to act as a word-finder and as such it identifies other words which are associated with the word being investigated and not just the meanings of that word and its synonyms. This approach is unique in my experience, in that instead of starting with a word and seeking its definition, as in a conventional dictionary, we can start with any element of the definition to find the word.

The dictionary does this by directing you from a familiar word you know is connected with the particular subject ("cue word") to the elusive word ("target word") which you are seeking. A target word may even be cued in this way by its **opposite** meaning.

Together with its 222 tables — from acids to Zodiacal signs — and diagrams, the *Reader's Digest Reverse Dictionary* is a very helpful reference work.

Reader's Digest Oxford Complete Wordfinder

Every crossword solver will find this combined volume a unique crossword aid. Here for the first time in one handy volume is a general purpose dictionary with a thesaurus fully integrated into the dictionary text.

The relevant material from each appears together on the same page, thus obviating the need to consult a second volume or, indeed, to search in other parts of the same volume. Because the thesaurus items are arranged directly below their corresponding dictionary entries, the user can go straight to a word and can move easily from dictionary to thesaurus and back again. The dictionary gives the meanings of a word while the thesaurus lists synonyms for each meaning. With 120 000 words and 200 000 synonyms, this book is a fund of information for the crossword solver.

There are also many reference books containing conventional tabulations of words (generally ranging from 3 to 9 letters) and phrases (generally from 8 to 15 letters) in alphabetical order. Unfortunately, my own favourite one is no longer in print but I have had my copy for twenty years and have added many additional phrases and words over that time. It is now dog-eared, stuck together by sellotape, but still invaluable! I suggest you look through the many good books that are available and select one as one of your main reference books since the phrases section, in particular, will provide key assistance to solvers of the more difficult cryptic crosswords.

What I do consider "cheating", and also a meaningless exercise from an educational point of view, is the use of PC computer-based aids. These are generally on CD ROM technology and one can feed in a few letters of the target word and let the PC search and display possible answers. At this point

I draw the line and can see no enjoyment, stimulus or benefit accruing to the genuine crossword puzzler.

This book is divided into two sections: Techniques and Glossary.

In the first section I cover some eleven approaches used by compilers of cryptic crossword puzzles. Each compiler is different, but I have tried to cover the basic techniques you will come across. There are plenty of examples of each and you should work through and understand them. This understanding has always been very important to me — I hate to have what is obviously the answer without knowing how it is arrived at from the given clue.

The Glossary section contains words commonly used by compilers which indicate either letters or other words in the form of synonyms or alternative meanings that go into the resolution of many clues. The alternative meanings given here are letters (WORDS TO LETTERS) and short or unusual words (WORDS TO WORDS) that both go to make up answers, or are answers in themselves. As such, these are not exhaustive lists, nor is this section meant to replace a full dictionary. It should, however, be your starting point in clue resolution and you should feel free to add your own words and their equivalent letters and words as you find them while doing your favourite puzzles.

Solving cryptic crosswords will often involve a combination of the given techniques, together with reference to the words and letters in the Glossary. This will become clear as you work through the various examples which I have included to explain compiler methods in the Techniques section.

I have felt for a considerable time the need for somebody to try to explain cryptic crossword compilation and resolution, if only to introduce others to a pastime that costs so little but gives so much pleasure and satisfaction. I hope this book goes some way towards that goal by placing the solver on more equal terms with the compiler.

This insight into how the compiler's mind works should enable the solver to arrive at answers that can always be justified logically. I am therefore trying to teach you **how** to fish, rather than giving you a fish. An understanding of this guide to cryptic crosswords will indeed reduce the time and effort required to complete a puzzle, as well as enhance the prospect and enjoyment of doing so.

The compilation of this book has taken many months of research into many sources of information, as well as the solving and analyses of hundreds of published crosswords. The data capture alone has been a massive exercise, and for her help with this task, I must thank my daughter Kellie. Above all I must commend the patience of my wife Kathleen, who must have tired of the incessant clatter of my PC keyboard in competition with her favourite TV programmes, but who was always supportive of my efforts to complete this my first book.

JACK DUNWOODY
Wynberg, Cape Town

SECTION 1
TECHNIQUES

ANAGRAMS

An ANAGRAM is the transposition of the letters of a word or number of words, to form a new word or phrase. This is probably the device most commonly used by compilers and the first task is to identify that a clue actually contains an ANAGRAM. This is seen from words in the text which indicate a movement or rearrangement of other letters and words. In the examples which follow the words in the clues which indicate the probable use of ANAGRAMS are underlined.

The key to determining which words and letters go to forming the ANAGRAM, and thus to solving it, is the number of letters given at the end of a clue that are contained in the answer. The logic of the clue should indicate what you are trying to find an answer for.

EXAMPLES

Dread becoming a crawler (5)

Dread (5) → adder crawler [snake]
= adder

Dread is the only (5) letter word and becoming is the ANAGRAM indicator. The answer we are looking for should obviously mean a **crawler** . The clue may have indicated **snake** but **crawler** requires that little bit more thought to resolve.

A horse staggered on the beach

A horse (6) → ashore (6) on the beach = ashore

A horse is the only combination of (6) letters and staggered is the ANAGRAM indicator. Another word for **on the beach** is what is required here.

Martina is playing like a monkey (7)

Martina (7) → tamarin
(7) monkey = tamarin

Martina has (7) letters, but so does **a monkey**. The key here is that the ANAGRAM indicator refers to **Martina**, leaving **a monkey** as the answer to determine.

May end up in the soup on court, possibly (7)

on court (7) → crouton
[bread] in the soup = crouton

Frail but has potential talent (5)

frail (5) → flair
talent = flair

Detest the start of theatrical play (4)

start of theatrical (4)
thea → hate
Detest = hate

The clue refers to the start of **theatrical** but (4) indicates the first four letters only are needed. This is a combination of an ANAGRAM with the techniques used in STARTS, MIDDLES AND ENDS.

3

Increase <u>possibility</u> of having a<u>r</u>gument   a<u>r</u>gument → agument (7)
right away (7)   agument → augment
                                                            increase = augment

This is a combination of DROPPING LETTERS FROM WORDS [**right = r**
from **argument**] and an ANAGRAM of the remaining letters. Again (7) letters in
the answer is the key and it should mean **Increase**.

Win two of the events in April, <u>maybe</u> (7)   April (5) → pr ail
                                                        (2) of the events = ev
                                                        Win = pr-ev-ail

The ANAGRAM is clearly of **April** which has (5) letters and the clue further
indicates that (2) of **the events** should be held in it. It's then a question of deciding
which two letters to choose to combine with the ANAGRAM to give a synonym
of **Win**.

Scenic <u>tour</u> to see Eastern technology (7)   Scenic + e [Eastern]
                                                        → science (7)
                                                        technology = science

This combines an ANAGRAM of **Scenic** with a final letter **e**, which is not part of
the ANAGRAM.

Knight gets lion <u>badly</u> cut (7)   Knight = sir (3)
                                             lion (4) → loin
                                             cut = sirloin (7)

This is a combination of a synonym for **Knight** [see WORDS TO WORDS] with
an ANAGRAM of **lion**. The synonym must be (3) letters for the answer to be
(7).

Did not concur with gluttony, <u>cook</u> said   said → disa (4)
originally (9)   gluttony = greed (5)
                                                      did not concur = disa-greed

The ANAGRAM of **said** (4) [**cook** is a frequent indicator] comes first [**originally**],
then a (5) letter synonym for **gluttony** is needed to complete the solution.

<u>Botched</u> raid in the borders produces   raid → irad (4)
outburst (6)   <u>the</u> borders = t . . . e (2)
                                                   irad <u>in</u> t . . . e = t(irad)e (6)
                                                   outburst = tirade

This is another combination of an ANAGRAM [of **raid**] with a variation of the
techniques used in STARTS, MIDDLES AND ENDS. The anagram should be in
the borders, i.e. **t . . . e**.

One who takes off <u>damaged</u> room panel   room panel (9) → lampooner
(9)   one who takes off [satirist]
                                                   = lampooner

The following three clues actually use parts of clue words as ANAGRAM indicators.

And a chip-<u>making</u> race (8)

And a chip (8) → handicap
race = handicap

Chemist discovered to use part-<u>exchange</u> (7)

use part (7) → pasteur
Chemist = Pasteur

Pardon the sailors when love<u>sick</u> (7)

sailors = abs (3)
love (4) → olve
Pardon = absolve (7)

This is a combination from WORDS TO LETTERS [**sailor = ab**] and an ANAGRAM [of **love**].

See great <u>changes</u> in overseas accommodation (8)

See great (8) → steerage
overseas accommodation = steerage

This is clearly an ANAGRAM but the clever meaning here of the word **overseas** could point in the wrong direction for a synonym!

Clipping the head with airy <u>carelessness</u> (7)

head = top (3)
airy (4) → iary
clipping (shrubs) = topiary

This is a combination from WORDS TO WORDS [**head = top**] and an ANAGRAM [of **airy**].

No points <u>arranged</u> when one **disappears** constantly (3–4)

No points → noponts (7)
noponts → non-stop
constantly = non-stop

This is a three-way combination of WORDS TO LETTERS [**one = i**], DROPPING LETTERS FROM WORDS [**i** from **No poi_n_ts**] and an ANAGRAM of the remaining letters.

Difficult to install chips or <u>bits</u> in this instrument (11)

Difficult = hard (4)
chips or (7) → psichor
instrument = har-psichor-d

WORDS TO WORDS gives us **difficult = hard**. We then install an ANAGRAM of **chips or** in **hard** to give us our **instrument**.

Fit for the sea, canoe <u>somehow</u>'s meeting race conditions (5–5)

canoe (5) → ocean
race conditions = going (5)
fit for the sea = ocean-going

Our ANAGRAM produces **canoe** and WORDS TO WORDS gives us **going**.

Talks much, being sent art <u>noveau</u> (7)

sent art (7) → natters
Talks much = natters

This is a clever use of the term **art noveau** with the latter French word [= new] being our ANAGRAM indicator.

Beat up Miles in a scrimmage (7)

Here we have two possible ANAGRAM indicators which both refer to the correct number of letters. We can take <u>Beat up</u> as our indicator and look for an ANAGRAM of **Miles in** (7) to mean **scrimmage**; or we can take <u>in a scrimmage</u> and look for an ANAGRAM of **up Miles** (7) to mean **Beat**! Other letters in the target word will help, but the answer here is:

up Miles (7) → impulse
beat = impulse

Pauses in travels <u>abroad</u> (9)

in travels (9) → intervals
Pauses = intervals

The indicator <u>abroad</u> is not an obvious one and [from WORDS TO WORDS] could actually take us off at a tangent, looking for a word starting with **out**.

It's rejected by <u>terribly</u> angry swimmer (8)

It's <u>rejected</u> = sti (3)
angry (5) → ngray
swimmer = sti-ngray (8)

At first glance this may be taken as a double ANAGRAM but <u>rejected</u> rather points to reversing the letters to which it applies [from BACKWARD ANSWERS], hence **sti** in this clue.

<u>Suspect</u> I'm OK with no dressing-gown (6)

I'm OK (4) → kimo
Kimo + no (2) = kimono
dressing-gown = kimono (6)

Printer has <u>sort</u> of quiet alliance (11)

Printer has (10) → partnershi
quiet = p (1)
alliance = partner shi-p (11)

A lazy compiler will occasionally use no more than a ? for an ANAGRAM indicator. Care should be taken not to confuse this short-cut with clues in the form of QUESTIONS? which are covered later in this section.

Nice gal<u>?</u> She's just divine (7)

Nice gal (7) → angelic
divine = angelic

The extent of one's anger<u>?</u> (5)

anger (5) → range
extent = range

The above examples have been relatively simple. When long words or two words or more are indicated in the answer, a technique of placing the letters (identified as making up the ANAGRAM) into a circle is often employed. The letters, as

they are identified in the answer by completing other clues, can be crossed out to
concentrate on the remaining ones. This should help with the resolution of the
ANAGRAM.

EXAMPLES

Rotten shows <u>are performed</u> not far from
here (6, 5)

```
      T T
    O     E
    R       N
              S
    S     H
      W O
```

Rotten shows (11) → stones throw
not far from here = stones throw (6,5)

Guilty owner with thing <u>that's bent</u>
(2, 3, 5)

```
      N E
    W     R
    O
            T
    G     H
      N I
```

owner + thing (10) → in the wrong
guilty = in the wrong (2,3,5)

Grow a trifle <u>uneasy</u> when being held by
<u>frayed</u> rope (11)

```
      R I
    T     F
    A       L
              E
    E     R
      P O
```

a trifle + rope (11) → proliferate
Grow = proliferate (11)

The above clue is actually more helpful than the straight ANAGRAM we solved.
It indicates that an ANAGRAM of **a trifle** is actually held by another
ANAGRAM of **rope**. Hence we know that the beginning and end of the solution
will use the letters of **rope**. A basic grasp of English words should point you to
pro . . . e since other combinations of these letters are unlikely, since **per** and **pre**
starts would mean unlikely endings in **o**.

<u>Arrange</u> pets to guard a person of degree
(12)

```
      T S
    E     T
    P       O
    A       G
    D       U
      R A
```

pets to guard a (12) → postgraduate
person of degree = postgraduate (12)

Non-operatic company shortly <u>arranged</u>
this musical work (5,8)

```
      O P
    N     E
    O       R
    N       A
              T
    O       I
      C C
```

Non operatic <u>co</u> (13) → piano concerto
musical work = piano concerto (5,8)

A number of different ANAGRAM indicators are employed below:

In her case, finds <u>another way</u> to
withdraw vote (14)

In her case finds (14) → disenfranchise
withdraw vote = disenfranchise (14)

```
      E R
   H      C
 N          A
 I          S
 S          E
   D      F
      N I
```

Trust Len can <u>arrange</u> to have light
coming through (11)

Trust Len can (11) → translucent
have light coming through = translucent
(11)

```
      U S
   R      T
 T          L
              E
 N          N
   A      C
```

Lying dormant, breathing in <u>with
difficulty</u> (11)

breathing in (11) → hibernating
Lying dormant = hibernating (11)

```
     E A
   R      T
 B          H
              I
 N          N
   I G
```

For those with one bent, the bar offers aid
<u>freely</u> (5,2,1,7)

the bar offers aid (15) → birds of a feather
those of one bent = birds of a feather
(5,2,1,7)

```
      B A R
   E        O
 H            F
 T            F
 D            E
 I            R
   A        S
```

Pretentious, so it sent out a <u>different
version</u> (12)

so it sent out a (12) → ostentatious
Pretentious = ostentatious (12)

```
      T S
   I      E
 O          N
 S          T
 A          O
   T U
```

So Phil and Sophie, <u>when inclined</u>, can
talk sense (12)

so Phil (6) + Sophie (6) → philosophise
talk sense = philosophise (12)

```
      H I
   P      L
 O          S
 S          O
 E          P
   I H
```

Benevolent <u>type of</u> theatre grade (5–7)

theatre grade (12) → great-hearted
Benevolent = great-hearted (5–7)

```
        A T
   E         R
  H           E
  T           G
   E         R
        D A
```

If you're sceptical that one can just arrive at twelve or more letter ANAGRAMS as shown here, don't forget that you will be gradually building up a profile of the target word by solving other clues and thus getting letters in this one. You should also know from reading the clue for which word or phrase you are seeking a synonym or other alternative.

Stan can't trail <u>over</u> to America (13)

Stan can't trail (13) → transatlantic
to America = transatlantic (13)

```
      N C
    A     A
   T       N
   S        T
             T
     L     R
      I   A
```

Remember this is a British crossword book, so **to America**, which is the phrase for which you seeking an alternative, can correctly be construed as **transatlantic**.

Non-stop United Nations punter tired <u>out</u> (13)

United Nations = un
un punter tired (13) → uninterrupted
Non-stop = uninterrupted (13)

```
      U N
   P       T
  N         E
  U         R
             T
   D       I
      E R
```

WORDS TO LETTERS gives us **un** for **United Nations** and then we have the necessary (13) letters for our ANAGRAM. The target word must mean **non-stop**.

I compose Santa <u>by being</u> warm-hearted (13)

I compose Santa (13) → compassionate
warm-hearted = compassionate (13)

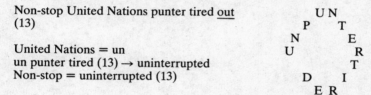

```
      M P
   O     O
  C       S
  I        E
            S
    A     A
     T N
```

It's very late to go under and love <u>swimming</u> (4,7)

go under + love (11) → long overdue
It's very late = long overdue (4,7)

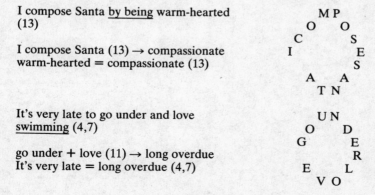

```
      U N
   O     D
  G       E
           R
   E       L
     V O
```

Red sea-power <u>potentially</u> tidier, by the
road (11)

Red sea-power (11) → roadsweeper
tidier by the road = roadsweeper (11)

```
      D S
     E   E
    R     A
           P
    R     O
     E W
```

A clever answer, don't you think?

NUMBERS

Numbers are used mainly in two ways: as their Roman equivalents or other associations and as references to other clues in the same puzzle. Since the latter uses the solution of the other clue in determining that for the clue in question, answers to both are often inter-dependent. The logic of the clue should point to which use of numbers is being employed by the compiler.

Numbers in clues may be written in both numeric digits and letters. When not referring to other clues, they have the following Roman equivalents and sometimes other associations (shown in brackets).

EXAMPLES

1 (one)	= i, (a, an, ace)
2 pints	= (quart)
3 feet	= (yard)
4 (four)	= iv
4 quarts	= (gallon)
5 (five)	= v
5th (fifth)	= (nones)
6 (six)	= vi
7 days	= (week)
7th (seventh)	= (nones)
8 gallons	= (bushel)
8 pints	= (gallon)
8 stones	= (cwt)
9 (nine)	= ix
10 (ten)	= x [cross], io
11 (eleven)	= xi, (side, team)
12 inches	= (foot)
12 months	= (year)
13th	= (ides)
14 pounds	= (stone)
15th	= (ides)
16 ounces	= (pound)
20 (twenty)	= xx [double-cross], (score)
20 cwt	= (ton)
22 yards	= (chain)
24 sheets	= (quire)
26 characters	= (az) [alphabet]
30 seconds	= (min) [half minute]
49 (fortynine)	= il
50 (fifty)	= l
50% (per cent)	= half
50–50 (fifty fifty)	= ll
51 (fiftyone)	= li
51 French	= lun(e)

11

99 (ninetynine)	= ic
100 (hundred)	= c, (ton)
101 (hundred and one)	= ci
101 French	= cun(e)
144	= (gross)
200 yards	= (cable)
220 yards	= (furlong)
400 (four hundred)	= p
480 sheets	= (ream)
499	= id
500 (five hundred)	= d
501 (five hundred and one)	= di
501 French	= dun(e)
999	= im
1000 (thousand)	= k, m
1000 dollars	= g [grand]
1000 kg	= (tonne)
1001 (thousand and one)	= mi
1001 French	= mun(e)
1760 yards	= (mile)

FOREIGN WORDS

Foreign words are frequently employed in the compilation of clues. This should not be of concern since the words used are from very basic school days and are mostly French. In the examples below I have shown the language before the word being translated. Often it is the other way round in clues, so look both before and after references to languages or nationalities.

Sometimes, the key words **continental, Gallic** or **Parisian** are used by the compiler instead of **French**. Also popular is the use of **agreement** or **approval** for **yes** and **denial** or **refusal** for **no**.

EXAMPLES

FRENCH	a	= un, une
FRENCH	above	= sur
FRENCH	all, every	= tout
FRENCH	and	= et
FRENCH	below	= sous
FRENCH	by	= par
FRENCH	day	= jour
FRENCH	father	= pere
FRENCH	friend	= ami, amie [lady]
FRENCH	girl, miss	= mme
FRENCH	good	= bon
FRENCH	head	= tete
FRENCH	here	= ici
FRENCH	how	= que
FRENCH	in	= dans, en
FRENCH	iron	= fer
FRENCH	is	= est
FRENCH	island	= ile
FRENCH	key	= clef
FRENCH	lady, woman	= mm
FRENCH	love	= amour
FRENCH	man	= m
FRENCH	morning	= matin
FRENCH	mother	= mere
FRENCH	name	= nom
FRENCH	night	= nuit
FRENCH	no	= non
FRENCH	of the	= de, des
FRENCH	on	= sur
FRENCH	one	= un, une
FRENCH	sea	= mer
FRENCH	station	= gare
FRENCH	the	= la, le, les
FRENCH	this	= ce

FRENCH	yes	= oui
FRENCH	you	= tu
FRENCH	water	= eau
FRENCH	way, street	= rue
FRENCH	well	= bien
FRENCH	where	= ou
FRENCH	wine	= vin
FRENCH	with	= avec, met
FRENCH	word	= mot

GERMAN	a	= ein
GERMAN	day	= tag
GERMAN	mister	= herr
GERMAN	mountain	= berg
GERMAN	my	= mein
GERMAN	no	= nein
GERMAN	one	= ein
GERMAN	please	= bitte
GERMAN	the	= das, der, die
GERMAN	with	= mit
GERMAN	woman	= frau
GERMAN	yes	= ja

ITALIAN	a	= un, una, uno
ITALIAN	evening	= sera
ITALIAN	good	= bene
ITALIAN	house	= casa
ITALIAN	no	= non
ITALIAN	the	= il, la, le, lo
ITALIAN	well	= bene
ITALIAN	wine	= vino
ITALIAN	with	= con
ITALIAN	yes	= si

RUSSIAN	yes	= da

SPANISH	a	= un, una, uno
SPANISH	day	= dias
SPANISH	the	= el, la, las, los
SPANISH	wine	= vino
SPANISH	yes	= si

STARTS, MIDDLES AND ENDS

Use is often made of first, middle and last letters of words in clues by clever association of two words or two syllables which go to form words. This is also extended to other letters by their positions in words or to parts of words.

EXAMPLES

beginning of April	= a
centre forward	= w
egg-**head**	= e
Gateshead	= g
last train	= n
leading lady	= l
Maiden**head**	= m
Middlesex	= e
safety **first**	= s
second half	= a
third of April	= r
west **end**	= t
youth **leader**	= y

The answer may actually use more than one letter . . .

borders of Essex	= e, x
half an hour	= ho or ur
half time	= ti or me
centrefold	= ol

. . . or be combined with other words directly or indirectly, e.g. using synonyms or ANAGRAMS.

Tool for fitting spring to **end of** runner (7)

    spring = spa (3)
    end of runner = nner (4)
    tool = spanner (7)

With **spa** being (3) letters, (4) more are needed from the end of **runner**.

Went in **last** thirty and made a score (6)

    last thirty = ty (2)
    score = t-went-y (6)

With **went** being (4) letters, only (2) are needed from last letters of **thirty**.

Onset of flu always causes high temperature (5)

    Onset of flu = f (1)
    always = ever (4)
    high temperature = fever (5)

It's sore if Paul never **starts** to realise (7)

    never **starts** = n (1)
    if + Paul + n → painful (7)
    sore = painful

Married and **middle**-aged club (5)

> Married = wed (3)
> **middle** ag<u>e</u>d = ge (2)
> club = wed-ge (5)

We use WORDS TO WORDS to get **wed** and the middle of **ag<u>e</u>d** to form our (5) letter answer.

Killing time after **first half** of the carnival (7)

> first half <u>carn</u>ival = carn (4)
> time = age (3)
> killing = carn-age (7)

The first half of **carnival** is (4) letters, so we need a synonym of **time** in WORDS TO WORDS of (3) letters. The logic is similar in the next clue.

Complained when woken up after **mid**night (7)

> **mid** ni<u>g</u>ht = g (1)
> woken up = roused (6)
> Complained = g-roused (7)

It's used to steer up to the **end** of the water (6)

> up to = till (4)
> **end** of wat<u>er</u> = er (2)
> It's used to steer = tiller

This is another combination from WORDS TO WORDS with this time the end of **water**. Because **till** is (4) letters, we only need the last (2) of **wat<u>er</u>**.

Cautious about **end** of the race, showing signs of fatigue (5)

> Cautious = wary (4)
> **end** of the rac<u>e</u> = e (1)
> showing signs of fatigue
> = w-e-ary (5)

WORDS TO WORDS gives us **wary** (4), leaving (1) only needed from the end of **rac<u>e</u>**. **Wary** should be about **e** according to the clue, giving **weary** as our answer.

At sun-up, move **half** the planet (5)

> move **half** = ve (2)
> sun <u>up</u> = nus (3)
> planet = ve-nus (5)

An excess of gold and grey **borders** (4)

> gold = or (2)
> gr<u>ey</u> **borders** = gy (2)
> excess = or-gy (4)

Touch **both ends** and hold up a beating (5)

> <u>Touch</u> **both ends** = th (2)
> <u>h</u>old up = rob (3)
> beating = th-rob (5)

As can be seen from the above examples, STARTS, MIDDLES AND ENDS generally provide letters to go in conjunction with other compiler techniques in determining target words.

Whilst key words in STARTS usually refer to the initial or first letter of one word only, they can apply to a number of consecutive words in order to form the answer. The following are some examples:

Firework **initially** shows quite unusual ignition blast (5)

Firework = s-q-u-i-b (5)

At first, English lupins may seem to be trees (4)

trees = E-l-m-s (4)

Merit excitement as rowdy noise **starts** (4)

merit = e-a-r-n (4)

Country **starts** to emerge near Germany, later around Northern Denmark (7)

Country = e-n-G-l-a-N-D (7)

Use new lining in tent **when beginning** to get dark (5)

dark = U-n-l-i-t (5)

Spin **starts** to work in Red Lion (5)

Spin = t-w-i-R-L (5)

Starts to diet, eats tuna and cheese, has to break off (6)

break off = d-e-t-a-c-h (6)

Puts up shoots round ivy leaves, **at first** (6)

ivy leaves **first** = il (2)
shoots = buds (4)
shoots round il = bu(il)ds (6)
Puts up = builds

Heartbroken lover, yet **initially** of this world (7)

Heart → earth (5)
lover, yet initially = ly (2)
of this world = earth-ly (7)

There are a number of compiler techniques to better hide what I have called MIDDLES, i.e. letters already inside clue words, [e.g. middle aged = ge], that are needed to determine target words or letters that are actually required to be put into the target words.

Medal I'll be wearing is on its way out (5)

Medal = gong (4)
I **wearing** gong → go(i)ng (5)
on its way out = going

Hungry chap has cause to complain (4)

chap = man (3)
[Hungry means has nothing inside]
Hungry man → m(o)an (4)
complain = moan

DROPPING LETTERS FROM WORDS

Another compiler technique is to drop letters from words in the clues. The answers are then found in the remaining letters (often by ANAGRAM).

Generally clues will include terms such as:

. . . hasn't finished
without . . .
headless . . .
. . . doesn't start
no . . .
. . . away

An interesting ploy is used where reference is made to **Cockney**. This will mean that the letter **h** will be dropped from the word in question, just as a Cockney does in his speech.

EXAMPLES

Tipster <u>without notice</u> of cover (5)

Tipster = advisor (7)
notice = ad (2)
<u>advisor</u> → visor (5)
cover = visor

<u>No con</u> artist in firm (6)

artist = Constable
Constable → stable (6)
firm = stable

<u>Don't pat</u> knee if it's a girl (4)

knee = patella
patella → ella (4)
girl ('s name) = Ella

Drug dealer <u>loses his head</u> but he shows the way in (5)

Drug dealer = pusher
pusher → usher (5)
he shows the way in = usher

<u>Head off</u> landowner <u>holding</u> AGM in bog (8)

landowner = squire
quire (5) → qu-agm-ire (8)
bog = quagmire

<u>Unfinished</u> melod<u>y</u> composed for the mannequin (5)

melod → model (5)
mannequin = model

Here we also have an ANAGRAM [indicated by **composed**] and in the next clue [indicated by **treatment**].

No hesitation in solarium treatment for Jack (6)

    hesitation = um (2)
    solarium (8) → solari (6)
    solari → sailor
    Jack = sailor

Money lost in official garment (8)

    money = investment
    investment → vestment (8)
    garment = vestment

Once more in vanishing, the chief appears (3)

    Once more = again
    again → aga (3)
    chief = Aga

Also a Cockney member (3)

    member = hand
    Cockney member → and
    Also = and (3)

Name lady losing heart in flat (6)

    flat = even (4)
    lady → ly (2)
    name = eve-ly-n (6)

Agreement to drop second marriage (5)

    Agreement = unison
    second = s
    unison → union (5)
    marriage = union

Here **second** = s from WORDS TO LETTERS is dropped from **unison**.

Part of the inn is almost stripped (3)

    stripped = bare
    almost bare → bar (4)
    Part of the inn = bar

WORDS TO WORDS gives us **bare**, while **almost** indicates we should drop a small part of it. The (3) shows it need only be one letter.

Repeat: unable to read, but not ill (7)

    unable to read = illiterate
    illiterate → iterate (7)
    Repeat = iterate

Japan has no right to disappear! (6)

    Japan = varnish
    varnish → vanish (6)
    disappear = vanish

Looked for top off figure (5)

    looked for = sought
    sought → ought (5)
    figure = ought

Protected from that Cockney fellow and 1001 French (6)

    Cockney fellow = him (2)
    1000 = m (1)
    1 French = une (3)
    protected = immune (6)

This is a clever clue, involving examples from DROPPING LETTERS FROM WORDS, NUMBERS and FOREIGN WORDS!

Patrick mainly has incomplete idea of murder (9)

Patrick mainly → patric (6)
incomplete idea → ide (3)
murder = patric-ide (9)

Here we have two lots of DROPPING LETTERS in the one clue.

Sagacious, well-mannered for the most part and in charge (7)

well-mannered = polite
the most part → polit (5)
in charge = ic (2)
Sagacious = polit-ic (7)

We combine DROPPING LETTERS with WORDS TO LETTERS to solve this clue.

Ran out of orange while raising morale (3)

orange → oge (3)
oge → ego
morale = ego

This solution involves DROPPING LETTERS and BACKWARD ANSWERS.

Try out commerce on the river (5)

commerce = industry (8)
industry → indus (5)
river [India] = indus

Declare the girl's fallen for a lightweight (5)

Declare = announce (8)
girl = Ann (3)
announce → ounce (5)
light weight = ounce

Notice the clever use of **lightweight** in this clue.

There's endless talk about sport equipment (6)

talk = discuss (6)
endless talk → discus (5)
sport equipment = discus

In the context of the clue, **talk** is a noun. The synonym of **talk**, however, used in the solution is a verb. This exchange of the grammar of a clue word is very often used by compilers and always needs to be considered as an option.

All-powerful when almost eighty so turned Lawrence out (8)

so turned = os (2)
Lawrence = te (2)
almost eighty → alm-ighty
All-powerful = almighty (8)

Understanding this clue and the following one augurs well for LOGICAL ANSWERS!

In other words, superfluous underwear causes delay! (6)

in other words = ie (2)
underwear = lingerie (8)
linger<u>ie</u> → linger (6)
delay = linger

Flower vessel <u>losing</u> business (5)

vessel = coaster (7)
business = co (2)
<u>co</u>aster → aster (5)
Flower = aster

Crazy admiral's <u>first</u> to leave nautical snafu (7)

admiral's first = <u>a</u>
a <u>to leave</u> nautical = n utical
nutical (7) → lunatic
crazy [person] = lunatic

Here, <u>snafu</u> indicates an ANAGRAM which needs to be applied after we have dropped the **a** from **nautical**.

Complete, <u>losing</u> nothing from end to end (7)

Complete = thorough (8)
nothing = o (1)
th<u>o</u>rough <u>losing</u> o = through (7)
from end to end = through

Greek centre <u>replaced by</u> French in Polish port (6)

Greek centre = ree
French in = dans
ree <u>replaced by</u> dans = G(dans)k
Polish port = Gdansk (6)

Talk <u>endlessly</u> about a plate (6)

Talk = discuss (7)
discus<u>s</u> <u>endlessly</u> = discus (6)
plate = discus

Fish has <u>no tail</u> — built differently! (7)

has <u>no tail</u> → ha (2)
built <u>differently</u> = libut (5)
Fish = ha-libut (7)

Besides DROPPING LETTERS we have an ANAGRAM indicator to consider.

Open it up in June, having got the <u>tip off</u> (5)

June, having <u>tip off</u> → une
it <u>up</u> / <u>in</u> une = un(ti)e (5)
Open = untie

<u>Not entirely</u> unwanted points (7)

unwanted = needless (8)
<u>Not entirely</u> needles<u>s</u> = needles
points = needles (7)

Heavy of French <u>extraction</u> not fat (4)

Heavy = leaden (6)
of <u>French</u> = de (2)
de <u>extraction</u> = lea n (4)
not fat = lean

Test for divorcee — a help<u>less</u> maid (4)

divorcee = ex (2)
a **help**<u>less</u> **maid** = a m
Test = ex-a m (4)

DOUBLE MEANINGS

The compiler often selects target words for which he gives two alternative meanings in his clue, one of which may be relatively obscure. This technique I will refer to as SIMPLE DOUBLE MEANINGS. In a variation of this approach we first have to determine interim words which are then taken together, or punctuated differently, to give another meaning. This I will call COMPLEX DOUBLE MEANINGS.

EXAMPLES OF SIMPLE DOUBLE MEANINGS

Swerve cut people down (4)

swerve = slew (4)
cut people down = slew

It's a question of investigation (7)

question = inquiry (7)
investigation = inquiry

Recovered and played a series of shots (7)

Recovered = rallied (7)
played a series of shots
= rallied [tennis]

Opening for hire (4)

Opening = rent [tear] (4)
hire = rent

Conditions prevailing in countries (6)

Conditions = states (6)
countries = states

Mockery of a defence (7)

Mockery = apology (7)
defence = apology

Here both meanings of **apology** are relatively obscure ones.

Enjoy the sauce (6)

Enjoy = relish (6)
sauce = relish

Scorch the cleaner (4)

Scorch = char (4)
cleaner = char

Become cracked like a man (4)

Become cracked = chap (4)
man = chap

Found worthless (4)

Found = base (4)
worthless = base

Took up permanent residence and paid the bill (7)

Took up permanent residence
= settled (7)
paid the bill = settled

23

Make a statement non-stop (7)

Make a statement = express (7)
non-stop = express

Very inclined to soak (5)

Very inclined = steep (5)
soak = steep

Loaf of bread for the swan (3)

[round-headed] loaf = cob (3)
[male] swan = cob

Soon to be shortly nameless (4)

Soon = anon (4)
nameless = anon[ymous]

Train set (5)

Train [retinue] = suite (5)
set = suite

Stock letter (7)

Stock = capital (7)
letter = capital

Smart cheat (5)

Smart [hurt] = sting (5)
cheat = sting

Don't eat quickly (4)

Don't eat = fast (4)
quickly = fast

Work the register (4)

Work [the land] = till (4)
register = till

Scientific equipment will produce the answer (6)

Scientific equipment = retort
answer = retort (6)

Loose change found on a beat (7)

Loose change = coppers [money]
found on a beat = coppers (7)

They show you approve of bloodsuckers! (5)

They show you approve = ticks [marked as being correct]
bloodsuckers = ticks (5)

Occasionally, we may find two plausible answers, as in the following example. Other clues, which provide letters to this clue, will help determine which is the correct one in any particular instance.

Sharp sweet (4)

Sharp = tart (4)
sweet = tart

or:

Sharp [sour]= acid (4)
sweet = acid [drop]

River sport (4)

River = Wear (4)
sport = wear

It's not easy to get out of this clothing (5)

It's not easy to get out of
= habit (5)
clothing = habit

Return to surrender (5)

return [financial] = yield (5)
surrender = yield

They dress in blue — not silver! (7)

They dress in blue
= coppers (7) [policemen]
not silver = coppers [coins]

Went at speed and also came nowhere (3)

Went at speed = ran (3)
also came nowhere = [also] ran

Divided up into billets (9)

Divided up = quartered (9)
into billets = quartered

Not forthcoming, but found at the fair (3)

Not forthcoming = shy (3)
found at the fair
= [coconut] shy

Prompt essential to potter (3)

Prompt = cue (3)
essential to potter
= [snooker] cue

Carpenter commonly accompanied by fish (5)

accompanied by fish = chips
[Ship's] Carpenter = Chips (5)

Extension of time inside (7)

Extension = stretch (7)
time inside [gaol] = stretch

First class letter (7)

First class = capital (7)
letter = capital

Pin used to catch a fish (7)

[freshwater] fish = gudgeon
[metal] pin = gudgeon (7)

Affixed in an unnatural way (3,2)

Affixed = put on (3,2)
in an unnatural way = put on

Start to show to advantage (3,3)

Start = set off (3,3)
show to advantage = set off

Lets try some final examples of SIMPLE DOUBLE MEANINGS.

Questions the daily (5)

[exam] Questions = paper (5)
daily = [news]paper

He'll send the bill (6)

He'll send [post] = poster (6)
bill = poster

Destined for a title (7)	Destined [for] = heading [for] title = heading (7)
Presides over furniture (6)	Presides over = chairs (6) furniture = chairs
Force bloomers under this hat (6)	[bell shaped] hat = cloche (6) glass cover to help grow young plants [bloomers] = cloche
Withdraw from taking a particular kick (4,3)	Withdraw = drop out (4,3) [particular] kick = drop out
Hide in shower (4)	[animal] Hide = pelt (4) shower = pelt
Original letter (7)	Original = initial (7) letter = initial
Course for a singer (5)	Course [drift] = tenor (5) singer = tenor
Common name put on door (6)	Common name = handle (6) put on door = handle
Top quality beginners at school (5–5)	beginners at school = first class (10) Top quality = first-class
Get on a plane and scarper (4,6)	Get on a plane = take flight scarper = take flight (4,6)

Here the compiler gets carried away and goes for a TRIPLE MEANING!

Even the accommodation is dull (4)	Even = flat (4) accommodation = flat dull = flat

Now that you have the idea with SIMPLE DOUBLE MEANINGS we'll move on to COMPLEX DOUBLE MEANINGS. In these examples we are looking at interim words which combine to give us our target meanings.

EXAMPLES OF COMPLEX DOUBLE MEANINGS

Generally when key words such as **again, another** or **further** appear in a clue we can expect **re** to figure in the solution. This is the simplest (sounds Irish again!) form of COMPLEX DOUBLE MEANINGS:

Take objection to being posted <u>again</u> (6)

posted = sent
posted <u>again</u> = re-sent
take objection to = resent (6)

<u>Again</u> have to take back (9)

have = possess
<u>Again</u> have = re-possess
take back = repossess (9)

Touch up and put in stock <u>again</u> (7)

put in stock = store
put in stock <u>again</u> = re-store
touch up = restore (7)

Free to let the property <u>again</u> (7)

let the property <u>again</u>
= re-lease
Free = release (7)

Decline to connect up the circuit <u>again</u> (6)

connect up the circuit <u>again</u>
= re-fuse
Decline = refuse (6)

Determine to do the puzzle <u>again</u> (7)

do the puzzle <u>again</u> = re-solve
Determine = resolve (7)

Feeling discomfort <u>again</u>, stretching (8)

feeling discomfort <u>again</u>
= re-aching
stretching = reaching (8)

Start work <u>again</u> on potted version (6)

Start work <u>again</u> = resume
potted version = resume (6)

Withdraw to buy <u>another</u> round of drinks (7)

buy <u>another</u> round of drinks
= re-treat
Withdraw = retreat (7)

Go back and make a <u>further</u> concession (6)

make a <u>further</u> concession
= re-cede
Go back = recede (6)

We can now move on to more clever uses of COMPLEX DOUBLE MEANINGS:

Can't be a person of distinction (7)

Can't = not able (7)
person of distinction = notable

Come to grief at sea — it depends how big-headed one is! (7)

how big-headed one is
= cap size (7)
Come to grief at sea = capsize

How big-headed one is is indicated by one's **cap size**. These words together give us **capsize**, our target meaning.

Diligence of acting tutor (5–5)

acting tutor = stage coach
Diligence = stage-coach (10)

The clever interpretation of **acting tutor** gives us our interim words, while our target word is an obscure meaning of **diligence**.

Uniform passed — just (4–6)

Uniform = even (4)
passed = handed (6)
just = even-handed

Solemn measure appropriate for cemetery (9)

Solemn = grave (5)
measure = yard (4)
cemetery = graveyard (9)

Rider has a job writing (10)

job = post (4)
writing = script (6)
Rider = postscript (10)

Uniform rise (3,2)

Uniform = get up
rise = get up

Another view of clairvoyance (6–5)

Another = second (6)
view = sight (5)
clairvoyance = second-sight (6–5)

Most important, although of equal quantity (9)

equal = par (3)
quantity = amount (6)
Most important = paramount (9)

Undertaking to go in by force (10)

to go in = enter (5)
force = prise (5)
Undertaking = enterprise (10)

Little money needed for biscuits (10)

Little = short (5)
money = bread (5)
biscuits = shortbread (10)

Major engagement: dresser running across (7,7)

dresser = cabinet (7)
running across = meeting (7)
Major engagement
= cabinet meeting (7,7)

Did you spot that **Major** here is Prime Minister John **Major**?

Point to a church in London (11)

Point = west (4)
church = minster (7)
in London = Westminster (11)

Escape route is a jetty into the sea (7)

Escape = slip (4)
route = way (3)
jetty = slipway (7)

Outline of study trip (7)

study = con (3)
trip = tour (4)
outline = contour (7)

Cut more obsolete type of fuel container (9)

Cut = gash (4)
more obsolete = older (5)
container = gasholder (9)

They can't lose undoubted restrictions (11)

undoubted = certain (7)
restrictions = ties (4)
They can't lose = certainties (11)

Piece of harness to pinch a little (7–3)

pinch [steal] = snaffle (7)
little = bit (3)
Piece of harness = snaffle-bit

Occasionally, the punctuation in the combination of the interim words will need to be taken differently:

A fabric produced to order (2,4)

a fabric = a twill (6)
produced to order = at will

Baseball player's trousers and cap (5–4)

trousers = shorts (6)
cap = top (3)
Baseball player = short-stop

Get funny — find a sleeping bag (3–4)

Get funny = be droll (7)
sleeping bag = bed-roll

Act like a bird and get lost (4,2)

Act like = be (2)
a bird = a tit (4)
get lost = beat it!

QUESTIONS?

We've seen that a **?** can be a lazy compiler's ANAGRAM indicator. More often, when a clue is phrased in the form of a question this indicates that the answer is possible, given another meaning of the word or other context in which it may be used. It's best to try and illustrate this clever technique with examples and explanations as we go along.

EXAMPLES

Pudding that's no good? (4)

Pudding = [plum] duff
no good = duff (4)

Duff in one sense means no good but this doesn't mean that a **duff** as a **pudding** is no good. It can be so, hence the **?**

Eye make-up used by passengers at sea? (5)

Eye make-up = liner (5)
used by passengers at sea
= liner

Liner is part of a lady's eye make-up and **passengers at sea** can use a liner, but in a liner = boat sense.

Board game? (5,6)

Board = table (5)
game = tennis (6)
Board game? = table tennis

Board game will normally conjure up "Monopoly", "Ludo", etc., or some such game played on a board. However, the **?** indicates another possibility. This is separately arrived at via **Board = table** [see WORDS TO WORDS] and **game = tennis**.

Stock check? (4)

Stock = stem (4) [of plant]
check = stem [= stop]

Without the **?** we may look for a synonym of, say, **audit**. The logic with the **?** however is completely different, as we can see from the solution.

Criminal involved in demolition? (12)

criminal = housebreaker (12)
involved in demolition?
= housebreaker

A **house breaker** may be conceived to **be involved in demolition** while a **housebreaker** is certainly a **criminal**.

Find the record's finished? (8)

record = disc (4)
finished = over (4)
find = discover (8)

30

Here we have a combination of two words, separately arrived at, which together can mean **find**.

Disagree on type of arrow used? (7) | Disagree = quarrel (7)
type of arrow = quarrel

A **quarrel** is a bolt for a crossbow but you can **disagree** as in **quarrel** on its use.

Cross footballers? (6) | footballers = Celtic (6)
[upright] cross = celtic

[Glasgow] Celtic footballers can be **cross** in an angry sense, but celtic is also an upright cross on a circle in a religious context.

Not a troublesome stretch of water? (7) | Not troublesome = pacific (7)
stretch of water = Pacific

Not troublesome is certainly **pacific**, but the **Pacific** [ocean] won't necessarily be so.

Disorder causing bitterness? (8) | Disorder [medical] = jaundice
causing bitterness = jaundice

Jaundice as a disease may well affect one with **jaundice** at one's plight.

Hammer? New title is not enough (3,6) | Hammer? = tool (4)
New title (5) → ittle
not enough = too little

Hammer is just one type of tool and the **?** should start us looking in this direction. The ANAGRAM and the clever combination of **tool** and **ittle** make this an interesting clue to solve.

Flags waved by a singer? (7) | Flags = bunting (7)
singer [bird] = bunting

Singer is one of the compiler's clever uses of words and can set you off in the wrong direction. Also, **bunting** is an unusual type of bird in crossword terms, making this a fairly testing clue.

Old king in the ant world? (7) | Old king = Pharaoh (7)
[type of] ant = pharaoh

An **Old king** in Egypt was a **Pharaoh** while pharaohs can also be found **in the ant world**.

The above QUESTIONS? clues have produced answers with two meanings, one usually directly related and the other by possible inference. Next we'll look at another form of answers to QUESTIONS? which are one-shot solutions and thus generally more difficult.

By now the **?** should stimulate the mind to look a bit beyond the obvious. Often you are in a DOUBLE MEANINGS situation as in the preceding examples, but there are also clever "one liners" to tax your ingenuity some more.

Key personnel employed in an   skeleton staff! (8,5)
emergency? (8,5)

The **?** is our indicator to look for another meaning or other context in which the answer may be applicable. A **skeleton** is a form of **key** while **staff** is a synonym for **personnel**.

Twin cats? (7)   Siamese! (7)

Both **Twin** and **cats** can be Siamese.

Food for flyers? (8)   birdseed! (8)

Birdseed is a sort of food and birds can be **flyers**.

Drinking hole? (10)   nineteenth!

The **?** sets us looking for a more unusual answer that just another word for, say, a **bar** or **dive**.

Where astronauts are delighted to be?   over the moon!
(4,3,4)

Over the moon is a good phrase for one being **delighted** and **astronauts** can physically be there as well.

Spring water? (5,7)   April showers!

Beware the **?**. Without it, we can go looking for other words involving **spring** as in **well**, particularly with the reference to **water**. We have to stretch our thoughts to **spring** as in **season** and **water** as in **rain**.

Not just ugly? (6)   unfair!

Not just is certainly **unfair** and if you are **ugly** as well, that can be doubly unfair!

Capital growth arrangement? (9)   hairstyle!

WORDS TO WORDS helps here with **Capital = head** and then, of course, we have our **?** pointer to look for the unusual. **Head growth = hair** is the next logical step and some thought given to **hair arrangement** should get us our answer.

Corrected when the clock struck noon?   am-ended!
(7)

When the clock strikes noon morning [**am**] has certainly **ended** while together they give **amended** as a possible alternative for **Corrected**.

The last of the stock for soup? (6)   oxtail!

Stock here is in the sense of **cattle**, which gives us **ox**. **The last of the ox** is its **tail** and together they make a possible **soup**.

Male midwife doing the rounds (8,3)   delivery man!

A **Male midwife** could well be described as a **delivery man**, but more usually the latter would be **doing the rounds** with his client deliveries.

Permissive characters? (7)   letters!

Alphabetic **characters** are **letters** but you could also describe **permissive** people as **letters** — people who let things happen.

Musical painter? (8)   Whistler!

Whistler is a famous painter but a **whistler** could be a **musical** painter as well.

Jacky? (7)   knavish!

The key here is to see **Jacky** with a **?** as an adjective of **jack** and not go chasing after some person's surname that will fit, such as Kennedy. **Jack** is a playing card, also referred to as a **knave**. If one were Jack-like, then **knavish** is another way of expressing this.

Loudspeaker making bird-like noises? (7)   tweeter!

A **tweeter** is a type of **loudspeaker**, while something making bird-like noises can be referred to as a **tweet-er**.

Grandfather clock? (3,5)   old timer!

A **Grandfather clock** can well be described as an **old timer**, while a **grandfather** can also claim to be an **old timer** because of his age.

Now you know that in solving QUESTIONS? you must treat the **?** as a flag to look for an answer with two possible connections to the clue.

INSERTS

The answers to a number of clues are actually hidden in the text of the questions, the letters being spread through a number of adjacent words.

INSERTS contain indicators (underlined below) in the wording of the clues which are generally obvious. Both FORWARD and BACKWARD INSERT techniques are used and are best illustrated by the examples below.

EXAMPLES OF FORWARD INSERTS

Poe's lurid poem <u>involves</u> imputation (4)

imputation = slur (4)

<u>Some</u> steaming beverage (3)

beverage = tea (3)

Ancient <u>part of</u> golden wedding (3)

ancient = old (3)

Girl <u>in</u> car — a Chelsea fan? (6)

girl = Rachel (6)

Allow Cyril licence <u>to hold</u> foreign alphabet (8)

foreign alphabet = cyrillic (8)

It's convenient <u>being within</u> reach and you love it (5)

convenient = handy (5)

Took a picture of animals, <u>including</u> this one (5)

animal = okapi (5)

Maiden voyage <u>carries</u> messenger (5)

messenger = envoy (5)

Primate <u>some</u> find ribald (5)

primate [lemur] = indri (5)

<u>Part of</u> a petrol engine (4)

Part = role (4)

Cleverly, here, the insert indicator and the word for which we are seeking a synonym are one and the same.

Garbo's career would be incomplete <u>without</u> it (5)

oscar (5)

This is not so obviously an INSERT as the other clues above, since the indicator is well disguised in the wording. It is actually **without** but in this case it means **on the outside of**.

Very often, as is the case in the following two examples, such clues are split over two lines to better conceal the INSERT.

Quiver <u>detected in</u> quiet
remorse (6)

quiver = tremor (6)

34

Made of clay <u>from</u> **near The** Needles (7)	Made of clay = earthen (7)
<u>Some</u> people send **a te**lex for an appointment (4)	appointment = date (4)
Are **the m**any <u>hiding</u> the others? (4)	the others = them (4)
Operas **oft**en have quiet <u>part</u> (4)	quiet = soft (4)
Ste**p up p**yramid <u>carrying</u> young Barker (5)	young barker [dog] = puppy (5)
Passageway <u>through</u> the **va**lleys (5)	Passageway = alley (5)
Story <u>of</u> Ptolemy **the** first (4)	Story = myth (4)
It might keep afloat <u>some</u> stock mar**ket** characters (5)	It might keep afloat = ketch (5)
Lavender <u>entered</u> **as pick** of the bunch (5)	Lavender [preserve for future use] = aspic (5)
Woman left <u>in</u> sorrow **I do w**ant to meet (5)	Woman left = widow (5)
Hardly the shout <u>that contributes to</u> laug**h**ter (3)	shout [of disgust] = ugh (3)
They are chosen <u>to be in</u> the Israeli team (5)	They are chosen = elite (5)
<u>A bit of</u> rot**ten ch**eese and some fish (5)	fish = tench (5)

We'll now move on from FORWARD to BACKWARD INSERTS.

EXAMPLES OF BACKWARD INSERTS

Lea**d a ven**ture to <u>reverse</u> state involvement (6)	state = Nevada (6)
Name <u>backwards in</u> alpha**beti**cal order (4)	name = cite (4)
Leave Man**ch**ester and call <u>in on the way</u> <u>back</u> (4)	call = name (4)

Again very often, as is the case in the following three examples, such clues are split over two lines to better conceal the BACKWARD INSERT.

Frequently <u>arises in</u> argument, **fort**unately (3)	Frequently = oft (3)
Skilful <u>backing in</u> efficient **fed**eral government (4)	skilful = deft (4)
<u>In backing</u> army **CO I di**splayed stupidity (6)	stupidity = idiocy (6)
Bird on i**ceberg** suffering a <u>bit</u> of a setback (5)	Bird = grebe (5)
A couple <u>will get up</u> in **low** turn-out (3)	couple = two (3)

All too easy? Sometimes a combination of techniques makes for a more difficult clue:

Artillery has to <u>retreat</u> to a desert area (6)	Artillery = ra (2) ra has → sahar (5) sahar **to a** = sahar-a (6) desert area = sahara

This is a clever combination from WORDS TO LETTERS (**artillery = ra**), then a BACKWARD (indicator <u>retreat</u>) reading of **ra has** to indicate **sahar** and finally **sahar** with **a** from the clue to give **sahara**, a desert area.

This clue leads us to look at BACKWARD ANSWERS as another compiler technique covered in the next pages.

BACKWARD ANSWERS

Another compiler technique is for the end answers to be found by reversing the sequence of interim solutions. Generally BACKWARD ANSWERS clues will include indicators such as:

. . . in the ascendant
. . . backward . . .
brings up . . .
. . . coming back . . .
reversing . . .
. . . returning . . .

EXAMPLES

Well-fitting weapons are <u>in the ascendant</u> (4)

Well-fitting = snug (4)
snug → guns
weapons = guns

Inventor <u>brings up</u> end of rugby (6)

end of rugby [match] = no side
no side → edison (6)
Inventor = Edison

Mediterranean mount which <u>returns</u> one's stake (4)

stake = ante (4)
ante → etna
Mediterranean mount = Etna

Wicked person led <u>backward</u> existence (5)

led existence = lived (5)
lived → devil
Wicked person = devil

The pace of <u>returning</u> animals (4)

animals = pets (4)
pets → step
pace = step

One faint <u>reflection</u> from part of France (4)

One faint = i dim (4)
i dim → midi
part of France = Midi

Drink can go cold <u>coming back</u> (6)

cold = c (1)
can go c → cognac (6)
Drink = cognac

Swallow when <u>returning</u> the stopper (4)

swallow = gulp (4)
gulp → plug
stopper = plug

37

Fill <u>up</u> pockets (4)

pockets = pots (4)
pots → stop
Fill [plug] = stop

<u>Return</u> after putting scripture lesson in another test (7)

after = later (5)
later → retal
scripture lesson = ri (2)
retal / putting ri <u>in</u>
= ret(ri)al = another test

For now, just be aware of the "wrong" sequence of the wording of the insertion. This technique is explained later in LOGICAL ANSWERS.

Party's means of exerting influence <u>on the way up</u> (5)

party = revel (5)
revel → lever
= means of exerting influence

Mistake <u>over</u> eye parts (4–2)

eye parts = pupils (6)
pupils → slipup
Mistake = slip up

Hands <u>back</u> an exchange (4)

Hands = paws (4)
paws → swap
exchange = swap

Catch when a bit <u>elevated</u> (4)

bit = part (4)
part → trap
Catch = trap

Shout "silver <u>put back</u> in ship's kitchen" (6)

shout = yell (4)
silver = ag (2)
yell-ag → ga-lley (6)
ship's kitchen = galley

When in taxi, is <u>going backwards</u> fundamental? (5)

taxi = cab (3)
in taxi / is = c(is)ab (5)
cisab → basic
fundamental = basic

Merchant's colourful craft, <u>if you look back</u> (6)

colourful = red (3)
craft = art (3)
red-art → trader (6)
Merchant = trader

The Queen going to America <u>will turn up</u> safe (4)

The Queen = er (2)
America = us (2)
er-us → sure (4)
safe = sure

Laugh when a king <u>turns up</u> the joker (6)

Laugh when a = ho-a (3)
king = rex (3)
rex → xer
joker = ho-a-xer (6)

SOUNDS LIKE

Homonyms are often used in crossword puzzles where the word indicated by a particular clue still needs to be substituted by another word, pronounced in exactly the same way. This provides the actual answer.

Generally SOUNDS LIKE clues will use terms such as:

sounds like
. . . sounding
one hears
by the sound of it
reported
said

EXAMPLES

Periods of bewilderment, <u>we're told</u> (4)	bewilderment = daze daze → days (4) periods = days
Bigger <u>sounding</u> kitchen implement (6)	bigger = greater greater → grater (6) implement = grater
Distribute plenty, <u>by the sound of it</u> (5)	plenty = a lot a lot → allot (5) distribute = allot
The place, <u>we hear</u>, is an eyesore (5)	place = site site → sight (5) eyesore = sight
Story on armistice <u>reported</u> in supplement (9)	Story = tale tale → tail (4) armistice = peace peace → piece (5) supplement = tailpiece

This is a clever example of a double SOUNDS LIKE, with **tale** and **tail** as well as **peace** and **piece**. The following clue uses the same technique:

<u>Verbally</u> crossed swords with old soldier in this period (9)	crossed swords = fought fought → fort (4) old soldier = knight knight → night (5) period = fortnight

One might argue that **fought** and **fort** are not very good homonyms, certainly not as good as **knight** and **night**, but remember that the compiler also has poetic licence!

It takes two seasons, <u>say</u>, to go head over heels (10)

season [1] = summer
summer → somer (5)
season [2] = salt
salt → sault (5)
go head over heels = somersault

Here we also have a double SOUNDS LIKE but with the added disguise of a DOUBLE MEANING for the word **season**.

Farewell to a bargain, <u>we hear</u> (7)

bargain = good buy
good buy → goodbye (7)
farewell = goodbye

<u>Said</u> to have stumbled over a criminal (5)

stumbled over = fell on
fell on → felon (5)
criminal = felon

<u>Heard</u> the crowd gather (5)

crowd = horde
horde → hoard (5)
gather = hoard

Sweet but bolder, <u>we hear</u> (4)

bolder → boulder
boulder = rock (4)
[type of] sweet = rock

Church singers <u>heard</u> needing a number of sheets (5)

Church singers = choir
choir → quire (5)
number of sheets = quire

Missile used by a cricketer, <u>by the sound of it</u> (4)

cricketer = bowler
bowler → bola (4)
bola = missile

<u>Sounds like</u> a necessity to make some dough (5)

necessity = need
need → knead (5)
make dough = knead

Gladly, <u>we hear</u> two pages (4)

two pages = leaf
leaf → lief (4)
Gladly = lief

Angler, <u>say</u>, on land. That's cracked! (7)

angler = fisher
fisher → fissure (7)
land that's cracked = fissure

Rubbish you <u>heard</u> during <u>disorderly</u> retreat (4)

Rubbish you → rot u (4)
rot u → rout (4)
retreat = rout

Dog is <u>pronouncedly</u> less refined (7)

less refined = coarser
coarser → courser (7)
dog [breed] = courser

<u>Sounds like</u> the fat of the land (6)

fat = grease
grease → greece (6)
land = Greece

Bird to hide <u>said</u> fruit (10)

Bird = goose (5)
hide = bury
bury → berry (5)
fruit = goose-berry

Which person, <u>say</u>, with a beam gives a word of cheer? (6)

Which person = who
who → hoo (3)
beam = ray (3)
word of cheer = hoo-ray

Benefit afforded by a valley, <u>we are told</u> (5)

valley = vale
vale → vail (4)
a-vail = benefit

Pulse no longer present, <u>it's said</u> (4)

no longer present = been
been → bean (4)
Pulse = bean

A rest for feet, <u>we're told</u> (5)

feet = paws
paws → pause (5)
rest = pause

Aim always, <u>say</u>, to do one's best (9)

Aim = end (3)
always = ever
ever → eavour (6)
do one's best = end-eavour (9)

Reduce the instruction, <u>it's said</u> (6)

instruction = lesson
lesson → lessen (6)
Reduce = lessen

Note that the SOUNDS LIKE indicator applies to **instruction** and not to **Reduce**. Therefore our answer cannot be **Reduce** = **lessen** → **lesson** = **instruction**.

Miser, <u>say</u>, turns out to be an agent (8)

This example shows that you can't take your compiler for granted! We seem to have a SOUNDS LIKE indicator, <u>say</u>, but we have an ANAGRAM indicator as

well, <u>turns out to be</u>, and we have the correct number of letters for the answer:
Miser, say (8) → **emissary** = **agent**.

List in parts of ship, <u>we are told</u> (5)	parts of ship = decks decks → dex (3) in-dex (5) = List
Platform in harbour locker, <u>we hear</u> (4)	locker = key key → quay (4) Platform in harbour = quay
Early period of grieving, <u>say</u> (7)	grieving = mourning mourning → morning (7) Early period = morning
Spot a cat, <u>we hear</u>, or some other animal (7)	Spot = see cat = lion see lion → sealion (7) animal = sealion
Fruit given as soiled present, <u>by the sound of it</u> (12)	soiled = black (5) present = current current → currant (7) Fruit = black-currant (12)
Underwear intended, <u>say</u>, to be worn as robe (8)	Underwear = vest (4) intended = meant meant → ment (4) robe = vest-ment (8)
<u>Sounds like</u> a smoke backfires (5)	a smoke = cigar cigar → segar (5) segar <u>back</u> → rages fires = rages

This is a clever clue, involving SOUNDS LIKE and BACKWARD ANSWERS.

Help with correcting <u>sound</u> script (11)	Help = hand (4) correcting = righting righting → writing (7) script = hand-writing (11)
<u>Sounds like</u> a pesky worker won't do shift (7)	a pesky = a damn a damn → a-dam (4) worker = ant (3) won't do shift = a-dam-ant (7)
<u>Sound</u> ring for a young bird (6)	ring = signet signet → cygnet (6) young bird [swan] = cygnet

You should have found SOUNDS LIKE clues are generally easily solved.

LOGICAL ANSWERS

"Above all, resolution of a cryptic crossword clue is a process of logic." This quote from my preface can best be illustrated by the following examples.

EXAMPLES

Smooth, top journalist with common sense (5–6)

1. Smooth = level (5)
2. top = head (4)
3. journalist = ed (2)
4. with common sense
   = level-head-ed (11)

The answer comes from WORDS TO WORDS and WORDS TO LETTERS and a pure logical approach to the wording of the clue. The same applies to the next two clues.

Affected a refusal to record winning position as a ringer (13)

1. Affected = camp (4)
2. a refusal = a no (3)
3. record = log (3)
4. winning position = ist (3)
5. camp-a no-log-ist (13)
   = [bell] ringer

Smart, fashionable count and single man (11)

1. fashionable = in (2)
2. count = tell (4)
3. single = i (1)
4. man = gent (4)
5. in-tell-i-gent (11) = smart

With the next clue we use WORDS TO WORDS and WORDS TO LETTERS, but we logically create an INSERT as well.

Having got back managed to get round people to make a change (13)

1. back = rear (4)
2. managed = ran (3)
3. people = men (3)
4. get (3) round men = ge(men)t
5. rear-ran-gement = change

Again we use our logic and WORDS TO LETTERS and WORDS TO WORDS, but with an ANAGRAM thrown in for good measure!

Person of religion given the ring as a bribe — this is wrong! (11)

1. the ring = the o (4)
2. bribe = sop (3)
3. this → hist (4)
4. the o-sop-hist (11)
   = person of religion

44

Author uninspiring when <u>rewriting</u> rest of verses (11)

1. Author = pen (3)
2. uninspiring = tame (4)
3. rest → ters
4. pen-tame-ters (11) = verses

Marks made in spheres of sophistication (11)

1. Marks = lines (5)
2. spheres = worlds (6)
3. lines <u>made in</u> worlds = world(lines)s (11)
4. = sophistication

News of Tom, perhaps, and I, being in agreement (13)

1. Tom and I = cat+i (4)
2. agreement = communion (9)
3. cat + i <u>being in</u> agreement = communi(cati)on (13)
4. = news

Compilers are devious people, so you would be forgiven if your first approach to this clue was to look for an ANAGRAM of **News of Tom and I** (13) [taking <u>perhaps</u> as your indicator] to mean **agreement**.

However, the **perhaps** has not been applied to the whole phrase, which it should be if an anagram was intended. In fact, it refers only to **Tom** which points us to **cat** in WORDS TO WORDS.

Harness part of market in stormy weather (10)

1. market = mart (4)
2. in stormy weather = in gale
3. mart-in gale = Harness part

We get both **mart** and **gale** from WORDS TO WORDS and insert **in** between them as shown in the clue.

You may have first looked at a synonym of **market** to put **in** a synonym of **stormy weather.** This was my initial thought as well, so logic does offer a number of options!

One underweight hen discovers it's gradually disappearing (5,5)

1. weight = oz [ounce] (2)
2. one (3) <u>underweight</u> = oz-one
3. hen = layer (5)
4. it's gradually disappearing = ozone layer (10)

Plan withdrawn due to what çat did (7)

1. Plan = aim (3)
2. Plan <u>withdrawn</u> = mia
3. due to = owed (4)
4. mia-owed (7) = what cat did

Crooned a tune in return for a drink in Spain (7)

1. Crooned = sang (4)
2. tune = air (3)
3. tune <u>in return</u> = ria
4. sang-ria (7) = drink

Discreetly work round rude book (9)

1. work = ply (3)
2. rude book = rude nt (6)
3. work <u>round</u> rude nt
   = p(rude-nt)ly (9)
4. = Discreetly

Mark left a model in a fever (10)

1. Mark = scar (4)
2. left a = l a (2)
3. model in a = t in a (4)
4. = scar-l a-t-in-a (10)
5. scarlatina = fever

A day in France not available to catalogue writer (10)

1. A day in France = jour (4)
2. not available = na (2)
3. catalogue = list (4)
4. jour-na-list (10) = writer

Drink agent consumes cold drink (7)

1. agent = spy (3)
2. cold = c (1)
3. drink = rum (3)
4. agent <u>consumes</u> c rum
   = s(c-rum)py (7) = Drink

We back the majority being farthest to the left (11)

1. We (2)
2. back = stern (5)
3. the majority = most (4)
4. we-stern-most (11)
   = farthest to the left

Security pass the Parisian <u>replaced</u> later (10)

1. pass = col (3)
2. the Parisian = la (2)
3. later → teral (5)
4. col-la-teral (11) = security

That is not Kylie in view of the window (8)

1. view = sight (5)
2. That is = ie
3. That is <u>not</u> Kylie = kyl (3)
4. kyl <u>in</u> view = s(kyl)ight (8)
5. skylight = window

Listen to a row that's more robust (8)

1. Listen to = hear (4)
2. row = tier (4)
3. hear-tier (8) = more robust

You're forgiven if you took <u>Listen to</u> as a SOUNDS LIKE indicator!

Even if in a lake throws no lines (8)

1. a lake = a lough (6)
2. lines = rows
3. <u>throws no</u> lines = th (2)
4. <u>in a lake</u> / th
   = a l(th)ough (8) = even if

Notice the sequence of the wording of the insertion. This is the compiler's lateral thinking to the fore and you need to beware that clue wording is not always straightforward. You have to think of the clue in component parts and not just in serial order. There will be further such examples, indicated by the / mark in the explanations.

Now that you have the idea with LOGICAL ANSWERS the following further examples should help cement your lateral thinking.

Scottish one got back round by fiddling (6)

1. Scottish one = yin (3)
2. got back = tog (3)
3. Scottish one / tog round
   = to(yin)g (6) = fiddling

Vulgar chat when woman drops round without guard (8)

1. Vulgar chat (4) → atch
2. round = o
3. woman drops round = wman (4)
4. atch / wman / without
   = w(atch)man (8) = guard

Here we have a clue with three lots of component parts and where **without** means **on the outside of.**

Remarkable occurrences every year include bird writing on the wall (9)

1. every year = p a (2)
2. bird = hen (3)
3. writing on the wall = omen
4. p a include hen omen
   = p(hen-omen)a (9)
5. = Remarkable occurrences

Point to artist among friends on the bench (11)

1. Point = gist (4)
2. artist = ra (2)
3. friends = mates (5)
4. gist to ra among mates
   = ma(gist-ra)tes (11)
5. = on the bench

Batting, inform a chap, Bright (11)

1. Batting = in (2)
2. inform = tell (4)
3. a chap = i gent (5)
4. in-tell-i gent (11) = Bright

Carrying on when pair of monsters give voice (11)

1. pair = pr (2)
2. monsters = ogres (5)
3. give voice = sing (4)
4. pr-ogres-sing (11) = Carrying on

Small moan by Edward, lacking judgement (5–7)

1. Small = short (5)
2. moan = sigh (4)
3. Edward = ted (3)
4. short-sigh-ted (12)
   = lacking judgement

Vulgar show featuring English apprentice (10)	1. show = indicate (8) 2. English apprentice = e l (2) 3. ind(e l)icate (10) = vulgar

| Choose right, and one urban couple will make current charge (11,4) | 1. Choose right = elect r (6)
2. one urban = i city (5)
3. couple = bi (2)
4. will = 'll (2)
5. = elect r-i city-bi'll (15)
    = current charge |

| Am upset and unhappy about the flag's position (8) | 1. Am upset = ma (2)
2. unhappy = sad (3)
3. sad about the (3) = s(the)ad
4. = ma-s-the-ad (8)
    = the flag's position |

| Quiet inhabitant needs one friend acting as head of state (14) | 1. Quiet = p (1)
2. inhabitant = resident (8)
3. one friend = i ally (5)
4. = p-resident-i ally (14)
    = acting as head of state |

| In finishing hunter is excited —it's a tight race (5–3,5) | 1. finishing = closing (7)
2. hunter (6) → erunth
3. erunth in closing
    = clos(e-run th)ing (13)
4. = a tight race |

| Short old Indian wears everything for bow to audience (7,4) | 1. Short = curt (4)
2. old Indian = inca (4)
3. everything = all (3)
4. inca wears all = a(inca)ll
5. = curt-a(in-ca)ll (11)
    = bow to audience |

| Theft of gown with black lining on track (7) | 1. gown = robe (4)
2. black = b (1)
3. robe with b lining = ro(b)be
4. track = ry (2)
5. Theft = ro(b)bery (7) |

Just when you thought it was safe . . . I have to say that applying logic can occasionally lead to two perfectly correct answers to the same clue:

| Companion of an American star (6) | 1. Companion [knight] = sir (3)
2. an = i (1)
3. American = us (2)
4. sir-i-us (6) = star |

Companion of an American star (6)

Stripe (6) [stars and stripes]

Obviously, the letters which other clues have placed in this target word will get you to the right answer in a particular instance.

Legal obstruction for one vehicle entering turning lane (10)

1. one vehicle = i bus (4)
2. turning lane = filter (6)
3. i bus entering filter
   = fil(i bus)ter (10)
4. = Legal obstruction

Anger has broken out in the company (9)

1. Anger = enrage (6)
2. broken out (3) = tou
3. enrage has tou in
   = en(tou)rage (9) = company

It produces strong scent and is a necessity outside (7)

1. a necessity = a need (5)
2. is (2) / a need outside
3. a n(is)eed (7)
   = it produces strong scent

Exercise resulting in castle seizure (4,3)

1. castle = keep (4)
2. seizure = fit (3)
3. Exercise = keep fit

No harm in having the sense to carry copper ring (9)

1. sense = nous (4)
2. in having nous = in-nous (6)
3. copper ring = cu o (3)
4. innous to carry cuo
   = inno(cuo)us (9) = no harm

Sailors fish, catch last of salmon, and do a bunk (7)

1. Sailors = abs (3)
2. fish = cod (3)
3. cod / catch last of salmon
   = co(n)d (4)
4. do a bunk = abs-co(n)d (7)

Just delivered first uniform (4–6)

1. delivered = handed (6)
2. uniform = even (4)
3. handed / first even
   = even handed (10)
4. Just = even-handed

Notice vehicle will join together with forward movement (11)

1. Notice = ad (2)
2. vehicle = van (3)
3. join together = cement (6)
4. forward movement
   = ad-van-cement (11)

Scholar has object to fit diving gear (7–4)

1. Scholar = ba (2)
2. object = thing (5)
3. fit = suit (4)
4. diving gear = ba-thing-suit

So far so good. Now we'll take a different look at LOGICAL ANSWERS.

LOGIC often involves how a clue is read. Other letters in the target solution will help in arriving at the answer, but we need to think through the wording options before, perhaps, chasing a red herring.

EXAMPLES

Do without women (4,5)

If the emphasis is placed on <u>Do without</u> women we will start to look for a different answer, say **stay unwed**, than if the emphasis is on <u>Do</u> without women, say **stag party**.

Not a single female will wear it (9)

Again, we can read this as <u>Not a single female</u> and go chasing after something that only men will wear, say **dungarees**. Or we can read it as <u>not a single</u> female, as in an unmarried female, and get the answer, say **trousseau**.

A great man in history (9)

We would have lots of possibilities if we focus on <u>A great man</u>, say **Churchill**. If however we home in on <u>great</u> as the key word, we'll more likely get to **Alexander** [the Great].

In bid to stop one doing wrong (8)

If our emphasis is placed on <u>In bid to stop one</u> leading to a probable past participle answer meaning <u>doing wrong</u>, we will be after a red herring. The logic of this clue is rather:

In bid to stop <u>one doing wrong</u> (8)

1. bid = offer (5)
2. to stop = end (3)
3. <u>In bid</u> / to stop
   = off-end-er (8)
4. one doing wrong = offender

Without leaving, will try entering measure consumed (9)

Where the comma is placed in the clue will tend to start us looking for an answer from the second part of the clue which means <u>Without leaving</u>. However, if we ignore the punctuation we get a very different target to aim for:

<u>Without leaving will</u> try entering measure consumed (9)

1. measure = in [inch] (2)
2. consumed = ate (3)
3. try = test (4)
4. test <u>entering</u> in ate
5. = in-test-ate (9)
   = Without leaving will

Write first section of book: no time to act as escort (9)

<u>Write</u> is our red herring here, probably causing us to look for an answer involving **pen**. In fact, we are being encouraged to write <u>first section of book</u> = **chapter one**. No **time = t** reduces this to **chap er one** (9) which gives us **act as escort**.

Tropic island having business with sailors (9)

An emphasis in this clue on <u>Tropic island</u> will take us off at a tangent. We need here to focus on <u>Tropic</u> only:

Tropic island having business with sailors (9)

1. island = Capri (5)
2. business = co (2)
3. sailors = rn (2)
4. Tropic = Capri-co-rn (9)

Tasteful additions in shanties round (10)

There are two traps here. Firstly, the clue appears to indicate an ANAGRAM of **in shanties** (10) with **round** as our indicator and a target word meaning **Tasteful additions**. Secondly, even if we give up in despair at what the ANAGRAM holds and start trying to put a synonym of **shanties** <u>round</u> **in**, we're still likely to look in the wrong direction.

Here, in fact, we're not after another word for **huts, cabins**, etc. but rather for **shanties** as in **sea songs**. We then arrive at **sea son-in-g** as our answer.

Paper hat for a dunce (8)

If our emphasis is on <u>Paper hat</u> we'll have a merry chase after a name for a **dunce's hat** made of **paper**. With our focus, however, on <u>Paper</u> only we may well arrive at **fool's cap** for **dunce's hat**. Written another way, **foolscap**, we get a size of writing paper.

Put down in the correct order (5)   = preen! (5)

Here you may well start looking for a synonym of **Put down** in an anagram of **order**. The clue is much cleverer than that and the connection we need is one of **down** as in **feathers**. To put feathers **in the correct order** is to **preen**.

_____

This completes our look at the techniques used by the compilers of cryptic crosswords. Hopefully, working through the various examples given will have lifted some of the mystique involved and allayed your fears of tackling this great pastime for yourself.

SECTION 2
GLOSSARY

WORDS TO LETTERS

In this section we look at words commonly used by compilers which actually indicate letters to go into the resolution of clues. This list has been compiled from my own experience and is not exhaustive, nor is it meant to replace a proper dictionary. The alternative meanings given here are letters that go into the **make-up** of our answers, rather than answers by themselves. This section should be one of your two starting points (the other being WORDS TO WORDS) and you should add your own words and their equivalent letters as you find them while solving your favourite puzzles.

When you come across the clue words on the left below, look to the adjacent letters on the right to go into your answers. Often there will be more than one possible answer as different compilers use their own connotations.

Where there is an overlap with WORDS TO WORDS, the words are also included on the right below, but in round brackets. Square brackets give an explanation, where appropriate.

A

a, an	=	i [Roman], (one)
able-bodied seaman	=	ab
aboard	=	s . . . s [in steamship], (on)
about	=	c, ca [circa], re, (anent, apropos, around, circa, on, over, round)
abridged	=	abr, (cut)
absent	=	abs, awol [absent without leave], ia [in absentia], (away, gone, off, out, truant)
absolute	=	abs, (entire, pure, sheer, total, utter)
abstainer	=	aa [alcoholics anonymous], tt [teetotaller]
academy	=	a
acceptable	=	ok, (adequate, fair, fine, welcome)
account	=	ac, acc, (bill, invoice, record, relation, story, tab, tale)
accountant	=	ac, ca [chief accountant]
acre	=	a
acreage	=	a (farm, land, ranch)
acting	=	a, (temporary)
additional thought	=	ps [postscript]
address system	=	pa [public address], (tannoy)
adult	=	a
adverb(ial)	=	adv
advert(isement)	=	advt, (ad, bill, blurb, copy, plug, poster)
a follower	=	b [ABC]
afternoon	=	aft, pm
afterthought	=	ps [postscript]
again	=	re, (also, anew, over)
against	=	v [versus], (anti, con, versus)
agreed	=	ok, (ay, yes)

55

aide	= adc [aide-de-camp], (adjutant, assistant, helper)
air corps	= raf [Royal Air Force]
aircraftman	= ac
(leading) aircraftman	= lac
air force	= af, raf [Royal Air Force]
(British) airmen	= raf [Royal Air Force]
Alcoholics Anonymous	= aa
alien	= et [ET], (foreign(er), outsider, strange(r))
all right	= ok, (fair, safe)
alphabet	= az [A to Z]
also known as	= aka, (alias)
aluminium	= al [element]
alumnus	= ob [old boy]
amateur	= a, l, learner [see], (layman)
ambassador	= he [His Excellency], (consul, diplomat, envoy, legate, nuncio)
America(n)	= a, am, us, usa [United States], (yank, yankee)
American city	= la [Los Angeles]
amount	= amt, (bulk, lot, mass, sum, total, whole)
and so on	= etc [et cetera]
Anglican	= ce [Church of England]
Anglo-French	= af
anonymous	= a, anon, (nameless, unnamed)
another	= ano [A N Other]
another name	= aka [also known as], (alias, nickname, pseudonym, sobriquet)
answer	= a, (fill, key, meet, reply, retort, riposte, solution)
anti-aircraft	= aa
antiballistic missile	= abm
any other business	= aob
apartment	= apt, (flat, pad, room, suite, tenement)
apostrophe	= o
appeal	= o, (allure, ask, beg, charm, implore, plead, pray, request)
(sex) appeal	= sa, (it, oomph)
appendix	= ps [postscript], (addendum, codicil, rider)
(not) applicable	= na
appreciation	= ta, (esteem, gain, praise, thanks, tribute)
apprentice	= l, learner [see]
approval, approving	= ok, (ay, yes)
apropos of	= re, (about, anent, on, over)
archbishop	= abp, arch
archdeacon	= ven [Venerable]
are unable	= cant [can't]
army	= ta [Territorial Army], (crowd, force, horde, host, legion, militia)
(Dad's) Army	= hg [Home Guard], ta [Territorial Army]
(Salvation) Army	= sa

arrival time	=	eta [estimated time of arrival]
artist	=	ra [Royal Academy of Arts], (drawer, painter, sculptor; name of [see])
asian	=	e [eastern], (asiatic, eastern, indian)
(sound) asleep	=	z, zz
assistant	=	pa, (aide, batman, deputy, factotum, helper)
assumed name	=	aka [also known as], (alias, nickname, pseudonym, sobriquet)
attorney	=	da [District Attorney], (lawyer [see])
attorney-general	=	ag
audio frequency	=	af
Australian territory	=	act [Australian Capital Territory]
automobile association	=	aa, rac [Royal Automobile Club]
(not) available	=	na
award	=	mbe, obe [Member, Order of British Empire], om [Order of Merit], (adjudge, gong, grant, medal, oscar, prize, trophy)

B

bachelor	=	b, ba, barch, bcom, bd, bed, beng, bsc [Bachelor of Arts, Architecture, Commerce, Divinity, Education, Engineering, Science]
balance	=	bal, (equilibrium, poise, remainder, rest, scale(s), weigh)
ball	=	o, (dance, globe, hop, orb, sphere)
barium	=	ba [element]
battalion	=	bat, bn
bearing	=	e, n, ne, nw, s, se, sw, w, (air, aspect, birth, carriage, gait, manner, mien, port, pose, posture)
before	=	a [ante], (afore, ahead, ante, ere, pre, prior)
before Christ	=	bc
beginner	=	l, learner [see]
bend	=	s, u, (arc, bias, bow, curve, flex, helix, incline, ogee, turn, yield)
beryllium	=	be [element]
betting odds	=	sp [Starting Price]
bible	=	b, bib, nt, ot [New, Old Testament]
(very) big	=	os [outsize], (colossal, gigantic, huge, jumbo, titanic)
Big Apple	=	ny [New York]
bigwig	=	vip [very important person], (nabob, nob, pot)
bill	=	ac [account], be [bill of entry, exchange], (account, beak, invoice, neb, nib, note, poster, tab)
bisexual	=	acdc [AC/DC], bi
bishop	=	b [chess], rr [Right Reverend]
bismuth	=	bi [element]
black	=	b, (dark, ebony, jet, night, sable)

blood type	= a, ab, a, o
(winning) blow	= ko [knockout]
board	= bb [bed & breakfast], (dash, embark, lodge, panel, plank, slat, table, wood [see])
(on) board	= s . . . s [in steamship]
boat	= ss [steamship], (ship, vessel; name of [see])
(old) Bob	= s [shilling]
(international) body	= un [United Nations]
bone	= t, (steal; name of [see])
book	= b, nt, ot [New, Old Testament], (ledger, novel, order, reserve, tome)
(good) book	= nt, ot [New, Old Testament], (bible)
born	= b, (nee)
(in) both hands	= l . . . r, r . . . l [in left and right, right and left]
bowled	= b [cricket], (out)
boxing body	= aba [Amateur Boxing Association]
bridge partners	= ew, ns [east-west, north-south]
bridge player	= e, n, s, w [east, north, south, west]
British	= b, br, bri, brit
British airmen	= raf [Royal Air Force]
British detectives	= cid [Criminal Investigation Dept], (yard)
(outside) broadcast	= ob
brother	= br, (brer, cleric, comrade, friar, monk)
brought forward	= bf [accounting]
business	= co [company], (company, concern, firm)
bye	= b [cricket]

C

calcium	= ca [element]
calendar	= cal, (almanac, list, menology, register, schedule, table; name of [see])
California	= ca, cal [US State]
Californian city	= la [Los Angeles]
Canada, Canadian	= can
cannot	= cant [can't]
(measure of) capacity	= cc, gal, l, pt, qu, (bushel, gallon, gill, litre, noggin, peck, pint, quart, quarter)
capital	= cap, (cash, chief, fine, head, letter, main, money, prime, stock; name of city [see])
car	= gt, mg, rr, vw, (coach, coupe, estate, limo, limousine, motor, saloon, sedan; name of [see])
car club	= aa, rac [Automobile Association, Royal Automobile Club]
car firm	= bl [British Leyland]
car test	= mot [Ministry of Transport]
carat	= c, car, ct
carbon	= c [element]
carbon copy	= cc
care of	= co

cash on delivery	= cod
catalogue	= cat, (file, index, inventory, list, roll, roster)
catapult	= cat, (launch, sling)
catholic	= rc [Roman Catholic], (general, jesuit, papist, universal)
caught	= c, ct [cricket], (out)
cavity	= o, (hole, hollow, sinus)
cent	= c
centimetre	= cm
central heating	= ch
century	= c, (ton)
(double) century	= cc
Channel Islands	= ci
chapter	= c, cap [caput], ch, (branch)
chapters	= cc
(in) charge	= ic
childless	= sp [sine prole = without issue]
church	= c, ce [Church of England], ch, ec [Established Church], rc [Roman Catholic], (basilica, cathedral, chapel, kirk, minster)
circa	= c, ca, (about, around, round)
circle	= o, (clique, coterie, disc, halo, ring, round, set)
circles	= oo
circular	= o, (notice, round)
citizens' band	= cb
city	= la, (municipal, urban; name of [see])
(American, US) city	= la [Los Angeles]
Civil Defence	= cd
classy	= u [upper]
clear-air turbulence	= cat
clergy(man)	= dd [Doctor of Divinity], rev [Reverend], (name of [see])
(car) club	= aa, rac
(cricket) club	= cc
(football) club	= fc
cold	= c, (algid, chill, cool, frigid, icy, nip)
colonel	= co [commanding officer], col
commander	= cbe [Commander of British Empire], cdr
Common Market	= ec [European Community]
companion	= cb, ch [Companion of the Bath, Honour], (buddy, crony, mate, pal, sir [Knight])
company	= co, (business, concern, crew, firm, group, set)
compare	= cf [confer], cp
compass point	= e, n, s, w, (rhumb)
compere	= mc [master of ceremonies], (host)
concerned with	= re, (about, anent, apropos, on, over)
concerning	= re, (about, anent, apropos, on, over)
condition	= asis [as is], (case, rider, rule, shape, state)
(in) connection with	= re, (about, anent, apropos, on, over)

consent	= ok, (accede, agree, leave, permit, yes)
conservationist(s)	= nt [National Trust]
Conservative	= c, con, (blue, right, tory)
consumption	= tb [tuberculosis], (use)
copper	= cu [element], d [old penny], p [penny]
(old) copper	= d, (denarius)
coppers	= cid, p [pence]
cops	= cid [Criminal Investigation Department]
copyright	= c
corner	= l, ne, nw, se, sw, (angle, bend, crook, niche, nook)
Cornwall	= sw [south west England]
(air) corps	= raf [Royal Air Force]
(county) council	= cc
country	= uk [United Kingdom], (land, nation, rural, state; name of [see])
county	= co, (shire; name of [see])
county council	= cc
(home) counties	= se [south east England]
couple	= pr [pair], (articulate, both, brace, duo, hitch, join, pair, span, twain, two(some), wed)
court	= ct, (date, woo)
craft	= ss [steamship], (art, guile, knack, skill, trade; name of [see])
credit	= cr, (belief, believe, loan, tick, trust)
credit note	= cn, iou [I owe you]
credit notes	= ious
creed	= ism, (belief, canon, dogma, tenet)
cricket club	= cc
cricket opponents	= wi [West Indies]
cross	= x, (angry, crucifix, hybrid, irate, kiss, mad, mongrel, thwart, trial, vexed; name of [see])
crusade	= me [military expedition], (cause, expedition, war)
cup	= a, b, c, d, dd, (beaker, bleed, chalice, drink, fate, trophy)
currency	= c, dr, ecu, fr, l, mk, p, sh, (bill, note; name of money [see])
current	= ac, dc, [alternating, direct current], (amp(ere)s, flow, electricity, river, tide)
(measure of) current	= v, w, (amp, volt, watt)
current month	= inst [instant]

D

Dad's Army	= hg [Home Guard], ta [Territorial Army]
daily	= ft [Financial Times], (char, cleaner, maid, (news)paper; name of [see])
daughter	= d

day	= d, name of [fri, mon, sat, sun, wed; etc.]
(half a) day	= am, pm
(present) day	= ad [anno domini], (anniversary, birthday, christmas, now, xmas)
(these, this) day(s)	= ad [anno domini]
dealing with	= re, (about, anent, apropos, on, over)
dear departed	= rip [rest in peace], (dead, late)
debt	= iou, (bill, due, hock, red, score)
debts	= ious
(in) debt	= r . . . ed [in the red], (owed, owes)
deceased	= rip [rest in peace], (dead, late)
decoration	= mbe, obe [Member, Order of British Empire], om [Order of Merit], (award, badge, gong, medal)
Democrat	= d
detective	= cid, di [detective inspector], pi [private investigator], (cop, ferret, shamus, spotter, tracer)
(British) detectives	= cid [Criminal Investigation Department], (yard)
detective sergeant	= ds
dial	= o, (face, ring)
dictionary	= oed [Oxford English Dictionary], (glossary, lexicon)
died	= d
diplomats	= cd [corps diplomatique], (mission)
direction	= e, n, s, w, (angle, slant, trend)
disc	= ep, lp, o, (record)
disciple	= l, (learner [see])
district attorney	= da
ditto	= do, (copy, duplicate, same)
divine	= dd [Doctor of Divinity], (clergy [see], guess, holy, hot, sacred, see, swell)
doctor	= doc, dr, gp [general practitioner], mb, md [Bachelor, Doctor of Medicine], mo [Medical Officer], (alter, fix, mend, rig, spike, treat; name of [see])
document	= ms [manuscript], (cite, deed, file, paper, record)
double	= di, (clone, dual, fold, image, run, twice, twin, two(fold))
double century	= cc
doughboy	= gi [general infantryman]
draw	= x, (attract, depict, describe, lure, paint, pull, sketch, stalemate, suck, tie, tow, trace)
drill	= pe, pt [physical education, training], (bore, exercise, furrow, practice, row, train)
(not) drinking	= aa [alcoholics anonymous], tt [teetotal], (dry, sober)
(new) driver	= l [learner]
dry	= aa, tt, (arid, barren, droll, sec)

duck	=	o, (bob, bow, nil, nothing, wet, zero; name of [see])
ducks	=	oo
dud	=	rd [refer to drawer]
duplicate keys	=	aa, bb, cc, dd, ee, ff, gg

E

each	=	ea, (apiece, every, per)
earth	=	e, (bury, clay, dirt, globe, ground, land, soil)
East(ern)	=	e, (orient(al))
East Indian, Indies	=	ei
east-north-east	=	ene
east-south-east	=	ese
editor	=	ed
egg	=	o, (goad, nit, spur, urge)
eggs	=	oo, (clutch, ova, roe)
Egypt, Egyptian	=	eg
electric current	=	ac, dc [alternating, direct current]
electricity	=	ac, dc, elec, (amp(ere)s, current, volts, watts)
electrocardiogram	=	ecg
electron	=	e
eleven	=	xi, (legs [bingo], side, team)
emergency	=	sos, (crisis, crunch, exigency)
emperor	=	emp, (king, ruler; name of [see])
enclosure	=	encl, (fence, pen, sty, wall, wrapper)
energy	=	e, (beans, brio, elan, erg, force, go, pep, power, vigour)
engineer(s)	=	re [Royal Engineers]
English	=	e, eng
(early) English	=	ee
epitaph	=	rip [rest in peace]
errors excepted	=	ee
Established Church	=	ec
estimated time of — arrival	=	eta
— departure	=	etd
et cetera	=	etc
European	=	eur, (name of [see])
even	=	een [e'en], (flat, just, level, plain, plumb, quits, smooth, stable, still, uniform, yet)
evening	=	een [e'en], evg, (dusk, sunset, twilight)
ever	=	eer [e'er], (always)
every body	=	u [universal], (all, each, lot)
everyone	=	u [universal], (all, each, lot)
everything	=	u [universal], (all, each, lot)
every year	=	pa [per annum], (annual)
(for) example	=	eg, (as, say)
excellent	=	ai, (banner, fine, great, prime, top)
exchange	=	lse, se [(London) Stock Exchange], (barter, bourse, repartee, swap, swop, switch, trade)

exclusive	= excl, (scoop, select, single, sole)
exercise	= pe, pt, (drill, lesson, practice, sport(s), stretch, study, use
(physical) exercise(s)	= pe, pt [physical education, training]
(military) expedition	= me, (crusade, incursion, invasion)
explosive	= he [high explosive], tnt, (amatol, dynamite, semtec)
ex-pupil	= ob [old boy], (alumnus)
external	= ext, (alien, exterior, out(er), outside)

F

factor	= rh [rhesus], (agent, deputy, element, item, steward)
Fahrenheit	= f
fashionable	= u, (in, chic, hip)
father	= fr, (abba, clergy [see], da, dad, pa, papa, pater, pop, sire)
feet	= f, ft
fellow	= f, fba [Fellow of British Academy], (chap, he, gent, guy, man, sport; name of [see])
(learned) fellow	= ba, ma [Bachelor, Master of Arts], (don, sage)
female	= f, fem, (dam, doe, girl [see])
field officer	= col [colonel], fo, (colonel, major)
fine	= f [pencil], ok, (amerce, capital, clear, fair, forfeit, good, mulct, narrow, nice, penalty, rare, slender)
finish	= fin, (cease, close, complete, die, end, halt, perfect, polish)
Finland, Finnish	= fin
fire hydrant	= fh
firm	= co [company], (business, company, concern, fast, fix(ed), hard, house, set, solid, sound, stable, staunch, steady, strict, tight)
first	= ist, noi [No 1], (alpha, initial, maiden, opening, premier, prime, top)
first-class, rate	= a, ai [A1], (capital, crack, excellent, prime)
fleet	= rn [Royal Navy], (armada, fast, quick, rapid, swift)
Florida	= fla
florin	= fl, fn
fluid	= fl, (flowing, liquid, mobile, pliable)
fluorine	= f [element]
flyers	= raf [Royal Air Force]
flying officer	= fo
folio	= f, fo
folios	= ff
(a) follower	= b [ABC]
following	= ff, (after, later, next, retinue, train)
foot	= f, ft, (base, bottom, pay, rear, step)

football club	= fc
footballers	= fa [Football Association]
footnote	= ps [postscript]
for	= pp [per pro], (as, pro)
for example, instance	= eg, (as, say)
force	= g [gravity], (army, coerse, constrain, dragoon, impetus, make, militia, posse, press, prise, thrust, vis)
foreign office	= fo, (bureau)
former pupil, student	= ob [old boy], (alumnus)
forte	= f, (loud, strong)
fortissimo	= ff
fourth class, rate	= d
free on board	= fob
French	= f, fr
Frenchman	= m [monsieur], (breton, gaul, norman; name of [see])
(audio) frequency	= af
further education	= fe

G

gallon	= g, gal
gazette	= gaz, (journal, (news)paper)
gender	= g, (sex; name of [common, feminine, masculine, natural, neuter])
general infantryman	= gi, (joe, serviceman, soldier)
general staff	= gs
George Cross	= gc
George Medal	= gm
gentle	= p [musical], (clement, kind, lenient, mild, soft, tender)
(very) gentle	= pp [musical]
Georgia	= ga [US State]
German(y)	= d [IVR], ger
Gestapo	= ss
Gibraltar	= gib
gilded	= o . . . r [in gold = or]
glamour	= sa [sex appeal], (allure, charm, it)
globe	= o, (ball, earth, orb, round, sphere)
G-man	= fed
God willing	= dv [deo volente]
gold	= au, or [element, French], (aurum)
gone off	= awol, (absent, away, out, sour)
gong	= bem, mc, mm, (award, medal)
(no) good	= nbg, ng [no (bloody) good], us [unserviceable], (useless)
good book	= nt, ot [New, Old Testament], (bible)
good man	= st [saint]
gospels	= nt [New Testament]

government	=	gov, govt, (oligarchy, province, ruling, state)
governor	=	gov, (beg, bey, dey, pasha, regent, satrap)
graduate	=	ba, ma, (bachelor, master, pass)
grand	=	g [1000 dollars]
grandmother	=	gran
Grand Old Man	=	gom
Grand Old Party	=	gop [Republican Party]
Grand Prix	=	gp
gran turismo	=	gt
gravity	=	g
great	=	gt, (big, fab, famous, fat, large, noted)
great dozens	=	ggr
Greece	=	gr [IVR]
Greek	=	gk, gr
group	=	gr, (batch, bevy, bloc, cluster, crowd, number, pack, sect, set, team; name of number [see])
guaranteed	=	gtd, guar
(Home) Guard	=	hg
guide	=	g, (direct, escort, lead, pilot, steer, usher; name of [see])
guinea(s)	=	g
gunmen, gunner(s)	=	ra [Royal Artillery], (artillery)
gymnastics	=	pe, pt [physical education, training]

H

haemoglobin	=	hb
half a day	=	am, pm
hand	=	l, r [left, right], (help, pass, paw, sailor [see])
hard	=	h [pencil], (adamant, brittle, difficult, firm, rigid, set, solid, stiff, tough)
(medium) hard	=	hb [pencil]
Hawaiian Islands	=	hi
head office	=	ho, (base)
headquarters	=	ho, hq, (base, depot)
(central) heating	=	ch
Hebrew	=	heb, (israelite, jew, semite; name of [see])
hectare	=	ha
he had	=	hed [he'd]
he has, is	=	hes [he's]
helium	=	he [element]
help	=	sos, (abet, aid, assist, back, hand, second)
Henry	=	h, (hal)
Her Majesty	=	er [Elizabeth Regina]
hesitation	=	er, um
he will	=	hell [he'll]
he would	=	hed [he'd]
high-class	=	a, ai [A1], u [upper]
high explosive	=	he
high frequency	=	hf

high tension	=	ht
hire purchase	=	hp
His Excellency	=	he
His Highness, Holiness	=	hh
hole	=	o, (aperture, cavity, eye, fix, gap, hovel, orifice, pit, scrape, vent, void)
Hollywood	=	la [Los Angeles]
holy man	=	st, (clergy [see], prophet, saint)
home counties	=	se [south east England]
Home Guard	=	hg
home improvements	=	diy [do-it-yourself]
honour	=	mbe, obe, om, (award, badge, glory, homage, kudos, pay, respect)
honourable	=	hon, (honest, just, noble, upright, worthy)
hoop	=	band, circle, ring, (o)
horse	=	gg, (bronco, charger, colt, filly, gelding, hack, hunter, jade, mare, mount, mule, mustang, nag, pony, ride, runner, steed, stud; name of [see])
horseshoe	=	u
hospital	=	h
host	=	mc [master of ceremonies], (army, entertainer, horde, lot, many, treat)
hot	=	h, (angry, ardent, fiery, keen, warm, torrid)
hotel	=	h, (hostel, inn, lodge, motel, tavern)
hour	=	h, hr
house	=	hc, hl [House of Commons, Lords], ho, (bungalow, chalet, firm, home, lodge, manor, semi, villa; name of [see])
hundred	=	c, (ton)
huge	=	os [outsize], (colossal, gigantic, jumbo, titanic)

I

I am	=	im [I'm]
idem	=	id, (same)
identity	=	id, ka, (name)
I had	=	id [I'd]
I have	=	ive [I've]
illustration	=	ill, (case, diagram, example, picture, sketch)
important person	=	vip, (bigwig, nabob, nob, pot)
(home) improvements	=	diy [do-it-yourself]
inactive	=	dido [did nothing], doo [do nothing]
inch	=	in, (crawl, creep, edge)
in charge	=	ic
including, inclusive	=	inc(l)
income	=	inc, (earnings, money, pay, revenue, salary, stipend, wage(s))
in connection with	=	re, (about, anent, apropos, on, over)
incorporated	=	inc

increase	=	inc, (add, boost, enlarge, extra, grow, more, rise, up, wax)
in debt	=	r . . . ed [in the red], (owed, owes)
indeed	=	de . . . ed [in deed]
indefinite number	=	n
independent	=	ind, (autonomous, free, separate, sovereign)
Indian	=	ind, (asian, brave, hindu; name of [see])
individual	=	i, (being, entity, one, single, special)
industry	=	ind, (effort, labour, trade, zeal)
infantryman	=	gi, (joe, serviceman, soldier)
inferior	=	b, inf, (less(er), lower, minor, under, worse)
info(rmation)	=	inf, (data, dope, facts, gen, news, word)
in other words	=	ie [that is]
insane	=	sa . . . ne [in sane], (crazy, daft, loco, mad, mental, nuts)
inscription	=	rip [Rest in Peace], (epitaph)
inside	=	si . . . de [in side], (in, inner)
instalment	=	hp [hire purchase]
(for) instance	=	eg, (as, say)
intelligence	=	mi [military intelligence], (acumen, brains, gen, news, nous, sense, wit)
interest	=	i, int, (bias, concern, engross, hobby, profit, return, share, stake)
international	=	i, int, (cap, global, test, universal, worldwide)
international body	=	un, uno [United Nations (Organisation)]
interval	=	int, (break, lull, pause, space)
in the manner of	=	ala [a la]
investigators	=	cid [Criminal Investigation Department]
iodine	=	i [element]
iron	=	fe [element], (club, press, smooth)
I see	=	ic [phonetic]
island	=	i, is, (ait, atoll, inch, isle; name of [see])
isle	=	i, iom, iow [Man, Wight], (ait,inch, man)
is not	=	aint [ain't], isnt [isn't]
is unable	=	cant [can't]
(without) issue	=	sp [sine prole], (childless)
Italian	=	i, it, (latin, roman)
Italian man	=	s, (signor)
I will	=	ill [I'll]
I would	=	id [I'd]

J

jack	=	j, (card, hoist, knave, lift, raise, sailor, seaman, salt, tar)
joe	=	gi [general infantryman], (sweetheart)
joint	=	jt, (cut, dive, hinge, knot, seam, shared; name of [see])
joint account	=	ja
journalist	=	ed, (editor, hack, scribe)

judge	=	ja, jag [Judge Advocate, General], (arbiter, assess, critic, expert, rate, reckon(er), ref(eree), settler, trier, try, umpire; name of [see])
junction	=	t, (angle, joint, seam, union)
(road) junction	=	t [T-junction]
junior	=	jnr, jr, jun, (lesser, lower, minor, subordinate, under, younger)
justice	=	jp [justice of the peace], (fairness, judge [see], law, right)
juvenile	=	juv, (boy, child, girl, immature, infant, minor, young, youth)
(bad) juvenile	=	jd [juvenile delinquent]

K

kangaroo	=	roo
keep quiet	=	sh
Kent	=	se [south east England]
Kenya	=	eak [IVR]
key	=	a, b, c, d, e, g, (basic, chief, main, ivory)
(duplicate) keys	=	aa, bb, cc, dd, ee, ff, gg
kick off	=	ko
kilo(gram)	=	k, kg
kilometre	=	km
kilovolt	=	kv
kilowatt	=	kw
king	=	hm [His Majesty], k, r [Rex], (emperor, monarch, rex, ruler)
(old) king	=	gr [George Rex], (name of [see])
King Charles	=	cr [Charles Rex]
King Edward	=	er [Edward Rex]
King George	=	gr [George Rex]
king's bishop	=	kb
king's pawn	=	kp
king's rook	=	kr
King William	=	wr [William Rex]
kiss	=	x, (buss, caress, neck, peck, smooch)
(two) kisses	=	xx, (double-cross)
knight	=	ch [Companion of Honour], k, kb [knight bachelor], kt, (banneret, paladin, sir)
knock out	=	ko, (kayo, stun)
knot	=	kn, (bend, bond, hitch, link, lump, maze, node, nodule, reef, tangle, tie, web; name of [see])
known	=	a, b [1st, 2nd known quantity], (felt, had, kent, seen)
(also) known as	=	aka, (alias)
krypton	=	kr [element]

L

labour	=	lab, (effort, grind, job, left, pains, sweat, toil, travail, work)
ladies	=	wi [Women's Institute]
(old) lady	=	oap [old aged pensioner], dam(osel), dutch, gran, ma, mother, wife
lake	=	l [geographic], (loch, lough, mere, pond, tarn, water; name of [see])
large	=	l [size], os [outsize], (big, bulky, fat, great, major)
(very) large	=	os [outsize], (colossal, gigantic, huge, jumbo, titanic)
large number	=	c, d, m [Roman numerals], (army, host, nation)
last month	=	dec [December], ult [ultimo]
Latin	=	l, lat
latitude	=	lat, (extent, play, range, room, scope, width)
lawyer	=	da [District Attorney], (advocate, attorney, barrister, counsel, solicitor)
(US) lawyer	=	da [District Attorney]
Lawrence	=	te [T E Lawrence]
lead	=	pb [element], (clue, conduct, flex, guide, head, pencil, top, van)
leading aircraftman	=	lac
learned fellow, man	=	ba, ma [Bachelor, Master of Arts], (don, sage)
learner	=	l, (amateur, apprentice, beginner, disciple, novice, pupil, scholar, starter, student, tiro, trainee)
left	=	l, (gone, labour, let, over, port, quit, sinistral, went)
(measure of) length	=	cm, f, ft, in, m, mm, yd, (chain, cubit, ell, feet, foot, furlong, inch, league, metre, mile, pole, yard)
(scripture) lesson	=	re, ri [Religious Education, Instruction]
letter of credit	=	lc
liberal	=	l, lib, (ample, broad, free, generous, handsome)
limited (company)	=	ltd, plc [public limited company]
line	=	br [British Railways], l, ry [railway], (file, lineage [see], queue, rank, rope, row, string, tier, track, wire, wrinkle)
lines	=	br, ll, ry, (ode, poem, verse)
lithium	=	li [element]
litre	=	l
little relation	=	bro [brother], sis [sister]
little time	=	min [minute], mo [moment], sec [second]
Livingstone	=	dr [Dr David], (ken)
local area network	=	lan
London (area)	=	se [south east England]
(part of) London	=	ec, sw, wc, wi [districts], (bow, soho)
loop	=	o, (circle, circuit, curve, ring, round)

Los Angeles	= la
loud	= f [musical], (forte, noisy, strident)
(very) loud	= ff [musical]
Louisiana	= la [US State]
love	= o, (adore, amour, nil, nought, zero)
low	= p [musical]
(very) low	= pp [musical]
low frequency	= lf
low tension	= lt

M

mackintosh	= mac(k), (raincoat)
madame	= mme
mademoiselle	= mlle
magnesium	= mg [element]
(Her) Majesty	= er [Elizabeth Regina]
male	= m, (cock, gent, man, ram, stag)
male chauvinist (pig)	= mcp
man	= iom [Isle of Man], (chap, fellow, gent, he, isle, male; name of [see])
manager	= mgr, (boss, head, runner)
manganese	= mn [element]
(in the) manner of	= ala [a la]
manoeuvre	= op, (dodge, ploy, ruse, trick, wangle)
manufacture	= mfg, mfr, (build, create, erect, forge, make)
manuscript	= ms, (article, book, paper)
Manx cat	= pus [puss without tail]
many	= c, d, m [Roman numeral], (host, lot(s))
marine	= rm [Royal Marine]
(Royal) marine(s)	= rm [Royal Marines]
mark	= mk, x, (line, note, scar, smear, spot, stain, standard, stroke, weal)
market	= ec, [European Community], (mart, sell)
(Common) Market	= ec, eec [European (Economic) Community]
married	= m, (wed)
master	= ma, mba, msc [Master of Arts, Business Administration, Science], (control, digest, grasp, lad, learn, sir, sire, teacher)
master of ceremonies	= mc, (compere, host)
maximum	= max, (greatest, highest, most, top, utmost)
measure of capacity	= cc, gal, l, pt, qu, (bushel, gallon, gill, litre, noggin, peck, pint, quart, quarter)
measure of current	= v, w, (amp, volt, watt)
measure of length	= cm, f, ft, in, m, mm, yd, (chain, cubit, ell, feet, foot, furlong, inch, league, metre, mile, pole, yard)
measure of weight	= cwt, g, lb, oz, t, (drachm, dram, grain, gram, ounce, pound, quarter, quintal, scruple, stone, ton, tonne)

medal	= bem, gm, mm [British Empire, George, Military Medal], (award, badge, decoration, gong)
media	= tv [television], (means, press, radio)
medic(o)	= doc, dr, mo [medical officer], (doctor)
medium	= m [size], (average, fair, mean, organ, psychic, vehicle)
medium wave	= mw
meeting	= agm, (event, match, meet, rally, tryst)
megawatt	= mw
member	= m, mep, mp [Member of (European) Parliament], (arm, hand, leg, limb, man)
mentality	= iq [intelligence quotient], (mind, wit)
merchant navy, ships	= mn
mercury	= hg [element]
messieurs	= mm
metre	= m
Mexican, Mexico	= mex
Middle East(ern)	= me
Middle English	= me
middle-of-the-road	= mor, (moderate)
mile	= mi
military	= re [Royal Engineers]
Military Cross	= mm
military expedition	= me, (crusade, incursion, invasion)
military intelligence	= mi
Military Medal	= mm
millilitre	= ml
millimetre	= mm
million	= m
minimal, minimum	= min, (base, least, lowest, smallest)
minister	= dd, rev, (clergy [see])
ministry	= fo [Foreign Office], (service)
minute	= m, min, mo [moment], (exact, fine, little, small, tiny)
missile	= abm [antiballistic], sam [surface-to-air], (arrow, bolt, dart, javelin, rocket, weapon; name of [see])
model	= t [Model T Ford], (ideal, pose(r), sit(ter))
modern time(s)	= ad [anno domini], (now, present)
moment	= m, mo, sec, (flash, import(ance), instant, second, shake, tick, trice, weight, worth)
monarch	= k [King], r [Rex], (king, rex, ruler)
(old) monarch	= gr [George Rex], (name of [see])
money	= ecu [European Currency Unit], l [pound], (brass, bread, capital, cash, coin, currency, dough, income, lucre, note(s), proceeds, purse, tin, wealth)
money order	= mo, (cheque, draft)
monsieur	= m

month	= m, mo, name of [apr, aug, dec, feb, jan, jul, jun, mar, may, nov, oct, sep]
(current) month	= inst [instant]
(last) month	= dec [December], ult [ultimo]
(next) month	= prox [proximo]
(this) month	= inst [instant]
months	= mos, (moons)
moon	= o, (month, mope, satellite; name of [see])
morning	= am, (dawn, daybreak, sunrise)
motor car	= gt, mg, rr, vw, (coupe, estate, limo(ousine), saloon, sedan; name of car [see])
motoring organisation	= aa, rac [Automobile Association, Royal Automobile Club]
motor vessel	= mv
motorway	= m, mi [M1], (road)
mount(ain)	= mt, (alp, ben, fell, tor)
mum	= sh [quiet]
musical note	= a, b, c, d, e, f, g; (do(h), ray, re, me, mi, fa(h), so(h), la(h), te, ti; breve, flat, minim, music, natural, pitch, sharp, tone)
musical work	= op, (opus)

N

name	= n, (dub, call, label, term, title)
(another, assumed) name	= aka [also known as], (alias, nickname, pseudonym, sobriquet)
national	= nat, natl, (citizen, civic, civil, public, subject)
native	= nat, (aboriginal, endemic, home, inborn, innate, local, oyster)
natural	= nat, (artless, common, frank, inborn, innate, native, normal, usual)
naught	= o
navy	= mn, rn [Merchant, Royal Navy], (armada, fleet)
near	= nr, (akin, approach, by, close, handy, mean, miserly, nigh, stingy, tight)
neckline	= v
network	= lan [PC], (grid, grill, maze, mesh, web)
Newcastle (area)	= ne [north east England]
new driver	= l [learner]
new paragraph	= np
news(paper) man	= ed [editor]
New Testament	= nt
New York	= ny
next month	= prox [proximo]
nickel	= ni [element]
nil	= o, (love, nothing, nought, zero)
nitrogen	= n [element]
no good	= nbg, ng [no (bloody) good], us [unserviceable], (useless)

noncommissioned officer	=	nco
no date	=	nd
no one	=	noi [no 1]
noon	=	n
north(ern)	=	n
North America	=	na
north-east	=	ne
Northern Ireland	=	ni
north-west	=	nw
not applicable	=	na
not available	=	na
(musical) note	=	a, b, c, d, e, f, g; (do(h), ray, re, me, mi, fa(h), so(h), la(h), te, ti; breve, flat, minim, music, natural, pitch, sharp, tone)
note well	=	nb [nota bene]
nothing	=	o, (duck, free, love, nil, nix, nought, nowt, trifle)
notice	=	ad, (banns, observe, poster, review, sack, see, sign)
not out	=	no [cricket]
not permitted	=	nl [non licet]
novice	=	l, (learner [see])
now	=	ad [anno domini], (present)
number	=	no, (digit, ether, figure, integer, some; name of [see])
(indefinite) number	=	n
(large) number	=	c, d, m [Roman numerals], (army, host, nation)
(small) number	=	no, (few)
numbers	=	nos
nun	=	sh [sisterhood], (abbess, novice, prioress, sister)

O

observatory	=	obs
obsolete	=	obs, (archaic, bygone, dated, dead, ex, old, out, passe)
occupation	=	occ, (business, career, job, line, work)
ocean	=	o, oc, (deep, main, sea, water)
(betting) odds	=	sp [Starting Price]
(foreign) office	=	fo, (bureau)
(head) office	=	ho, (base)
(post) office	=	po
officer	=	co, nco, oc, od [commanding, noncommissioned officer, officer commanding, officer of the day], (capt(ain), col(onel), ensign, gen(eral), maj(or), ranker; name of [see])
(police) officers	=	cid, (yard)
okay	=	ok, (agree, approve, endorse, pass, ratify)
old	=	o, (aged, ex, past, senile, stale)
(very) old	=	vo, (aged, ancient, antique, elderly)

old boy	=	ob [old boy], (alumnus, man)
Old English	=	oe
old lady	=	oap [old aged pensioner], dam(osel), dutch, gran, ma, mother, wife
old man	=	oap [old aged pensioner], (codger, father, geezer, husband, pa)
Old Testament	=	ot
on board	=	s . . . s [in steamship]
on demand	=	od
one	=	i, (a, ace, an, any, single, some, unit)
only	=	o, (barely, but, just, simply, sole)
Open University	=	ou
operation	=	op, (action, exercise, play, surgery, use)
opposing	=	v [versus], (against, enemy, rival, versus)
opposite	=	opp, (adverse, antonym, contrary, converse, diverse, facing, inverse, reverse)
optimum	=	opt, (best)
order	=	o, obe, om [Order of British Empire, Merit], (bid, book, charge, class, command, decree, discipline, edict, instruction, row, sect, tell)
(money) order	=	mo, (cheque, draft)
(postal) order	=	po
Ordnance Survey	=	os
organisation	=	org, (agency, business, concern, group)
or near offer	=	ono
(in) other words	=	ie [that is]
ought	=	o, (must, nothing, owed, should, zero)
ounce	=	oz
out of stock	=	os
outside broadcast	=	ob
outstanding	=	ai [A1], (due, great, owing, special)
overcharge	=	oc, (clip, fleece, skin, soak, stick)
overdose	=	od [drug overdose]
overdraft	=	od
over-the-counter	=	otc
over the top	=	ott
overtime	=	ot
owing	=	iou, (due)
Oxford (University)	=	ou
(of) Oxford University	=	oxon
oxygen	=	o [element]

P

pacifist	=	co [conscientious objector]
page	=	p, (boy, folio, (fly)leaf, paper, sheet)
pages	=	pp
paid	=	pd
pair	=	oo [spectacles], pr, (brace, couple, duet, duo, dyad, two, twosome)

Palestinian (group)	=	plo [Palestine Liberation Organisation]
paper	=	ms [manuscript], (essay, exam, gazette, journal, page, quire, rag, ream, tabloid, test)
paragon	=	st [saint]
paragraph	=	par(a)
park(ing)	=	p
part of London	=	ec, sw, wc, wi [districts], (bow, soho)
party	=	lab, lib, (bash, beano, cabal, clique, do, faction, group, revel, sect, social, thrash, tory)
pawn	=	p, (hawk, pledge, puppet, stooge, tool)
peacemaker	=	un [United Nations], (dove)
pellet(s)	=	o, oo
pence, penny	=	p
Pennsylvania	=	pa [US State]
(old) penny	=	d, (copper, denarius)
per	=	ea [each], p, (by, each, via)
per annum	=	pa, (annually)
per cent	=	pc, pct
periodical	=	mag [magazine], (journal, magazine, organ, paper, review, serial, weekly)
(not) permitted	=	nl [non licet]
person	=	ist [first], (being, human, one, soul)
(important) person	=	vip, (bigwig, nabob, nob, pot)
personal assistant	=	pa, (aide, batman, secretary)
petty cash	=	pc
phosphorus	=	p [element]
phase	=	ph, (aspect, chapter, period, stage, step)
physical education	=	pe
physical exercise(s)	=	pe, pt [physical education, training]
physical training	=	pt
physician	=	dr [doctor], md [Doctor of Medicine], (doctor, healer, surgeon)
piano	=	p, (gentle, low, soft; name of [see])
piece	=	pc, (bit, bite, cut, morsel, part, portion, scrap, slab)
Pilot Officer(s)	=	po(s)
place	=	pl, (deposit, point, pop, put, set, site, stead, venue)
plug	=	pr [public relations], (ad(vert), bung, push, shoot, stop)
poet	=	pl, (bard, muse, rishi; name of [see])
poet laureate	=	pl
point	=	e, n, s, w [east, north, south, west], (aim, dart, dot, end, gist, matter, ness, prong, rhumb, tang, thorn, tine, tip, top, train)
pole	=	n, s [north, south], (anode, mast, perch, rod, spar, staff)
policemen	=	cid [Criminal Investigation Department], (yard)
police officers	=	cid, (yard)

politician	=	mep, mp, (democrat, labourite, liberal, republican, senator, tory, whig)
porn	=	x [rated]
port	=	l [left], (air, harbour, haven, left, mien, wine; name of [see])
postcard	=	pc
post-mortem	=	pm
post office	=	po
postal order	=	po
pound	=	l, lb, (beat, drub, lam, pen, quid)
power of attorney	=	pa
preferred	=	pf, (chosen, favourite, select)
present	=	ad [anno domini], (deliver, donate, gift, give, here, now, offer, tender, there)
present day, time	=	ad [anno domini], (anniversary, birthday, christmas, now, xmas)
president	=	p, (abe)
presiding figure	=	mc [master of ceremonies]
press agent	=	pa
press chief, man	=	ed [editor]
press officer, spokesman	=	pro [public relations officer]
price	=	sp [Starting Price], (charge, cost, fee, ransom, rate, tariff, toll, value)
(starting) price	=	sp, (odds)
priest	=	fr [Father], pr, (abbe, clergy [see], lama, rabbi; name of [see])
prime minister	=	pm, (premier; name of [see])
princess	=	di [Princess Diana]
prosecutor	=	da [District Attorney]
provisional(s)	=	ira [Irish Republican Army]
public address	=	pa, (tannoy)
public company	=	plc
public prosecutor	=	da [District Attorney]
public relations	=	pr
public transport	=	br [British Rail], ry [railway], (bus, cab, coach, taxi, train, tram, tube)
publicity	=	pr [public relations], (ad, hype, plug)
pupil	=	l, (eye, learner [see])

Q

qualification	=	ba, ma [Bachelor, Master of Arts], (but, caveat, degree, proviso, skill)
qualified	=	ba, ma, (able, adept, expert, fit, skilful)
quarter	=	e, n, q, qr, s, w, (area, billet, fourth, mercy, pity, region, side, zone)
quartet	=	iv [Roman numeral]
queen	=	er [Elizabeth Regina], hm [Her Majesty] q, r [Regina], (belle, empress, regina)
queen's bishop	=	qb

queen's pawn	= qp
queen's rook	= qr
question	= q, qu, (ask, eh, how, pose(r), pump, query, quiz, what, when, why)
queuing up	= li . . . ne [in line], (inline)
quiet	= p [musical], qt, sh [shush], (pacific, peace silence, silent, soft, still)
(keep) quiet	= sh
(very) quiet	= pp [musical]
quintet	= v [Roman numeral]
quotation	= quot, (bid, motto, tag, tender)

R

race	= tt [tourist trophy], (folk, hurry, nation, people, relay, run, rush, tribe; name of [see])
radio	= cb [citizens' band], (set)
RAF man	= lac [leading aircraftsman]
railway	= br [British Rail], lms [London Midland South], ry, (line, metro, track, tube)
rate	= kph, mph [kilometres, miles per hour], (charge, cost, count, earn, fee, judge, lecture, price, rail, rant, regard, scold, speed, tariff, tax)
rate of progress	= kph, mph [kilometres, miles per hour]
ray	= x, (beam, light, radiate, radius, skate; name of [alpha, beta, gamma, delta])
Rechabite	= tt [teetotaller]
recipe	= r, (formula)
record	= cd [compact disk], ep, lp [extended, long player], (diary, disc, enter, entry, file, journal, ledger, list, log, tape, transcribe)
recorder	= vcr, (judge, magistrate, video)
(with) regard, regarding	= re, (about, anent, apropos, on, over)
regiment	= re, rm [Royal Engineers, Marines]
relation	= bro [brother], sis [sister], (bond, pi, ratio, relative [see], respect)
(little) relation	= bro, sis [brother, sister abbreviated]
relative	= bro, sis, (aunt, brother, cousin, father, kin, mother, niece, sister, uncle)
religion	= rc [Roman Catholic], (creed, cult, faith, sect; name of [see])
religious education	= re
religious instruction	= ri
reporter	= ed, (editor, journalist, journo)
representative	= mp, (agent, delegate, deputy, rep)
reserve	= ta [Terr. Army], (book, spare, sub(stitute))
resistance	= r, (hindrance, opposition, refusal)
rider	= ps [postscript], (addendum, appendix, clause, codicil, condition, cossack, equestrian, horseman, hussar, jockey)

right	= r, rt, (apt, correct, due, exact, fit, lien, just, meet, proper, tick, true)
ring	= o, (arena, band, bell, call, circle, contact, disc, halo, hoop, loop, peal, round, toll)
rings	= oo
river	= r, (banker, flower, runner, stream; name of [see])
road	= m [motorway], mi [M1], rd, st, (avenue, lane, motorway, route, street, way)
road-junction	= t [T-junction]
rock	= gib [Gibraltar], (gem, reel, stone, shake, sway, swing)
roughly	= c, (about, almost, around, circa, nearly
round	= o, (about, almost, circle, lap, near, ring, rotund)
Royal Marines, Navy	= rm, rn
Royalty	= k [King], r [Regina]
run	= r [cricket], (bye, canter, control, double, flee, gallop, hie, hurry, jog, ladder, lope, manage, play, roll, rule, single, smuggle, speed, sprint, trot)

S

sailor	= ab [able-bodied seaman], po [petty officer], (hand, jack, lascar, matelot, rating, salt, seaman, tar)
sailors	= rn [Royal Navy]
saint	= st, (name of [see])
salt	= ab, (corn, sailor [see])
Salvation Army	= sa
same	= do, (alike, ditto, equal, idem, twin, very)
Sandhurst	= rma [Royal Military Academy]
sapper(s)	= re [Royal Engineers]
say	= eg [for example], (declare, speak, state, tell, utter, voice)
scholar	= ba [Bachelor of Arts], l [learner], ma [Master of Arts], (learner [see])
science fiction	= sf
scripture	= nt, ot [New, Old Testament], (bible, granth, koran, talmud, tantra, torah)
scripture (lesson)	= re, ri [religious education, instruction],
second	= mo [moment], s, sec, (back, instant, moment, sponsor, support, transfer)
second class, rate	= b
secret service	= mi [Military Intelligence]
(top) secretary	= pa [personal assistant]
semi	= bi, (demi, half, house)
sergeant-major	= sm

service	=	raf, rm, rn [Royal Air Force, Marines, Navy], (ace, duty, fault, force, let, ministry, rite, teaset, use; name of [see])
(secret) service	=	mi [Military Intelligence]
serviceman	=	nco [non-commissioned officer]
servicewoman	=	ats [Auxiliary Territorial Service], (wren)
sex appeal	=	sa, (it, oomph)
shamus	=	pi [private investigator], (detective, policeman)
she had, would	=	shed [she'd]
she will	=	shell [she'll]
shilling	=	s, sh
ship	=	ss [steamship], (boat [see], remit, route, send)
shirt	=	t [T-shirt]
(short) time	=	min [minute], mo [moment], sec [second]
side	=	l, r [left, right], (bias, edge, eleven, flank, lateral, team, wing)
silence	=	sh, (calm, hush, peace, quiet, stifle, still)
silver	=	ag [element]
signal for help	=	sos
single	=	i [1], (one, lone, mono, run, unit)
size	=	l, m, s [large, medium, small], (bulk, extent, height, volume, width)
small	=	s [size], (dwarf, little, midget, minor, petty, tad, tiny, wee)
small number	=	no, (few)
smell	=	bo [body odour], (aroma, nose, odour, reek, scent, stench, stink, tang)
sober (minded)	=	aa [Alcoholics Anonymous], tt [teetotaller], (dry, grave, sedate, staid)
society	=	s, (body, club, gentry, guild, league, people, public, union)
sodium	=	na [element]
soft	=	p [musical], (easy, gentle, lax, mild, piano, quiet, weak, simple)
softly	=	p [musical]
soldier	=	gi [general infantryman], nco [non-commissioned officer], or [other ranks], re [Royal Engineer], (para, private, ranker, recruit, regular, rookie, trooper)
soldiers	=	re [Royal Engineers], (army, battalion, brigade, division, legion, men, platoon, troops, unit)
solution	=	soln, (answer, liquid, remedy, result, solvent)
somebody, someone	=	vip [very important person], (name, one)
son	=	s, (issue)
sound asleep	=	z, zz
south(ern)	=	s, (austral)
South Africa, America	=	sa
South African	=	sa, (cape)
south-east	=	se

south-west	= sw
sovereign	= l [pound], (expound [ex pound], free, king, lofty, monarch, regal, royal, ruler, supreme)
Spain	= e [IVR]
specifically	= ie [that is]
spectacles	= oo
speed	= kph, mph [kilometres, miles per hour], (gait, haste, hurry, knot, pace, rate, run, tempo, ton)
splendid	= ai, (fine, good, grand, great, super)
(press) spokesman	= pro [public relations officer]
sport	= ru [rugby union], (exercise, fellow, game, toy, wear; name of [see])
square	= sq, t [T-square], (buffer, equal, even, fair, fogy, level, plaza, quits)
standard	= std, (example, flag [see], mark, norm, par, rule, set)
standard procedure	= sop [standard operating procedure]
starter	= l, (crank, novice, runner, soup, tiro)
starting price	= sp, (odds)
state	= ca, cal, ga, ma, va [US States], (air, aver, country, express, kingdom, mode, mood, nation, pomp, realm, say, tell, utter; name of [see])
station	= st, (base, depot, place, post, rank, site, stop)
statistics	= stat(s), (data, facts, info)
steamship	= ss
stock exchange	= lse, se [(London) Stock Exchange], (bourse)
stone	= st [weight], (boulder, cobble, granite, marble, ore, pebble, rock)
street	= st, (avenue, crescent, road, way)
string	= g, (chain, cord, fibre, rope, row, series, stable, strand, twine)
student	= l, (learner [see])
(former) student	= alumnus, (ob)
stumped	= st [cricket]
sulphur	= s [element]
sun	= s, (bask, sol, tan)
super	= ai [A1], (extra, great, petrol, swell, top)
superior	= u, (better, over, top, up, upper)
Switzerland	= ch [IVR]

T

taxmen, tax people	= ir [Internal Revenue]
tea	= t, (cha, char)
tea-time	= iv [four o'clock]
team	= xi, (eleven, group, side)
temperature	= c [Celsius], f [Fahrenheit], (heat)
terrier	= ta, (name of [see])

terrorists	=	ira [Irish Republican Army], oas, plo [Palestine Liberation Organisation]
test	=	mot [Ministry of Transport], (assay, check, examine, match, oral, prove, sample, trial, try)
(car) test	=	mot [Ministry of Transport]
testament	=	nt, ot [New, Old Testament], (proof, tribute, will, witness)
that is	=	ie
theologian	=	bd, dd [Bachelor, Doctor of Divinity]
these days	=	ad [anno domini], (now, present)
third class, rate	=	c
this day	=	ad [anno domini], (now, present)
this month	=	inst [instant]
thoroughfare	=	rd, st, (road, street, way)
thousand dollars	=	g, (grand)
three(some)	=	tri, (ternary, thrice, treble, triple)
time	=	t, (age, date, epoch, era, period, spell, term; name of [see])
(arrival) time	=	eta [estimated time of arrival]
(little) time	=	min [minute], mo [moment], sec [second)
(modern) time(s)	=	ad [anno domini], (now, present)
(present) time	=	ad [anno domini], (anniversary, birthday, christmas, now, xmas)
(short) time	=	min [minute], mo [moment], sec [second)
times	=	x [multiplied by]
tin	=	sn [element], (can, loaf)
tip-top	=	ai [A1]
ton	=	c [hundred], (century, fashion, hundred, mode, fashion, style)
top	=	t, (apex, best, brow, cap, ceiling, head, hat, lid, peak, spinner)
top class	=	u [upper]
top journalist	=	ed [editor]
track	=	ry, (course, follow, lane, line, orbit, path, rail, scent, spoor, tail, trail, way)
track(s)	=	ry [railway]
trade union	=	num, nur [National Union of Mineworkers, National Union of Railwaymen], tu
trainee	=	l, (learner [see])
(physical) training	=	pe, pt [physical education, training]
(public) transport	=	br [British Railways], ry [railway], (bus, cab, coach, taxi, train, tram, tube)
tungsten	=	w [element], (wolfram)
turn	=	s, u, (addle, alter, bend, curd(le), fit, go, pivot, plough, rev, rot, twist, veer)
turn over	=	to, (roll, tip, topple, upset)
twice	=	di, (double, doubly, twofold)
two(some)	=	bi, (brace, couple, duet, duo, pair)
Tyneside	=	ne [north east England]

(blood) type	= a, ab, a, o
tyro, tiro	= l, learner [see]

U

Ulster	= ni [Northern Ireland]
ultimate	= ult, (acme, end, epitome, final, last)
ultraviolet	= uv
(is) unable	= cant [can't]
underwriter	= uw, (backer, guarantor, insurer, sponsor)
union	= num, nur [National Union of Mineworkers, National Union of Railwaymen], tu, (club, guild, joint, league, merger)
unit	= u, (cadre, entity, item, one, troop, whole)
United Nations	= un, uno [United Nations Organisation]
United States	= us, usa, (america)
universal	= u, (cosmic, generic, global)
universal time	= ut
university	= u, univ, (name of [see])
university person	= ba, bed [Bachelor of Arts, Education], ma [Master of Arts], (blue, freshman, graduate, sophomore)
unknown	= x, y [1st, 2nd unknown quantity], (anon)
upper case	= uc
upper(-class)	= u
uranium	= u [element]
useless	= ng [no good]
US lawyer	= da [District Attorney]
US soldier	= gi [general infantryman]
US uncle	= name of [sam]

V

vacancy	= o, (gap, job, post, room, space, void)
vacation	= vac, (holiday, leave)
various	= var, (divers, many, several, varied [see])
various dates	= vd
verb	= vb
verse	= v, (poem, rhyme, stanza)
versus	= v, vs, (against)
very big	= os [outsize], (colossal, gigantic, huge, jumbo, titanic)
very gently	= pp [musical]
very large	= os [outsize], (colossal, gigantic, huge, jumbo, titanic)
very loud	= ff [musical]
very low	= pp [musical]
very old	= vo, (aged, ancient, antique, elderly)
very quiet	= pp [musical]

vessel = ss [steamship], (boat, container, craft, receptacle, ship, vein; name of [see])

vice admiral = va

Victoria Cross = vc

victory = v, ve [Victory in Europe], (conquest, triumph, win)

Virginia = va [US State]

volt = v

volume = v, vol, (amount, book, bulk, mass, tome, name of [see])

volunteers = ta [Territorial Army]

W

Washington (district) = dc [District of Columbia]

watt = w

way = ave, rd, st; e, n, s, w; mo [modus operandus], (avenue, how, lane, method, mode, path, road, route, street, track)

we had, would = wed [we'd]

we will = well [we'll]

weight = wt, (mass, power, tare, ton, troy)

(measure of) weight = cwt, g, lb, oz, t, (drachm, dram, grain, gram, ounce, pound, quarter, quintal, scruple, stone, ton, tonne)

west(ern) = w, (occident(al))

West Africa(n) = wa

West Indies, Indian = wi

wheel = o, (circle, deal, disc, helm, pivot, roll, spin, tiller, trade, turn)

wheels = oo

wide = w [cricket], (ample, broad, vast)

win = v [victory], (earn, gain, land, prevail, succeed, success, victory)

winner, winning position = ist [1st], (first)

winning blow = ko [knockout]

with = w, (among, and, by, for, per, pro, via)

without = wo, (beyond, ex, lacking, less, minus, outside, past, sine)

without issue = sp [sine prole], (childless)

wolfram = w [element], (tungsten)

women's institute = wi

(in other) words = ie [that is]

work = op [opus], (go, grind, labour, operate, opus, ply, slog, sweat, task, toil, travail; name of [see])

(musical) work = op, (opus)

workers = tu [trade union], (labour, men, staff, union)

writing = ms, (hand, print, prose, scrawl, script)

written matter = ms [manuscript]

wrong	=	x [wrong mark], (amiss, bad, crime, cross, evil, sin, tort)
Wye	=	y [phonetic]

Y

yard	=	cid [Scotland Yard], y, yd [measure]
year	=	ad [anno domini], y, yr
yearly	=	pa [per annum], (annual)
yellow	=	or [gold]
yew, you	=	u [phonetic]
you see	=	uc [phonetic]
yours truly	=	i, me

Z

zero	=	o, (cipher, duck, love, nil, nought)

WORDS TO WORDS

In this section we look at words commonly used by compilers and their synonyms or alternative meanings that go into the resolution of many clues. This collection has been compiled from my own experience and includes words that I have catalogued as being utilised over and over again. It is not an exhaustive list nor is it intended to replace a proper dictionary. The alternative meanings given here are both short words that go to make up answers and other words that are answers by themselves. This section should be one of your two starting points (the other being WORDS TO LETTERS) and you should add your own words as you find them while solving your favourite puzzles.

When you come across the clue words on the left below, look to the adjacent words on the right to go into your answers. Often there will be more than one possible answer as different compilers use their own connotations. Generally, plurals and past and past participle tenses of verbs have not been listed separately unless they take meanings that are different in context or spelling from their singular and present tense words.

Where there is an overlap with WORDS TO LETTERS, the letters are also included on the right below, but in round brackets. Square brackets include explanations, where appropriate.

A

a, an	= one, (i)
abandon	= cede, desert, leave, quit, waive
abandoned	= left, outcast, quit, wild
abate	= calm, dull, ease, ebb, fade, wane
abduct	= kidnap, nobble, seize, shanghai
abet	= aid, assist, back, help, incite, second
abetter	= backer, helper, second
abhor	= detest, hate, loathe
abide	= dwell, endure, stay, suffer
abiding	= permanent
ability	= ear, gift, knack, knowhow, might, power, prowess, skill
abject	= base, craven, menial, servile, slavish,
able	= adept, can, clever, fit, skilled
ablin(g)s	= maybe, perchance, perhaps, possibly
aboard	= on, (s . . . s)
about	= anent, apropos, around, circa, on, over, round, (c, ca, re)
above	= atop, beyond, over
abridge	= clip, cut, shorten, trim
abridged	= cut, (abr)
abroad	= away, far, out, overseas
abrupt	= curt, hasty, short, steep, sudden

absent	= away, gone, off, out, truant, (abs, awol, ia)
absolute	= entire, pure, sheer, total, utter, (abs)
absolute ruler	= autocrat, despot, dictator, tyrant
absolve	= acquit, assoil, clear, excuse, pardon
absorb	= fill, fix, hold, occupy, rivet
absorbed	= fixed, held, lost, rapt
abstruse	= arcane, esoteric, recondite, secret
abuse	= blame, curse, harm, hurt, rail, smear, tirade
abut	= adjoin, border, touch, verge
abysmal	= bad, deep, rank
(senior) academic	= don, prof
accede	= adhere, agree, assent, consent
accelerator	= throttle
accent	= acute, grave, stress, tone
accept	= acquire, admit, agree, brook, gain, get, have, swallow
acceptable	= adequate, fair, fine, welcome, (ok)
accepted	= in, normal, routine, usual
accessory	= aid, bag, frill, partner
accident	= chance, collision, crash, mishap, prang, smash
acclaim	= applaud, applause, commend, hail, plaudit, praise
accommodation	= board, digs, flat, house, pad, tenement
(temporary) accommodation	= camp(er), tent, tepee, wigwam
accomplish	= achieve, do, finish, fulfil, gain, win
accomplished	= done, over, perfect, won
accord	= agree, grant, harmony, suit, tally
accordingly	= ergo, hence, so
according to	= after, per
accost	= address, approach, confront, face, greet, solicit
account	= bill, invoice, record, relation, story, tab, tale, (ac, acc)
(give an) account	= relate, tell
(on) account of	= over
accuse	= blame, charge, impeach, indict
accusation	= charge, indictment
(false) accusation	= calumny, libel, slander
accustomed	= normal, used, usual
ace	= champion, expert, master, one, pro, spot, star
ache	= hurt, long, pain, smart, throb, yearn
achieve	= do, earn, gain, get
achievement	= deed, exploit, feat
(sporting) achievement	= cap, colours
acid	= acrid, pungent, sharp, tart; name of [acetic, amino, ascorbic, carbolic, citric, formic, hydrochloric, lactic, malic, nitric, prussic, sulphuric, tannic, tartaric, uric]
acknowledge	= admit, agree, allow, concede, grant, own
acquire	= earn, gain, get, obtain, secure, win

acquit	=	absolve, act, behave, clear, conduct
acreage	=	farm, land, ranch, (a)
act	=	bill, decree, deed, do, edict, feat, law, statute
act badly	=	ham
acting	=	temporary, (a)
action	=	battle, deed, exploit, feat, fighting, fray
(legal) action	=	case, lawsuit, suit, trial
actor	=	agent, doer, performer, player, thespian
(bad, poor) actor	=	ham
(great, leading) actor	=	star
(minor, part) actor	=	extra
actors	=	cast, crew
actual	=	live, real, true, very
adamant	=	firm, hard, obdurate, resolute, rigid, set, stubborn
adapt	=	adjust, alter, change, convert, fit, modify, suit
add	=	annex, append, cast, count, join, sum, tot(al)
adder	=	summer, totter, viper
additional	=	extra, more, new, other, spare
addle	=	confuse, curd, muddle, rot, spoil, turn
address	=	abode, lecture, speak, speech, talk
address system	=	tannoy, (pa)
adept	=	able, clever, skilled
adequate	=	ample, decent, enough
adhere	=	attach, cling, fix, glue, paste, stick
adherent	=	cohort, disciple, follower, supporter
adhesive	=	cement, glue, gum, paste, sticky
adjourn	=	defer, delay, postpone, shelve
adjust	=	adapt, fit, fix, suit, settle, tailor
admiration	=	ah, esteem, regard, respect
admirer	=	beau, fan, lover
admit	=	agree, allow, concede, confess, enter, grant, own
admonish	=	berate, chide, rebuke, scold, warn
ado	=	action, bother, business, fuss, trouble
adopt	=	assume, choose, embrace, espouse
adore	=	love, revere, worship
adoration	=	homage, idolatry, respect, worship
adorn	=	(be)deck, dress, embellish, trim
adornment	=	decoration, frill, ornament
advance	=	cite, go, lend, loan, march, sub
advanced	=	ahead, lent, on
advent	=	arrival, coming
adventure	=	dare, exploit, feat, hazard, risk
advert(isement)	=	ad, bill, blurb, copy, plug, poster, (advt)
advertising jingle	=	slogan
advice	=	counsel, help, tip(s)
advocate	=	backer, champion, favour, justify, lawyer [see], notary, promote
aegis	=	defence, shield

aerial	=	antenna, dipole, dish, mast, wire
affable	=	cordial, genial, gentle, nice, pleasant
affair	=	amour, concern, event, fling, intrigue, matter, romance, thing
affect	=	feign, haunt, influence, pretend, sway
affected	=	camp, chichi, insincere, sham, stiff, stilted
affirm	=	allege, assert, aver, avow, posit, ratify, state, swear
affirmation	=	assertion, avowal, vow
affirmative	=	yes
affix	=	add, bind, glue, join, tack
affliction	=	name of [ague, fever, gout, measles]
afford	=	bear, give, grant, offer, spare
affray	=	brawl, clash, fracas, fight, melee
afraid	=	alarmed, awed, feared, scared, timid
African	=	bantu
African soldier	=	askari
African river	=	name of river [see]
afresh	=	again, anew, new
aft	=	behind, stern
after	=	behind, chasing, hinder, later, post
(just) after	=	on
(run) after	=	chase, pursue
after all	=	last, latest
afterwards	=	later, then
again	=	also, anew, over, (re)
against	=	anti, con, versus, (v)
(one) against war	=	dove
(those) against	=	cons, noes
age	=	(a)eon, epoch, era, mature, ripen, time
aged	=	ancient, grey, old(en), ripe
agency	=	channel, means, medium, organ, vehicle
agent	=	envoy, factor, medium, organ, proxy, rep, representative, vehicle
(fermenting) agent	=	yeast
(secret) agent	=	bond [James], spook, spy
aggregate	=	amount, ore, sum, total, unite, whole
agile	=	active, limber, nimble, sprightly, spry
ago	=	past
agony	=	anguish, distress, misery, pain, torment
agree	=	accede, accept, accord, admit, assent, check, concur, consent, correspond, fit, jibe, nod, settle, suit, tally, yes
(don't) agree	=	argue, differ, dissent, no
agreed	=	ay, yes, (ok)
agreement	=	accord, ay, bond, compact, contract, deal, pact, treaty, tune, unison, yes
ague	=	fever, quaking, shakes, shivers
ahead	=	ante, before, forward, onward

(went, were) ahead	= led
aid	= abet, back, help, relief, serve
(navigational) aid	= compass, dogstar, radar, sextant, star
aide	= adjutant, assistant, helper, (adc)
ail	= afflict, distress, trouble, upset
aim	= aspire, end, goal, intend, object, plan, seek, target, wish
air	= aura, breeze, broadcast, display, mien, mood, music [see], space, vent, wind
(open-)air	= alfresco
aircraft	= glider, jet, jumbo, plane; name of [boeing, comet, mig, mirage]
(old) aircraft	= crate
airless	= calm, still, stuffy
airway	= flue, hole, outlet, vent
airy	= fresh, gay, light, open
aisle	= corridor, lane, passage, path
akin	= agnate, like, related, similar
alarm	= arouse, awe, disturb, dread, fear, scare, warning
alarmed	= afraid, awed, scared
alcoholic	= drunk, lush, soak, sot, sponge, toper, wino
alcoholic spirit	= name of [arak, bourbon, brandy, cognac, gin, grog, hooch, irish, liqueur, liquor, meths, rum, rye, scotch, schnap(p)s, vodka, whisk(e)y]
ale	= beer, drink
alibi	= excuse, plea, pretext
alien	= foreign(er), outsider, strange(r), (et)
alight	= land, perch, settle
alike	= akin, equal, even, same
alive	= active, alert, awake, extant, quick
all	= entire, full, lot, total, whole
(after) all	= last, latest
all right	= fair, safe, (ok)
alllege	= adduce, affirm, avow, cite, claim
alley	= lane, passage, walk
alliance	= club, guild, league, union, order
allot	= assign, grant, mete, share
allotment	= portion, quota, ration, share
allow	= admit, give, grant, let, own, permit, sanction, suffer
allowed	= lawful, legal, let, licit
(not) allowed	= out
allowance	= annuity, grant, lot, quota, ration, stipend
allure	= charm, draw, seduce, tempt
ally	= combine, friend, join, unite
almost	= about, nearly, nigh
aloof	= apart, cold, cool, distant, remote
alphabet	= name of [arabic, celtic, cretan, cyrillic, greek, kana, roman, runes]

also	= and, item, likewise, too, plus
also known as	= alias, (aka)
alter	= adapt, amend, change, modify, vary
alternative	= choice, option, or, other
always	= ay, eer, ever
amass	= collect, compile, garner, gather
amateur	= layman, learner [see], (a, l)
(no) amateur	= pro[fessional]
ambassador	= consul, diplomat, envoy, legate, nuncio, (he)
ambit	= bounds, circuit, compass, extent
ambition	= aim, drive, goal, end, push, target
amend	= alter, better, change, correct
American	= yank, yankee, (a, am, us, usa)
American miss	= gal
amiable	= benign, friendly, genial, kind
amiss	= awry, false, faulty, wrong
amnesty	= oblivion, pardon, reprieve
amok, amuck	= frantic, frenzied, rabid, wild
amount	= bulk, lot, mass, sum, total, whole, (amt)
amuse	= cheer, disport, divert, regale, tickle
amusing	= comical, droll, funny, witty
anaemic	= ashen, pale, pallid, wan
anaesthetic	= ether, number
analogy	= metaphor, parallel, simile
analyse	= assay, dissect, sift, test, winnow
ancestor	= ascendant, for(e)bear, forefather, gran
ancestral knot	= granny
ancestry	= blood, line(age), origin, stock, strain
anchor	= fix, moor, secure; name of [bower, grapnel, kedge, killick, sheet]
anchorage	= bay, cove, harbour, haven, port
anchorite	= hermit, recluse
ancient	= aged, antique, archaic, bygone, old(en), passe, primeval
ancient city	= name of [pompeii, sparta, troy, tyre, ur]
ancient warship	= bireme, galley, trireme
and	= with
and not	= nor
anecdote	= story, tale, wheeze, yarn
angel	= backer, cherub(im), patron, seraphim, spirit [see], sponsor
angelic	= divine, godly, holy, saintly, spiritual
anger	= choler, ire, irk, fury, nettle, pique, rage, rankle, temper, vex, wrath
angle	= bend, cast, corner, elbow, fish, slant
angler	= bender, fisher, troller, trawler
angler's basket	= buck, creel
angry	= cross, irate, hot, livid, mad, red
(get) angry	= rage, rail, rant, rate

anguish	=	agony, distress, grief, sorrow, woe
anil	=	blue, indigo
anile	=	doting, imbecile, senile
anility	=	dotage, senility
animal	=	beast, brute, creature, pet, rodent [see], swine; name of [alpaca, antelope [see], ape, ass, badger, bat, bear, beaver, bison, bobcat, buffalo, bull, burro, camel, cow, donkey, deer [see], elephant, ferret, fox, goat, hare, horse [see], ibex, jackal, llama, marten, mole, monkey [see], mouse, mule, okapi, otter, ox, pig [see], platypus, polecat, rabbit, ram, rat, sable, sheep, sloth, stoat, weasel]
(bovine) animal(s)	=	cow(s), kine, neat, ox(en)
(cat-like) animal	=	name of [civet, cheetah, genet, leopard, lion, lynx, ocelot, ounce, panther, puma, tiger]
(domestic) animal	=	name of [cat, dog, hamster]
(little, young) animal	=	calf, cub, foal, kid, kitten, lamb, pup
(sea-)animal	=	name of [dolphin, dugong, morse, orc(a), porpoise, seal, sealion, walrus, whale]
animal cry	=	bleat, low, moo
animals	=	cattle, herd, stock
(young) animals	=	litter
animation	=	dash, elan, esprit, spirit, verve, vim
animated	=	alive, lively, living, pert, vital
annex	=	add, append, attach, seize
anniversary	=	name of [china, coral, crystal, diamond, emerald, golden, pearl, ruby, sapphire, silver]
announce	=	declare, divulge, publish, say, tell
annoy	=	anger, bug, irk, nark, peeve, pester, rankle, rile, vex
annoyance	=	anger, bother, nuisance, pest, pique
annoyed	=	angry, cross, irate, mad
annoying chap, person	=	blighter, nuisance, pain, pest
annul	=	cancel, delete, expunge, quash, void
anoint	=	anele, consecrate, oil, smear
anonymous	=	nameless, unnamed, (a, anon)
another name	=	alias, nickname, pseudonym, sobriquet, (aka)
answer	=	fill, key, meet, reply, retort, riposte, solution, (a)
ant	=	emmet, queen, termite, worker
Antarctic	=	polar
ante	=	before, bet, pot, stake, wager
antelope	=	name of [addax, ariel, blesbok, bongo, bubal, chamois, eland, gazelle, impala, nilgai, oryx, roan, springbok]
antenna	=	aerial, feeler, horn
anterior	=	earlier, former, forward, front, past, prior, previous
anthem	=	motet, hymn, psalm, song

anti	= against, counter, instead, opponent, opposite, rival
antic	= bizarre, caper, frolic, lark, prank
antique	= aged, ancient, archaic, old(en), relic
antler	= branch, horn
anxiety	= angst, care, concern, worry
anxious	= agog, ardent, avid, eager, keen, taut, tense
(not) anxious	= calm, relaxed, relieved, sedate
any	= one, some
anybody	= one
apace	= fast, quickly, swiftly
apart	= alone, aside, asunder, separate, single
apartment	= flat, pad, room, suite, tenement, (apt)
ape	= copy, echo, mimic, mock, monkey [see], primate
aperture	= gap, hole, opening, orifice, vent
apex	= acme, peak, summit, tip, top, vertex
aplomb	= assurance, confidence, coolness, phlegm
apostate	= defector, false, rat, renegade, traitor
apostle	= messenger, missionary, preacher
appal	= dismay, horrify, shock, terrify
apparel	= adorn, clothes [see]
apparent	= clear, evident, obvious, patent, plain
appeal	= allure, ask, beg, charm, implore, plea, plead, pray, request, (o)
(sex) appeal	= it, oomph, (sa)
appear	= emerge, look, loom, seem, show, sound
appearance	= aspect, face, guise, look, mien
append	= add, affix, annex, hang, join
appendage	= tail
appendix	= addendum, codicil, rider, (ps)
applaud	= cheer, clap, commend, extol, hail, praise
applause	= acclaim, clapping, plaudit
apple	= eater; name of [biffin, cox, crab, green, pippin, ribston]
application	= balm, cream, industry, lotion, salve, use
apply	= use, fit, pertain, refer, suit
appoint	= mote
appointment	= date, job, office, place, post, tryst
apposite	= apropos, apt, germane, relevant
appraisal	= estimate, opinion, valuation
appreciation	= esteem, gain, praise, thanks, tribute, (ta)
apprehension	= alarm, arrest, doubt, dread, fear
apprehensive	= afraid, anxious, nervous, uneasy
apprentice	= learner [see], (l)
approach	= accost, advent, begin, meet, near, reach
appropriate	= annex, apropos, apt, embezzle, filch, fit, germane, meet, peculate, pilfer, pinch, proper, right, seize, steal, usurp

approve	=	clear, commend, confirm, pass, sanction
approval, approving	=	ay, yes, (ok)
(sign of) approval	=	nod, tick
apron	=	pinafore, skirt
apropos	=	apt, correct, fit, meet, proper, right
apropos of	=	about, anent, on, over, (re)
apse	=	recess
aptitude	=	bent, flair, gift, knack, talent
arab	=	name of [bedouin, berber, moor]
arachnid	=	mite, scorpion, spider
arbiter	=	judge, referee, umpire
arbour	=	bower, pergola
arc	=	bend, bow, crescent, curve
arcane	=	abstruse, esoteric, recondite, secret
arch	=	bend, bow, chief, cunning, curve, dome, first, head, ogee, shrewd, sly, span, top, wily
archaeological site	=	dig, name of [olduvai, thebes, ur]
archer	=	bender, bowman, hood [Robin], tell [William]
architectural style	=	name of [baroque, classical, colonial, gothic, ionic, norman, regency, rococo, tudor]
Arctic	=	polar
ardent	=	avid, burning, eager, hot, keen, strong, true
ardent supporter	=	admirer, aficionado, devotee, fan(atic)
ardour	=	emotion, fervour, heat, zeal
arduous	=	hard, severe, steep, tough
are	=	exist, live, move
area	=	belt, district, region, sector, tract
arena	=	ring, scene, sphere, venue
argot	=	jargon, slang
argue	=	bicker, debate, dispute, hassle, rebut
argument	=	clash, feud, fight, row, quarrel, tiff, wrangle
aria	=	hymn, lay, solo, song
arid	=	barren, desert, dry, parched, sterile
aristocrat	=	grandee, lady, lord, noble, peer
aristocratic	=	elite, grand, lordly, noble, titled, up
arithmetic	=	algebra, cipher, numbers, sums
arm	=	limb, bough, branch, equip, tentacle, wing
armada	=	fleet, flotilla, navy
armlet	=	badge, band, emblem, inlet, insignia
armour	=	bard, helmet, mail, shield
arms	=	artillery, ordnance, weapons
arms store	=	armoury, arsenal, magazine
army	=	crowd, force, horde, host, legion, militia, (ta)
army canteen	=	mess, naafi
army unit	=	platoon, squad, troop
aroma	=	bouquet, fragrance, odour, perfume, scent, smell
aromatic	=	fragrant, scented, spicy, sweet
around	=	about, along, back, on, throughout

arouse	= awaken, stir, wake(n), whet
arraign	= accuse, charge, impeach, indict, tax
arrangement	= group, order, score, setup, version
array	= adorn, clothe, dress, order, outfit
arrest	= bag, catch, check, halt, nab, net, nick, seize, seizure, stop
arrive	= come, land, reach, succeed
arrived	= came, famous, successful
arrow	= bolt, dart, flight, index, pin, quarrel, shaft
arrowsmith	= fletcher
art	= craft, cunning, knack, paintings, skill, trade, wile
art movement, style	= name of [baroque, cubism, dada, deco, noveau, op, pop, realism, rococo]
artery	= name of [aorta, carotid]
article	= a, an, it, item, leader, object, the, thing
articulate	= clear, couple, fluent, join, lucid, say, speak,
artificial	= bogus, ersatz, fake, false, mock, sham, synthetic
artisan	= carpenter, craftsman, joiner, mechanic, worker
artist	= drawer, painter, sculptor; name of [cezanne, constable, dali, degas, holbein, manet, matisse, monet, picasso, renoir, titian, turner], (ra)
artist's model	= poser, sitter
artless	= honest, ingenuous, naive, simple
as	= for, like, since, when
as well	= also, and, besides, too
ascend	= climb, mount, rise, scale, soar
ascent	= climb, rise, rising, slope
ascetic	= austere, severe, stern, stylite
ascribe	= assign, attribute, credit, impute, lay
ash	= deposit, dust, ember, soot
ashamed	= abashed, humiliated
ashen	= grey, livid, pale, pallid, wan
ashram	= hermitage, retreat
asian	= asiatic, eastern, indian, (e)
aside	= apart, cue, slant
(put) aside	= forget, ignore, keep, save
(set) aside	= quash
asinine	= idiotic, silly, stupid
ask	= demand, inquire, query, quiz, request, require, plead, pray, solicit, why
ask for money	= beg, sponge
askance	= askew, awry, oblique
askew	= agley, askance, awry, oblique
asleep	= dormant, dozing, out
(half) asleep	= comatose
aspic	= jelly
aspire	= aim, desire, dream, hope, seek, wish, yearn
ass	= burro, dolt, donkey, fool, idiot, ninny

assassin	= bravo, killer, murderer, ninja, slayer
assault	= attack, beset, charge, onset, strike
assay	= attempt, go, strive, test, trial, try, value
assemble	= build, convene, gather, mass, meet, muster
assembly	= concourse, crowd, gathering, meeting, rally, synod
assent	= agree, grant, nod, permit, sanction
assert	= aver, avow, claim, maintain, state, swear
assess	= fix, gauge, judge, rate, value, weigh
assets	= capital, property, wealth
assign	= allot, ascribe, cede, refer, transfer
assignation	= date, tryst
assist	= abet, aid, back, boost, help
assistance	= aid, comfort, hand, help, succour, support
assistant	= aide, batman, deputy, factotum, helper, (pa)
associate	= ally, consort, friend, mate, pal
assorted	= mixed, motley, varied
assume	= adopt, don, guess, feign, posit, premise
assumed name	= alias, nickname, pseudonym, sobriquet, (aka)
assurance	= aplomb, confidence, pledge, promise, word
asterisk	= star
astern	= aft, behind
astringent	= austere, binding, bitter, severe, sharp, styptic
astrologer	= chaldean, magus, sorcerer, soothsayer
astute	= adroit, canny, clever, sharp, shrewd, sly, subtle, wily
asylum	= bedlam, haven, madhouse, refuge, retreat, sanctuary, shelter
at	= by, to
atheist	= heathen, infidel, pagan, sceptic
athlete	= competitor, gymnast, player, runner
athletic	= active, fit, muscular, robust
atmosphere	= air, aura, climate, mood
atom	= bit, drop, grain, jot, morsel, mote, particle, ray, speck, whit
atomic	= nuclear
atrophy	= decline, waste, wither
attach	= add, fasten, fix, join, link, nail, pin, tie
attached	= fixed, on, tied
attack	= assault, beset, blitz, bombard, bout, charge, fit, onset, polemic, raid, storm, strike, stroke, turn, waylay
attain	= achieve, gain, reach, win
attempt	= aim, bid, crack, essay, go, shot, stab, trial, try
attend	= hear, heed, listen, mind, nurse, wait
attendant	= aide, escort, keeper, maid, nurse, page, steward, usher, waiter
attendants	= cortege, retinue, suite, train
attention	= heed, interest, mark, note, notice

attest	= certify, swear, testify, vouch, witness
attic	= elegant, garret, greek, loft, refined
Attila	= hun [Attila the Hun]
attire	= clothes [see], foot-wear [see]
attitude	= air, bearing, carriage, mien, mood, pose, stance, view
attorney	= lawyer [see], (da)
attract	= charm, draw, entice, lure, pull, tempt
attractive	= comely, fair, lovely, pretty, winsome
attribute	= ascribe, assign, credit, lay, trait, virtue
auction	= sale, vendue
auction item	= lot
audacious	= bold, brave, daring, heroic, rash, stout
audit	= check, review, scrutiny, survey
auditor	= ear, listener
augment	= boost, grow, inflate, raise, swell
augur	= bode, divine(r), oracle, portend, predict, prophet, seer
augury	= omen, portent, sign, token, warning
august	= grand, imposing, noble, regal, solemn, sublime
aura	= air, feel(ing), mood, tone, vibes
auspice	= aegis, care, charge, control
auspicious	= bright, fortunate, lucky
austere	= bleak, grim, harsh, severe, stern
Australia	= oz
authentic	= genuine, real, true
author	= creator, doer, father, founder, pen, writer; name of writer [see]
authority	= command, control, expert, might, power
autumn	= fall
avail	= benefit, help, profit, use
available	= free, handy, on, ready, vacant
avarice	= avidity, cupidity, greed
avaricious	= avid, greedy, mean, stingy
avast	= cease, stay, stop
avaunt	= begone, scram
avenue	= road, path, street, way
aver	= affirm, assert, avow, declare, say, state, swear, tell
average	= fair, mean, norm, par, rule, usual
aversion	= dislike, distaste, hate, hatred, horror
aviator	= airman, flier, pilot
avid	= agog, ardent, eager, greedy, keen
avoid	= dodge, duck, escape, eschew, evade, shun
avow	= admit, affirm, assert, aver, confess
await	= abide, expect, stay
awake	= alive, aware, rouse, stir, vigilant
award	= adjudge, gong, grant, medal, oscar, prize, trophy, (mbe, obe, om)

(top) award	= alpha
aware	= alive, awake, conscious, knowing
away	= abroad, absent, off, out
(get) away	= escape, flee, run, start
(go) away	= avaunt, begone, depart, leave, scram
awe	= dread, fear, frighten, wonder
awful	= dire, dread, nasty, ugly
awkward	= gauche, inept, rude, stiff, stubborn
awning	= canvas, cover, roof, shelter
awry	= agley, amiss, askance, askew, oblique
axe	= cancel, chop, fell, fire, hatchet, hew, sack
axiom	= adage, gnome, maxim, moral, principle
axle	= axis, pin, pivot, rod, shaft, spindle

B

babble	= blab, chatter, gab(ble), mutter, prate
baboon	= monkey [see], primate
baby	= bairn, child, infant, tot
baby carriage	= pram
back	= abet, bet, end, endorse, hind, rear, tail
(ship's) back	= aft, counter, stern
backer	= angel, gambler, patron, punter, sponsor
backing	= aid, funds, subsidy, support
backbiting	= abuse, gossip, malice, spite
backbone	= basis, bottle, courage, guts, spine
back down	= accede, concede, yield
backfire	= boomerang, fail, flop
background	= culture, history, milieu
bacon	= rasher
bad	= base, evil, off, poor, sour, wrong
(go) bad	= addle, rot, spoil
(very) bad	= abysmal, rank
badge	= armlet, cockade, emblem, insignia, rosette
badger	= bait, brock, bully, chevy, chiv(v)y, goad, harass, harry, haunt, hawker, nag, tease, worry
badinage	= banter, jocularity, raillery, repartee
baffle	= amaze, astound, daze, foil, hoodwink, nonplus, puzzle, stump
bag	= catch, pouch, sac, sack, satchel, shoot, trap
bail	= bond, guarantee, ladle, scoop, surety
bail out	= jump, parachute, spring
bairn	= baby, child, infant
bait	= badger, bribe, decoy, gall, lure, snare, tease, worry
bake	= cook, dry, harden, heat, set, swelter
balance	= equilibrium, poise, remainder, rest, scale(s), weigh, (bal)
balanced	= fair, just, sane
bald	= bare, dull, hairless, meagre, smooth

baldness	= alopecia
ball	= dance, globe, hop, orb, sphere, (o)
ballad	= ditty, poem, song
ballot	= election, poll, ticket, vote
bam(boozle)	= cheat, hoax, mystify
ban	= bar, curse, forbid, outlaw, prevent, prohibit, taboo, veto
banal	= bland, flat, inane, trite, vapid
band	= armlet, belt, corps, crew, gang, girth, hoop, league, orchestra, ribbon, ring, strap, strip, stripe, tape, troop, unite
bandage	= bind, dress(ing), lint, swathe, tie, tourniquet
bandit	= brigand, crook, outlaw, robber, thief
bang	= blast, boom, crack, crash, fringe, hit, slam, thwack, wallop
banish	= deport, dismiss, dispel, exile
bank	= fund, heap, mound, nore, pile, rely, stack, tier
bankrupt	= bereft, broke, bust, insolvent, ruin
banner	= colour(s), ensign, flag, jack, pennant, pennon, standard
banquet	= beano, dinner, feast, fete, spread
bar	= ban, bench, block, bolt, counter, court, except, exclude, fasten, lever, loch, lounge, pole, prohibit, pub, rail, rod, streak, stripe
(seedy, sleazy) bar	= dive
bars	= air, melody, serenade, song, tune
barb	= beard, dart, hook, jag, sting
barbarian	= hun, savage; name of [attila]
barber	= figaro [Barber of Seville]
bard	= minstrel, muse, poet, singer
bare	= bald, empty, mere, naked, nude, reveal, scant, strip, uncover
bare back rider	= godiva [Lady Godiva]
barely	= just, merely, only, scarcely
bargain	= barter, deal, haggle, pact, sale, snip
barge	= bump, butt, intrude, lurch, push, scold; name of boat [lighter, scow, tug]
bark	= cough, skin, snap, snarl, tan, yap
barker	= cannon, dog, pistol, tout; name of dog [see]
baron	= beef, noble, peer
barrack	= boo, hoot, jeer
barrel	= butt, cask, drum, keg, tub, tun, vat
barren	= dull, infertile, meagre, sterile, waste
barren land	= desert
barricade	= bar(rier), block(ade), defence, fortify, obstruct(ion)
barrier	= bar, dam, ditch, fence, hedge, hurdle, wall
barrister	= lawyer [see]
barter	= bargain, exchange, haggle, trade, swap

base	=	cheap, foot, home, ignoble, inferior, low, mean, nadir, plinth, root, vile
bash	=	attempt, blow, go, try, wallop, whack
bashful	=	coy, demure, modest, shy, timid
basic	=	key, vital
basin	=	bowl, dish, dock, harbour, pan, valley
basket	=	goal [basket-ball], skep, skip, trug
(angler's) basket	=	buck, creel
bat	=	blink, club, racket, vampire, wink
bats	=	crazy, daft, insane, loco, mad, nuts
bath	=	sponge, tub, wash
bathe	=	bath, clean(se), sponge, swim, wash
baton	=	staff, stick, truncheon, wand
(first) batsman	=	opener [cricket]
(last, late) batsmen	=	tail [cricket]
batter	=	baste, beat, hammer, lam, paste, wallop
batting	=	in [cricket]
battle	=	action, combat, fight, fray, strife, struggle, war(fare)
baulk	=	hinder, jib, miss, shirk, shy, thwart
bawl	=	bellow, cry, howl, roar, shout
bay	=	alcove, bark, bight, cove, gulf, howl, inlet, laurel, niche, nook, recess, stall, yelp
BBC	=	auntie, beeb
be	=	abide, endure, exist, feel, happen, is, last, live, occur
beach	=	coast, pebbles, sand, seaside, shore, strand
beacon	=	guide, light, signal; name of [belisha]
bead	=	ball, bubble, drop, (fore)sight, prayer
beak	=	bill, neb, nib, nose, snout, spout
beam	=	glow, light, ray, shine, smile, spar, transom; name of [laser]
beaming	=	aglow, bright, lucent, lucid, radiant, shining
bean	=	coin, head; name of [broad, coffee, runner, soya, string]
bean stalk	=	halm, haulm
beans	=	energy, go, pep, pulse, vigour
bear	=	beget, breed, brook, bruin, carry, hold, stand, suffer, tolerate, tote, wield name of [pooh [Winnie], rupert, yogi]
beard	=	barb, defy, gill, oppose; name of [beaver, goatee, vandyke, ziff]
beard of grain	=	arista, awn
bearer	=	agent, carrier, payee, porter, runner
bearing	=	air, aspect, birth, carriage, gait, manner, mien, port, pose, posture, (e, n, ne, nw, s, se, sw, w)
beast	=	animal [see], brute, fiend, swine
(large) beast	=	behemoth, mammoth, mastodon, monster, ogre
(little) beast	=	calf, cub, foal, kid, kitten, lamb, pup

beast of burden	= ass, burro, camel, donkey, mule, ox
beat	= best, cane, clobber, drub, flog, fox, hit, lam, lash, leather, perplex, pulse, rhythm, surpass, tan, tired, thrash, throb, trounce, whip
beating	= cat [-o'-nine-tails], hiding
beau	= admirer, dandy, fop, lover
beauty	= charm, fairness, grace
because	= as, for, since
because of	= by, over, through
become	= adorn, (be)fit, get, grace, happen, suit
bed	= berth, bunk, cot, couch, crib, divan, mattress, plant, plot, row, strip
(straw) bed	= pallet
bedlam	= asylum, madhouse
bee	= poet; name of [drone, queen, worker]
beekeeper	= apiarist
beef	= baron, brawn, carp, complain(t), flesh, gripe, grouse, muscle, sinew
beer	= ale, draught, grog, lager, nog, pint, porter
(bad) beer	= swipes
(unfermented) beer	= wort
beetle	= brow, bug, insect, jut, overhang; name of [cockroach, ladybird, scarab, weevil]
befall	= ensue, happen, occur, pass
before(hand)	= afore, ahead, ante, ere, pre, prior, (a)
(day, night) before	= eve
before long	= anon, shortly, soon
beg	= ask, beseech, entreat, implore, plead, sponge
beggar	= cadger, mendicant, pauper, tramp, vagrant
beggarly	= abject, base, low, mean, poor, stingy
begin	= arise, commence, dawn, spring, start
beginner	= learner [see], (l)
beginning	= alpha, birth, genesis, onset, origin, outset, source
begone	= avaunt, scram
begrudge	= envy, resent
beguile	= amuse, charm, cheat, delude
behalf	= account, benefit, favour, interest, sake, side
behave	= act, do, perform
behaviour	= action, conduct, guise, manner(s)
behest	= charge, command, dictate, order
behind	= aft(er), astern, late, next, rump, seat
behold	= eye, lo, look, mark, see, view, watch
being	= human, mortal, person, soul, thing
belabour	= beat, berate, flay, flog, thrash, whip
belief	= credence, credit, faith, religion, trust
believe	= accept, credit, deem, feel, think, trust
(make-)believe	= charade, dream, fantasy, mock, sham
bell	= ben [Big Ben], buzz(er), call, chime, cry, ring, toll

bellow	= bawl, cry, roar, shout
belly	= abdomen, appetite, stomach, womb
below	= beneath, lower, inferior, sub, under
belt	= area, band, girdle, lam, sash, slam, smash, strap, tan, tract, zone, wallop; name of [baldric, bandoleer]
ben	= hur [Ben Hur], mount, peak, room [inner]
bench	= court, form, ledge, pew, seat, settle
bend	= arc, bias, bow, curve, flex, helix, incline, ogee, turn, yield; name of [carrick, common, fisherman's, sheet], (s, u)
bent	= bias, grass, heath, intent, tendency, twist
bender	= archer, orgy, spree
Benedictine	= dom [monk's title]
benefit	= advantage, avail, behalf, boon, favour, interest; kind of [allowance, pension]
benevolent	= big, generous, good, kind
benign	= gentle, gracious, kind(ly), mild
berate	= chide, rail, rant, rate, revile, scold
berserk	= mad, wild
berth	= bed, dock, jetty, moor, pier, quat, wharf
beset	= assail, attack, badger, harass, pester
beside	= besides [see], by, near(by), nigh
besides	= also, bar, beyond, but, else, except, more(over), otherwise, still, too, yet
best	= beat, cap, lay, right, utmost, worst
(very) best	= cream, elite, pick, prime, top
bestow	= award, confer, deposit, give, grant, lodge
bet	= ante, back, evens, flutter, odds, risk, stake, wager
betrothal	= engagement, espousal, promise
betrothed	= engaged, fiancee, intended
better	= beat, best, cap, defeat, gambler, outwit, punter, superior
(do) better	= cap, surpass, top
(feel, get) better	= improve, rally, recover, revive
bevy	= bunch, covey, crowd, flight, flock, group, pack
beware	= cave, fore, heed, mind
bewilder	= confuse, fox, perplex, puzzle
beyond	= above, besides, outside, over, past
bi	= doubly, twice, two
bias	= bent, drift, leaning, prejudice, side, slant, tendency
biblical king	= name of [herod]
bicker	= argue, brawl, dispute, quarrel, quibble
bid	= ask, attempt, command, offer, order, tell, told, try, venture
bide	= await, dwell, live, stay, tarry, wait
big	= fat, huge, large, major, tall, vast

(very) big	=	colossal, gigantic, huge, jumbo, titanic, (os)
bigwig	=	nabob, nob, pot, (vip)
bill	=	account, beak, invoice, neb, nib, note, poster, tab, (ac, be)
billiard-player	=	cueist
Billy	=	can, kid
bind	=	attach, fasten, glue, hitch, lash, oblige, tie, truss, wrap
binding	=	astringent, braid, obligatory, tying
birch	=	cane, flog, rod, stick, switch
bird	=	boo, catcall, chick, girl, hiss, woman = name of [aigrette, auk, barbet, bittern, bunting, crane, crow, daw, dove, egret, erne, finch, fowl, grouse, hen, jay, magpie, martin, peacock, pigeon, raven, rook, shank, snipe, sparrow, starling, stork, swallow, swift, tern, tit, turkey, warbler, wren]
(extinct) bird	=	dodo, moa, roc
(flightless) bird	=	bustard, cassowary, emu, kiwi, ostrich, rhea
(gull-like) bird	=	skua, tern
(sea)bird	=	albatross, auk, cormorant, gannet, gull, pelican, tern, skua
(song-)bird	=	bulbul, canary, lark, nightingale, thrush
(talking) bird	=	budgie, cockatoo, macaw, parrot
(water-)bird	=	avocet, coot, duck, eider, gannet, godwit, goose, gull, heron, mallard, pelican, pen, scooper, smew, stilt, swan, teal
(wise) bird	=	owl
bird group	=	aviary, colony, flock, gaggle, rookery
bird of prey	=	buzzard, eagle, falcon, harrier, hawk, kestrel, kite, osprey, owl, raptor, vulture
birth	=	alpha, dawn, genesis, origin, rise
(by, from, of) birth	=	natal
biscuit	=	cracker, farl, flapjack, pretzel
bishop	=	diocesan
bishop's office	=	bishopric, diocese, see
bit	=	bite, iota, jot, morsel, part, piece, portion, scrap, whit
bite	=	bit, burn, chomp, cut, eat, peck, nip, slice, smart, snack, snap, sting
biting	=	pungent, sarcastic, sharp, trenchant
bitter	=	acid, acrid, beer, cold, harsh, icy, sharp, sour
(not) bitter	=	mild, sweet
bitterness	=	gall, grudge, pique, rancour, venom
bivalve	=	mollusc, native, oyster
black	=	dark, ebony, jet, night, sable, (b)
black eye	=	mouse, shiner
blackguard	=	bounder, cad, knave, rogue, scoundrel
blade	=	bat, knife, leaf, oar, spade, sword

blame	=	accuse, censure, condemn, fault, rap
bland	=	boring, dull, flat, gentle, mild, smooth
blank	=	clean, empty, space, vacant, void
blast	=	bang, boom, clap, curse, gust, rout, slam, squall, storm
bleak	=	bare, chilly, dreary, grim, harsh
bleat	=	complain, cry, gripe, moan, whine
bleed	=	fleece, milk, ooze, seep, weep
bleep	=	beep, call, signal
blemish	=	blot, fault, flaw, mar, spoil, spot, stain, taint
blend	=	alloy, fuse, meld, merge, mingle, mix
bless	=	extol, hallow, laud, praise
blessing	=	benison, boon, favour, gift, grace
blimey	=	cor, crumbs, gosh
blimp	=	diehard, reactionary
bliss	=	ecstasy, euphoria, heaven, joy, rapture
block	=	anvil, bar, cake, choke, clog, jam, slab, thwart
blockage	=	dam, jam, let
blockhead	=	chump, dolt, dope, duffer, dunce, idiot, moron, mug, mutt, nitwit, oaf
bloke	=	chap, fellow, man
blond(e)	=	fair, flaxen, light
blood	=	anger, dandy, fop, gore, plasma, race
bloody	=	gory, rare, red, sanguine
bloodsucker	=	bug, extortioner, leech, tick, vampire
bloom	=	flourish, flower, flush, glow, prime
bloomer	=	blunder, bud, flower [see], mistake, plant [see], slip
blossom	=	bloom, burgeon, flower, grow
blot	=	blemish, mar, spot, stain, sully
blow	=	blast, fan, gust, pant, puff, wind
blow up	=	enlarge, inflate
blown	=	gone, wasted
blower	=	bugler, (tele)phone, trumpeter
blubber	=	cry, fat, sob, wail, weep
blue	=	glum, lewd, low, risque, sad, sportsman, tory, unhappy; shade of [anil, azure, cobalt, cyan, indigo, navy, royal, sapphire, saxe, saxon, sky, turquoise]
blue pencil	=	censor
blueprint	=	chart, design, draft, pilot, plan
blues	=	dumps, gloom
bluff	=	abrupt, blunt, frank, hearty
blunder	=	boob, err(or), fault, gaffe, slip
blunders	=	errata
board	=	dash, embark, lodge, panel, plank, slat, table, wood [see], (bb)
board game	=	name of [backgammon, chess, draughts, halma, ludo, monopoly, scrabble]

boarder	= lodger, guest, tenant
boast	= blow, brag, bray, crow, extol, vaunt
boat	= ship, vessel; name of [barge, canoe, coracle, dinghy, kayak, launch, liner, punt, scow, scull, steamer, tender, trawler, tug], (ss)
(mail)boat	= packet
(sailing) boat	= name of [bark, barque, brig(antine), corsair, dhow, galleon, galley, ketch, proa, schooner, sloop, smack, xebec, yacht, zebec(k)]
boat-crew	= eight
boatman	= cox(swain), gondolier, oarsman, rower
boatman's song	= barcarole
bob	= bound, curtsy, cut, dance, dock, jerk, rap, shilling
bode	= augur, foresee, foretell, omen, portend
body	= cadaver, corpse, society, stiff, torso, trunk
(heavenly) body	= asteroid, comet, meteor, planet, star
(military) body	= army, battalion, brigade, division, legion, platoon, soldiers, troop(s), unit
body of type	= form(e)
bog	= fen, marsh, morass, quagmire, swamp
bogus	= fake, false, phony, pseudo, sham
boil	= churn, decoct, seethe, simmer, stew
bold	= brave, clear, doughty, gallant, game
bole	= stem, trunk
bolt	= arrow, dart, escape, flee, jump, latch, rivet, run, snib, start, wolf
bombard	= attack, batter, blast, blitz, pound, shell, strafe
bombast	= bluster, brag, fustian, rant
bombastic	= fustian, pompous, turgid, verbose
bond	= bail, join, link, pact, surety, tie, union
bone	= steal; name of [clavicle, femur, fibula, rib, shin, sternum, tibia, ulna], (t)
book	= ledger, novel, order, reserve, tome, (b, nt, ot)
(good) book	= bible, (nt, ot)
(introductory) book	= primer
boom	= barrier, buzz, hum, spar, upsurge
boon	= blessing, favour, gift, godsend, request
boost	= help, hike, hoist, lift, plug, raise
boot	= fire, kick, punt, sack
booth	= stall, tent
bootless	= vain
booty	= haul, loot, spoil(s), swag
border	= abut, boundary, edge, fringe, frontier, hem, rim, side, verge
bore	= awl, calibre, drill, eagre, flood, hole, jade, mine, nuisance, pest, pierce, sink
boredom	= apathy, ennui, tedium
boring	= dead, dull, flat, humdrum, stale, tedious

born	=	nee, (b)
borrow	=	adopt, cadge, scrounge, touch, use
borrowed	=	out
boss	=	cock, head, knob, manager, master, nub, stud, umbo
both	=	couple, pair, two
bother	=	ado, fuss, nag, pester, trouble, vex, worry
bottle	=	drink; name of [carafe, carboy, flagon, flask, phial, vial]
bottom	=	base, beam, nadir, posterior, rear, seat
bounce	=	hop, evict, jump, leap, rebound
bouncer	=	ball, chucker, doorman, lie
bound	=	hedge, hop, jump, leap, limit, obliged, spring, strapped, tied, vault
boundary	=	four [cricket], edge, fence, hedge(row), limit, wall
bounder	=	cad, cur, heel, rat
bounty	=	gift, grant, gratuity, premium, reward
bouquet	=	aroma, bunch, flowers [see], nosegay, perfume, posy, scent
bout	=	fight, fit, match, spell, stint
(drinking) bout	=	bender, binge, spree, toot
bovine animal, creature(s)	=	cow(s), kine, neat, ox(en)
bow	=	arch, bend, curve, defer, prow, salute, stem, submit, yield
bower	=	arbour, boudoir, pergola
bowl	=	basin, pitch, spin, tureen, wood
bowled	=	out, (b)
bowler	=	hat, seamer, spinner [cricket]
bowman	=	archer, hood [Robin], tell [William]
box	=	carton, case, chest, crate, coffer, cuff, fight, slap, spar, trunk
boxer	=	bruiser, fighter, pugilist
(old) boxer	=	ali [Mohammed Ali], clay [Cassius Clay]
boy	=	lad, native, page, servant, son; name of [al, des, don, ed, bill, eric, les, mark, pete, ray, ron, stan, ted, tom]
(German) boy	=	name of [dieter, gunter, hans, heinz, helmut, karl, ulrich]
(homeless) boy	=	arab, waif
(Irish) boy	=	name of [connor, eamon, liam, mick, paddy, pat(rick), seamus, sean, spud]
(old) boy	=	alumnus, man, (ob)
(Russian) boy	=	name of [boris, igor, ivan, serge]
(small) boy	=	(abbreviated) name of boy [see]
brace	=	couple, pair, prop, stay, strut, truss
bracken	=	brake, fern
brag	=	bluster, blow, boast, crow, vaunt
brain	=	cerebrum, egghead, genius, pundit, sage, scholar

brainwave	=	idea
brainy	=	cerebral, clever, sharp, smart
branch	=	antler, arm, bough, chapter, limb, prong, sprig, wing
brand	=	burn, make, mark, stigma, sword, torch
brandy	=	cognac, spirit
brass	=	cheek, gall, money, nerve
brat	=	apron, bantling, child
brave	=	bold, defy, face, game, stout, vivid; name of [apache, cree, mohawk]
(young) brave	=	papoose
brave partner	=	squaw
brawl	=	clash, feud, fight, fray, row, scrap
brawling woman	=	scold, shrew, termagant, virago
bray	=	bawl, blare, boast, heehaw, trumpet
bread	=	cash, dough, loaf [see], money, pay
(slice of) bread	=	doorstep
break	=	chance, check, crack, crumble, dawn, gap, respite, rest, shatter, smash, snap
(short) break	=	hol[iday], vac[ation]
break down	=	analyse, crumble, decay, dissect, wilt
break open	=	burst, crack, force, split
break up	=	dissolve, divorce, rift, split
breaker	=	cask, comber, keg, roller, wave
breakfast	=	cereal, egg
breath	=	air, gasp, gulp, pant, puff, whiff
breathe	=	be, exhale, exist, inhale, live, whisper
breather	=	break, lung, nose, pause, rest
breed	=	bear, class, grow, ilk, race, raise, rear, sire, stock, strain
breeding	=	culture, education, manners, polish
breeze	=	air, cinch, quarrel, snap, wind
brew	=	concoct, ferment, fester, loom; name of [beer, coffee, punch, tea]
bribe	=	graft, lure, payola, sop
brickbat	=	criticism, missile
brick	=	adobe, block
brick-carrier	=	hod
bridge	=	arch, cross, link, span(ner)
brief	=	concise, crisp, curt, pithy, quick, short, terse
brigand	=	bandit, gangster, outlaw, robber
bright	=	alert, clever, gaudy, lucid, sharp, smart, vivid
brilliant	=	bright, clever, illustrious, lucent, luminous, smart, sparkling
brim	=	edge, lip
bring	=	bear, carry, conduct, convey, fetch
bring up	=	broach, raise, rear
brink	=	border, edge, fringe, rim, verge
brisk	=	active, lively, nimble

British detectives	=	yard, (cid)
brittle	=	fragile, frail, hard
broad	=	ample, large, risque, vast, wide
broadcast	=	air, beam, blazon, on, seed, sow
brochure	=	booklet, folder, leaflet, tract, pamphlet
broke(n)	=	bust, ruined, skint, stony
broker	=	agent, dealer
brooch	=	clip, pin
brood	=	crew, hatch, meditate, swarm
brook	=	beck, burn, gill, rill, stream
broom	=	besom, brush, sweep(er)
brother	=	brer, cleric, comrade, friar, monk, (br)
brothers' room	=	cell
brow	=	brim, crest, edge, peak, rim, top
browbeat	=	badger, bully, coerce, cow, hector
brown	=	auburn, bay, bistre, dun, sepia, tan
bruise	=	batter, contuse, dint, injure, pound
brunt	=	burden, force, shock, stress, thrust
brush	=	besom, broom, graze, loofah, sweep(er)
brusque	=	abrupt, curt, gruff, short, tart, terse
brute	=	animal, beast, fiend, ogre, swine
buck	=	dandy, dollar, dude, fop, jump, male, stag
bud	=	embryo, germ, shoot, sprout
buddy	=	crony, friend, mate, pal
buff	=	addict, fan, freak, polish, rub, shine
(in the) buff	=	bare, naked, nude
buffer	=	fogy, square
buffoon	=	clown, jester, mocker, wag
buggy	=	cart, trap
build	=	assemble, construct, create, erect, form, frame, raise
building	=	edifice, erection, fabric, frame, house
(farm) building	=	barn, byre, cote, shed, silo, stable, sty
building area, land	=	plot, site
built-up area	=	city, town
bulb	=	globe; name of [crocus, daffodil, iris, lily, narcissus, onion, tulip]
bulge	=	beetle, jut, lump, swell
bulk	=	body, cargo, mass, size, volume
bull	=	absurd, coerce, cow, edict
bull('s eye)	=	inner
bulls	=	stock
bullet	=	lead, run, scoot, shot, slug, speed, tracer
bullets	=	ammo
bulletin	=	news, report, story
bully	=	bluster, coerce, cow, oppress, tyrant
bump	=	barge, clash, collide, crash, jar, jolt
bumpkin	=	clown, fool, peasant, rustic, yokel
bunch	=	clump, cluster, group, knot, tuft

bunch of flowers	= bouquet, corsage, nosegay, posy, spray
bunk	= bed, berth, cot, flight, flummery, hokum, humbug, nonsense, vanish
burden	= cargo, duty, load, onus, oppress, tax, weight
(beast of) burden	= ass, burro, camel, donkey, mule, ox
burgeon	= bud, flourish, grow, sprout
burial mound	= barrow, tumulus
burn	= blaze, brook, char, flame, rill, sear, smart, sting, stream
burning	= ardent, eager, fiery, hot, intense
burrow	= den, dig, hole, lair
burst	= crack, erupt, pop, spate, split, surge
bury	= earth, embed, entomb, hide, inter, stash
bus	= coach
bush	= shrub [see]
business	= company, concern, firm, (co)
bust	= break, broke(n), crash, fail, fold, ruin(ed)
bustle	= ado, dash, fuss, rush, stir
but	= except, however, only, room [outer], save, yet
butcher	= kill, mutilate, slaughter, slay
butt	= barrel, cask, end, mound, object, stump
butte	= hill, knoll, mound
butter	= pat; name of [ram, shea, tup]
butterfly	= trifler; name of [adonis, brimstone, copper, skipper]
buy	= accept, believe, bribe, purchase
(good) buy	= bargain, snip
buy back	= ransom, redeem
buy shares	= invest, speculate
buyer	= bull, customer, purchaser, shopper
buzz	= drone, hiss, hum, ring, whir(r)
buzzer	= bee, bell
by	= at, beside(s), near, over, past, per
by way of	= via
by(e)	= secret, side
bygone	= former, late, old, once, past

C

cab	= carriage, hackney, limo, taxi
cabal	= circle, clique, faction, party, ring
cabbage	= cole, kail, kale, savoy
cabin	= berth, cot, crib, hut, lodge, room, shack, shed
cabinet	= case, commode, chest, closet, locker
cable	= chain, hawser, telegram, telex, wire
cable-car	= gondola, telpher
cache	= bury, conceal, hide, stash, store
cachet	= seal, stamp
cad	= bounder, cur, heel, rat, rotter, roue
cafe	= bar, bistro, diner, restaurant, shop

cage	=	confine, coop, fence, mew, pen, pound
cajole	=	coax, con, dupe, entice, lure, tempt
cake	=	encrust, harden; name of [angel, banbury, battenberg, bun, eccles, fruit, genoa, lardy, madeira, muffin, pound, queen, simnel, sponge]
Caledonian	=	scot, scotch
calendar	=	almanac, list, menology, register, schedule, table; name of [gregorian, julian], (cal)
call	=	bleep, contact, dub, hi, name, phone, ring, shout, style, summons, term, visit
call forth	=	educe, elicit, evoke
call on	=	see, visit
called	=	rang, rung
calling	=	art, job, line, metier, mission, trade, vocation, work
callow	=	downy, green, raw
calm	=	abate, cool, hush, mild, quiet, sedate, serene, still, tranquil
calumny	=	defamation, slander
Cambrian	=	welsh(man)
camp	=	bivouac, laager, outspan, tent(s)
can	=	able, billy, may, tin
canal	=	aqueduct, channel, conduit, duct, groove; name of [corinth, panama, suez]
cancel	=	annul, delete, drop, erase, quash, repeal, revoke, void
candid	=	blunt, fair, frank, just, open
candle	=	light, tallow, wax, wick; name of [roman]
cane	=	birch, punish, rod, stick, switch, whip; name of [bamboo, sugar]
canine	=	dog, tooth; name of dog [see]
cannabis	=	dope, hemp, pot
cannon	=	gun, ordnance
canon	=	clergy [see], decree, edict, law
cant	=	incline, jerk, slope, tilt, tip, toss
(army) canteen	=	mess, naafi
canter	=	amble, dogtrot, gallop, jog, lope, run
canvas	=	burlap, painting, picture, sail, tarpaulin, tent
canvas holder	=	easel
canvass	=	doorstep, poll, solicit, survey
cap	=	beat, better, crown, headgear [see], peak, top
(measure of) capacity	=	bushel, gallon, gill, litre, noggin, peck, pint, quart, quarter, (cc, gal, l, pt, qu)
cape	=	cloak, head, ness, point
caper	=	cavort, dance, frisk, frolic, gambol, hop, leap, jump, romp
capital	=	cash, chief, fine, head, letter, main, money, prime, stock; name of city [see], (cap)
capitalise	=	back, exploit, finance, stake

Capone	= al
caprice	= conceit, fancy, freak, vagary, whim
capsize	= overturn, sink, upset
captain	= boss, chief, foreman, lead(er), master, pilot, skip(per); name of [bligh, cook, hook, scott]
caption	= arrest, heading, legend, note, title
captious	= carping, critical
captivate	= charm, enchant, enthral, fascinate
captive	= charmed, confined, hostage, prisoner
capture	= arrest, bag, catch, collar, nab, net, seize, seizure, take
car	= coach, coupe, estate, limo, limousine, motor, sedan, saloon; name of [audi, austin, jag(uar), mini, rolls], (gt, mg, rr, vw)
(old) car	= banger, boneshaker, heap, jalopy
(police) car	= panda
card	= character, eccentric, tease, wag; name of [ace, deuce, jack, joker, king, knave, queen]
(honour) card	= name of [ace, jack, king, knave, queen]
(security) card	= pass, permit
card game	= name of [baccarat, basset, bezique, blackjack, brag, bridge, canasta, cribbage, ecarte, euchre, faro, gin, loo, nap, patience, poker, pontoon, ruff, rummy, snap, solitaire, solo, whist]
cardinal	= central, number, red, scarlet, vital; name of number [one, two, three, four, etc]
care	= anxiety, heed, nurse, tend, ward, woe
care for	= minister, nurse, protect
career	= calling, livelihood, profession, race, rush, speed, tear
careless	= casual, remiss, slipshod, sloppy
career	= course, job, progress, race, rush, tear
caress	= fondle, hug, kiss, pat, pet, stroke
caretaker	= concierge, janitor, keeper, porter
cargo	= freight, haul, lading, load, ware
carnage	= bloodshed, butchery, massacre, slaughter
carnival	= feast, fete, fiesta, jamboree
carp	= beef, bicker, complain, criticise
carping	= captious, critical
carpenter	= joiner, planer
carpet	= drugget, mat, rug, runner
carriage	= air, bearing, gait, manner, mien, port, posture, vehicle [see]
(baby) carriage	= pram
(funeral) carriage	= bier, hearse
(horse-drawn) carriage	= (horse-drawn) vehicle [see]
carrier	= bag, hod, pigeon, vector
carry	= bear, fetch, haul, lug, stock, tote
carry out	= do, effect, execute, fulfil

cart	= convey, dray, transport, wagon
carton	= box, case, package, packet
case	= action, bag, box, carton, cause, event, example, pod, portfolio, sheath, shell, suit, trial; name of [attache, vanity]
cash	= bread, coin(s), dough, money, specie
cash register	= till
cashier	= bursar, clerk, discard, dismiss, expel, paymaster, purser, sack, teller
cask	= anker, barrel, breaker, butt, firkin, keg, pin, tun
caskmaker	= cooper
cast	= add, fling, hue, mould, plaster, set, shade, shed, shy, sum, throw, tinge, toss
caste	= class, grade, order, race, rank, status; = name of [brahmin]
castigate	= berate, cane, criticize, rebuke, scold
castigation	= censure, criticism, rebuke, reproof
castle	= chateau, citadel, fort(ress), keep, peel, tower
casual	= chance, informal, irregular, offhand, temp
cat	= feline, moggy, mouser, puss(y), scourge, tabby, tom, whip
cat(-like animal)	= name of [civet, cheetah, genet, leopard, lion, lynx, ocelot, ounce, panther, puma, tiger]
catlike, catty	= feline, leonine
cats-paw	= breeze, dupe, stooge, tool
catalogue	= file, index, inventory, list, roll, roster, (cat)
catapult	= launch, sling, (cat)
catcall	= boo, gibe, hiss, jeer, mew
catch	= arrest, bag, bolt, capture, clasp, clip, land, nab, net, snag, snare, snib
catch fire	= burn, ignite, light
catchword	= byword, phrase, slogan
cater	= outfit, pander, provide, purvey, supply
cathedral	= church [see], dome
cathedral (city)	= name of [ayr, bangor, cobh, cork, derby, durham, ely, ennis, leeds, ripon, truro, wells, york]
Catherine	= kate, kay
catholic	= general, jesuit, papist, universal, (rc)
cattle	= kine, neat, oxen, stock
cattle farm, station	= ranch
caught	= out [cricket], (c, ct)
cause	= case, effect, ground, induce, motive, produce, reason, suit
caution	= care, caveat, prudence, reprove, warn(ing)
cautious	= alert, cagey, careful, prudent, wary
cavalier	= curt, escort, gallant, knight, offhand
cavalryman	= dragoon, hussar, lancer

cave	= beware, cavern, den, grotto, hollow, pothole
caveat	= caution, proviso, warning
cavity	= hole, hollow, sinus, (o)
cavort	= caper, frisk, frolic, gambol, romp
cease	= close, desist, end, halt, quit, stop
cede	= admit, assign, grant, surrender, transfer, yield
ceiling	= apex, limit, peak, roof, top
celebrate	= extol, honour, laud, praise, sing
celebrate noisily	= revel, roister
celebration	= do, fete, gala, party
celebrity	= lion, name, star
cell	= cottage, dungeon, grave, room
cemetery	= graveyard, necropolis
censure	= blame, criticise, knock, rap, reprove
census	= count, poll, register, tally
central	= chief, focal, inner, key, main, mean, mid(dle)
centre	= core, crux, heart, hub, inner, mid(dle)
(dead) centre	= cemetery, graveyard, necropolis
(finance) centre	= city
(shopping) centre	= arcade, mall, market, mart, plaza
century	= ton, (c)
cereal	= corn, maize, oat(s), rice, rye, wheat
ceremony	= pomp, rite, ritual, service
certain	= bound, firm, fixed, positive, real, some, sure, true, valid
certainly	= ay, firmly, really, surely, truly
certify	= assure, attest, vouch, warrant, witness
chaff	= banter, bracts, hay, husks, jest, joke, rib, rubbish, straw
chaffer	= bargain, dicker, haggle
chain	= fetters, links, row, series, set, string
chair	= bench, preside, run, seat, sedan, sofa
chalet	= cabin, cottage, house, hut, lodge
challenge	= brave, contest, dare, defy, impugn
champion	= ace, back, crack, expert, head, hero, paladin, top, victor
chance	= break, fortune, gamble, hazard, luck, risk
change	= adapt, alter, amend, coins, modify, vary
change place	= flit, move
change position	= shift
changes	= medley, variety
channel	= canal, duct, gut, medium, pipe, rut, strait
chant	= croon, sing, song, warble
chap	= crack, crevice, fissure, gent, guy, he, him, male, man
(annoying) chap	= blighter, nuisance, pain, pest
(eccentric) chap	= card, case, character, crackpot, nut, oddity, quiz, weirdo
(irritating) chap	= blighter, nuisance, pain, pest

(little) chap	=	dwarf, midget, pygmy
chaps	=	men
chaplain	=	clergy [see], father, padre, priest
chapel	=	chantry, church [see], oratory
chapter	=	branch, (c, cap, ch)
char	=	burn, cleaner, daily, maid, sear, tea
character	=	card, ethos, figure, initial, letter, logo, nature, part, role, sort, style
(Figaro) character	=	barber
(Greek) character	=	(Greek) letter [see]
(operatic) character	=	name of [figaro, igor, mimi]
(mischievous) character	=	imp
characteristic	=	feature, mark, trait, virtue
charge	=	attack, claim, cost, count, due, fee, impute, indictment, ion, mandate, mine, onus, order, price, prime, rap, rate, rent, rush, tariff, ward
(customs) charge	=	duty
(exorbitant) charge	=	earth
(spiritual) charge	=	cure [of souls]
(currently) charged	=	electric
charged particle	=	ion
charity	=	alms, fund, gift
charm	=	allure, amulet, bewitch, draw, enamour, enchant, entrance, hex, mascot, spell, talisman, trinket, wile
chart	=	diagram, graph, map, plan, table
chase	=	emboss, engrave, hound, hunt, tag
chasm	=	abyss, gap, gulf, ravine, schism, split
chasten	=	correct, punish, refine, subdue, temper
chastise	=	beat, chasten, punish, whip
chat(ter)	=	babble, jaw, prate, rabbit, talk, yak
chatty	=	garrulous, loquacious, talkative
cheap	=	base, common, low, mean, nasty, shoddy
cheat	=	bilk, con, do, rook, sting, swindle
check	=	audit, bit, break, contain, curb, halt, limit, rein, stay, stem, stop, stunt
(final) check	=	mate
cheek	=	gall, lip, nerve, sauce
cheer	=	applaud, fare, feast, food, hurrah, shout
cheer up	=	comfort, console, enliven, gladden
cheese	=	name of [blue, brie, cheddar, cottage, edam, feta, gouda, gruyere, roquefort, ricotta, stilton]
chemical	=	name of [nitre, phenol]
cheque	=	draft, order
cherish	=	comfort, cosset, foster, nurse, prize
cherished	=	dear, favourite, pet
chest	=	box, case, casket, coffer, crate, kist, trunk
chevy	=	badger, chase, cry, hunt, scamper, shout
chic	=	fashion, skill, smart, style, stylish

chichi	=	affected, elaborate, frilly, fussy
chicken	=	biddy, capon, coward, fowl, hen, pullet
chid, chide	=	admonish, rebuke, reprove, scold, wig
chief	=	arch, boss, central, foremost, head, main, major, prime
chieftain	=	lord, ruler, sultan, thane
child	=	babe, baby, heir, issue, kid, minor, nipper, scion, son, tot
(homeless) child	=	arab, waif
(ill-behaved) child	=	imp
(spoilt) child	=	bantling, brat
(young) child	=	bantling, infant, tot
childish	=	immature, jejune, juvenile, puerile
children	=	brood, progeny, issue, offspring, seed
chill	=	bite, cold, cool, nip
china	=	name of [belleek, delft, dresden, faience, goss, limoges, ming, sevres, spode, wedgwood]
Chinese	=	ming, sino
chip	=	banter, break, carve, crack, cut, flake, score
chiv(v)y	=	badger, chase, cry, hunt, scamper, shout
chocolate	=	brown
choice	=	best, elite, option, pick, select
choir	=	chorale, chorus, glee, singers, voices
choke	=	gag, splutter, stifle, strangle, throttle
choker	=	garotte, necklace
choose	=	adopt, desire, elect, list, opt, pick, select, wish
chosen	=	elect, elite
chop	=	axe, boot, cut, dismissal, hack, hew, lop, sack
choral	=	anthem, canticle, hymn, psalm
chore	=	burden, duty, fag, job, stint, task
chorus	=	accord, choir, chorale, concert, glee, harmony, refrain, sing(ers), tune
chorister	=	angel, chanter, choir-boy, precentor
Christmas	=	noel, yule
Christopher	=	kit
chum	=	buddy, crony, friend, mate, pal
church	=	basilica, cathedral, chapel, kirk, minster, (c, ce, ch, ec, rc)
(part of) church	=	altar, apse, chancel, nave, pew, pulpit, reredos
(prince of the) church	=	cardinal
church calendar	=	menology
church official	=	beadle, elder, verger, warden
church petition	=	litany
church service	=	worship; name of [mass, matin, vespers]
churchman	=	clergy [see]
cipher	=	code, digit, logo, nought, number, zero
(royal) cipher	=	muster
circa	=	about, around, round, (c, ca)
circle	=	clique, coterie, disc, halo, ring, round, set, (o)

(run) circles	= lap
circuit	= ambit, lap, loop, orbit, round
circular	= notice, round, (o)
circumvent	= defeat, dish, frustrate, ruin, thwart
citadel	= acropolis, castle, fort, keep, kremlin, redoubt, tower
cite	= call, name, quote, summon
citizen	= burgess, burgher, denizen, subject
(old) citizen	= roman, trojan
city	= municipal, urban, (la)
(ancient) city	= name of [pompeii, sparta, troy, tyre, ur]
(capital) city	name of [aden, athens, belfast, berlin, berne, bonn, cairo, delhi, dublin, helsinki, kiev, lagos, lima, lome, london, moscow, oslo, ottawa, paris, prague, rio, rome, tokyo, tripoli, tunis, vienna, warsaw, zagreb]
(cathedral) city	= name of [ayr, bangor, cobh, cork, derby, durham, ely, ennis, leeds, ripon, truro, wells, york]
(eternal) city	= rome
(French) city	= French city [see]
(German) city	= German city [see]
(Italian) city	= Italian city [see]
(old) city	= name of [pompeii, sparta, troy, tyre, ur]
claim	= argue, charge, contend, demand, maintain, title
clamp	= brace, clasp, fix, grip, hold, vice
clash	= collide, conflict, feud, fight, jar, quarrel, wrangle
class	= caste, form, genre, genus, kind, order, range, rate, type
claw	= fang, hammer, nail, pincer, pounce, scratch, talon, tear
clay	= earth, kaolin, mud, soil
clean	= blank, chaste, mop, pure, sponge, swab, sweep, wash, wipe
cleaner	= char, lye, soap
clear	= evacuate, evident, fade, free, limpid, lucid, net, obvious, patent, plain, release, vivid
clear up	= clarify, explain, solve
clearance	= approval, consent, leave, sanction
clearing	= glade
cleave	= adhere, chop, cling, cohere, rive, split, stick
cleft	= chink, crack, fissure, schism, split
clement	= gentle, lenient, mild
clenched hand	= fist
clergy(man)	= name of [canon, chaplain, cleric, curate, dean, divine, father, minister, padre, parson, pastor, prelate, priest, rector, vicar], (dd, rev)
(non-)clergy, clerical	= laic, laity, lay, secular

clever	= able, adept, astute, bright, cunning, fly, quick, sly, smart
cliff	= bluff, crag, face, scar(p)
climate	= atmosphere, weather
climb	= ascend, ascent, clamber, mount, rise, scale
cling	= adhere, grasp, stick
clique	= circle, clan, coterie, set
cloak	= cape, conceal, cover, disguise, mask, poncho
clobber	= beat, belt, clothes [see], wallop
clock	= ben [Big Ben], ticker, timer, watch
close	= by, end(ing), finish, mean, near, nigh, plug, seal, shut, tight
cloth	= fabric, material, nap, rag, rep, yarn name of [baize, brocade, broche, buckram, calico, cambric, chintz, cotton, crape, crepe, denim, felt, gingham, grogram, lace, lame, lawn, linen, nankeen, nylon, rayon, sateen, satin, silk, tulle, tweed, velvet, voile, wool]
(sample of) cloth	= swatch
clothe	= attire, drape, dress, endow, invest, rig, swathe
clothed	= clad, girt
clothes, clothing	= accoutre, apparel, array, attire, clobber, costume, dress, duds, garb, garment, gear, get-up, habit, kit, outfit, raiment, rig, robes, togs, vestment [see], weeds; name of [blouse, cloak, coat [see], doublet, dress, gown, jeans, jumper, robe, shirt, shorts, skirt, slacks, suit, sweater, trousers]
(of men's) clothes	= sartorial
(plain) clothes	= mufti
(under)clothes	= name of [bodice, bra, chemise, hose, shift, singlet, slip, vest]
cloud	= blur, dim, fog, host, pall, shadow
clout	= cuff, hit, influence, pull, slap, strike
clown	= buffoon, fool, jester, joker, wag; name of [coco]
cloy	= jade, pall, sate, tire, weary
club	= bat, beat, cosh, cudgel, guild, mace, union
(golf) club	= name of [baffy, brassie, iron, driver, niblick, putter, spoon, wedge, wood]
clubs	= league, suit
clue	= hint, inkling, lead, notion, sign, thread
cluster	= batch, bunch, clump, group, knot, set
cluster of flowers	= bouquet, corsage, nosegay, posy, spray
clutch	= brood, claw, grasp, hand, hold, seize
coach	= bus, car, drill, train, tutor
coal waste	= slag, soot
coarse	= crass, crude, rough, uncouth, vulgar
coat	= hide, fleece, fur, paint, skin, warm; name of [blazer, burberry, jacket]

coax	=	cajole, entice, persuade, wheedle
cob	=	hazel, horse, loaf, swan
cocaine	=	dope, drug, snow
cock	=	bird, fowl, prick, raise, rooster, tap
cockade	=	badge, rosette
code	=	canon, cipher, ethic, maxim, morse
codicil	=	addendum, appendix, rider
coerce	=	compel, force, make
coffer	=	box, caisson, chest, money-box
cognac	=	brandy, spirit
cohere	=	adhere, cling, knit, stick
coiffure	=	haircut, hair-do; name of [beehive, bun]
coil	=	curl, loop, spiral, twine, wind
coin	=	change, copper, create, forge, frame, invent, mint, shiner, silver, specie
(low-value) coin	=	cent, copper, dime, penny, sou
(old) coin	=	name of [angel, crown, denarius, doubloon, ducat, farthing, florin, groat, pistole, sovereign, talent, tester]
(US) coin	=	name of [cent, dime, eagle, nickel, quarter]
coins	=	change, money, snide, specie
coincide	=	agree, concur, match, tally
col	=	neck, pass, saddle
cold	=	algid, chill, cool, frigid, icy, nip, (c)
collapse	=	break, crash, drop, faint, fall, swoon, wilt
collapsed	=	broke, fell
colleague	=	ally, partner
collect	=	amass, gather, hoard, muster, prayer, raise, save
collected	=	calm, cool, placid, sedate, serene
collected works	=	omnibus, volume
collection	=	group, herd, hoard, muster, set, trove
collector	=	name of [antiquary, bibliophile, deltiologist, numismatist, philatelist, phillumenist]
(tax) collector	=	publican
college	=	academy, university; name of [balliol, downing, dulwich, eton, jesus, lincoln, merton, oriel, trinity, wolfson]
college servant	=	scout, skip
collide	=	clash, conflict, crash
colonise	=	inhabit, people, settle
colonist	=	migrant, pioneer, planter, settler
colonnade	=	porch, portico, stoa
colour	=	dye, hue, paint, pigment, red(den), shade, tan, tinge, tint
colour(ed)	=	name of [beige, black, blue, brown, cream, ecru, green, grey, indigo, maroon, mauve, orange, pink, purple, red, violet, yellow]
(off) colour	=	ashen, ill, pale, wan

colours	=	banner, ensign, flag, jack, standard
column	=	monolith, pier, pilaster, pillar
combine	=	cartel, chain, join, link, mix, pool, unite
come	=	arrive, happen, occur, reach
come back	=	echo, recur, reply, return
come down	=	fall, land, teem
coming	=	advent, arrival, next
comedian	=	card, comic, wag, wit
comedy	=	farce, fun, humour, sitcom
comely	=	attractive, fair, lovely, pretty
comfort	=	aid, cheer, ease, help, solace
comic	=	card, clown, droll, funny, wag, wit
comical	=	absurd, droll, funny, silly
command	=	behest, bid, edict, decree, order, rule, sway
commence	=	begin, open, start
commend	=	acclaim, applaud, approve, entrust, hail, praise
commendation	=	applause, compliment, praise
comment	=	note, opine, remark, say
commerce	=	trade, traffic, truck
commercial	=	ad, advert(isement), plug
commission	=	appoint, bonus, cut, empower, enable, licence
common	=	base, cheap, general, green, joint, mean, mutual, park, public, square, usual
commotion	=	ado, din, furore, fuss, racket, riot, row, uproar
commune	=	converse, division, kibbutz
communication	=	letter, link, message, report, word
communist	=	red, trot
compact	=	bond, concise, deal, dense, thick
companion	=	buddy, crony, mate, pal, sir [Knight], (cb, ch)
company	=	business, concern, crew, firm, group, set, (co)
(shipping) company	=	line; name of [cunard]
compass	=	(en)circle, contrive, hem, ring, surround
compass point	=	rhumb, (e, n, s, w)
compassion	=	empathy, pity, sympathy
compel	=	coerce, exact, force, impel, make, urge
compelling	=	cogent, pressing, urgent
compere	=	host, (mc)
compete	=	enter, race, rival, run, vie
competent	=	able, capable, clever, equal, fit
competition	=	contest, game, match, meet, quiz, race, rival
competitive	=	keen, rival, vying
competitor	=	athlete, entrant, rival, runner
compiler	=	me
complacent	=	conceited, priggish, smug
complain(t)	=	beef, bleat, carp, cry, grouse, moan, wail, whine
complaint	=	disease [see]
(skin) complaint	=	name of [acne, eczema, fungus, impetigo]
complete	=	all, cap, clear, entire, finish, full, intact, total, utter, whole

completely	=	fully, quite, totally, wholly
compliment	=	applaud, bouquet, hail, praise
compose	=	arrange, create, form, make, write
composed	=	calm, cool, placid, made, sedate, serene, wrote
composer	=	name of [bach, bart, bizet, berlin, brahms, britten, chopin, debussy, delius, dvorak, elgar, gershwin, grieg, handel, haydn, holst, liszt, massenet, mozart, puccini, ravel, schubert, strauss, verdi, wagner]
comprehend	=	catch, contain, grasp, include, see, twig
compress	=	cram, crush, jam, pad, shrink
compunction	=	guilt, regret, remorse, scruple
con	=	against, anti, cheat, do, hoax, learn, read, study, tory, trick
conceal	=	bury, hide, mask, screen, secrete
concealed	=	covert, hid, hidden, secret
concede	=	admit, allow, confess, grant, own
conceit	=	caprice, ego(tism), pride, vanity
conceited	=	clever, egotistical, vain, witty
concept	=	idea, image, notion, thought
concern	=	affair, business, care, company, firm, heed, interest, matter, pertain, regard, worry
concerned with	=	about, anent, apropos, on, over, (re)
concerning	=	about, anent, apropos, on, over, (re)
concert	=	agree, harmony, prom, recital, tune, uni(s)on
concise	=	brief, compact, pithy, short, terse
conclude	=	end, cease, close, finish, infer, settle
conclusion	=	amen, end, close, finale, stop, term
concourse	=	assembly, crowd, meeting, throng
condense	=	abridge, compress, digest, shrink, sum
condensation	=	digest, epitome, precis, resume
condition	=	case, rider, rule, shape, state, (asis)
(good) condition	=	mint
(on) condition	=	if
(race) conditions	=	going
conduct	=	act, bring, chair, lead, mien, run
conducted	=	led, ran
confection	=	bon-bon, dress, preserve, sweet(meat)
confederate	=	allied, ally, greycoat, unite(d)
confer	=	award, bestow, give, grant, talk
conference	=	combine, meeting, seminar, tutorial
confess	=	admit, allow, aver, avow, own, tell
confidence	=	belief, credit, faith, hope, trust
confine	=	bind, cage, cramp, limit, restrict
confinement	=	cage, cell, custody, gaol, jail, pen, prison
confirm	=	endorse, fix, nod, ratify, yes
confirmed	=	actual, chronic, inured, sworn
confiscate	=	annex, appropriate, impound, seize
conflict	=	battle, clash, discord, fight, strife, war

confuse	= addle, cloud, faze, fog, ravel, twist
confusion	= chaos, flap, havoc, mess, muddle
conifer	= fir, pine
connection	= joint, link, relative, seam, union
(in) connection with	= about, apropos, anent, on, over, (re)
connote	= mean, imply, intend, signify, spell
conscious	= alert, awake, aware, wilful
(not) conscious	= asleep, comatose, out
conscript	= draft, enlist, enrol
consecrated	= holy, sacred
consent	= accede, agree, leave, permit, yes, (ok)
consequence	= aftermath, import, moment, outcome, pith, result, upshot
Conservative	= blue, right, tory, (c, con)
conserve	= hoard, jam, keep, nurse, save
consider	= believe, deem, reckon, think, weigh
consideration	= belief, fee, issue, point, study, tact, thought
consolidate	= cement, firm, fuse, join, unify, unite
conspiracy	= cabal, intrigue, plot, scheme
conspire	= connive, devise, plan, plot, scheme
constant	= even, fast, fixed, loyal, same, true
constant expense	= drain
constellation	= name of [bull, crab, orion, plough]
constituency	= district, seat
constrain	= check, coerce, compel, curb, force, make
construct	= build, create, erect, make, raise
consume	= devour, eat, scoff, use, waste
consumed	= ate, eaten, used
consumption	= use, (tb)
contact	= call, get, meet, reach, ring, touch
contain	= comprise, enclose, hold, include, restrain
container	= vessel; name of [barrel [see], bin, bottle [see], box [see], dish, flagon, flask, hopper, jar, pot, tank, urn]
contemptible	= base, cheap, low, mean, vile
contemptible type	= bounder, cad, cur, rat, rotter, sneak
content	= gist, happy, load, pleased, satisfied, text, willing
contest	= duel, fight, meet, race, rival, struggle, vie
continue	= abide, goon [go on], endure, last, proceed, resume
contort	= distort, twist, warp
contract	= agree(ment), bond, incur, lease, pledge, purse, reduce, shorten, shrink
contrary	= difficult, opposed, opposite, perverse
contrite	= humble, sorry
control	= boss, curb, direct, govern, limit, manage, master(y), rein, run
(Government) control	= authority, law, order, rule

convention	= bond, custom, form, pact, treaty, usage
converse	= counter, opposite, outre, talk [see]
convert	= adapt, alter, change, exchange, turn
conveyance	= carriage, transport [see], vehicle [see]
convict	= con, felon, jailbird, lag
cook	= bake, boil, braise, broil, falsify, fry, poach, roast, stew
cooker	= griddle, grill, hob, oven, plate
cool	= aloof, calm, chill, cold, frigid, poise
coolness	= aplomb, composure, indifference, phlegm
coolant	= air, fan, ice, water
cooler	= fan, gaol, jail, jug, ice, prison, stir
(old) copper	= denarius, (d)
copy	= ape, crib, draft, imitate, match, mimic, plagiarise, replica, roneo, trace, xerox
copier	= ape, mimic
(document) copier	= roneo, scribe, xerox
cor	= blimey, crumbs, gosh
cord	= flex, rope, string
cordon	= barrier, chain, fence, picket, ring
core	= centre, crux, heart, kernel, middle, nub, pith
corn	= cereal, grain, maize, salt
corner	= angle, bend, crook, niche, nook, (l, ne, nw, se, sw)
corporation	= council, firm, paunch, pot
correct	= amend, edit, emend, revise, right, sic, so, tick, true
correspond	= accord, agree, check, fit, jibe, match, tally, write
correspondence	= epistle, harmony, letter, mail, missive, note, post
corrie	= cirque, cauldron, hollow, whirlpool
corrode	= decay, rust
corsage	= bodice, bouquet, waist
cost	= charge, damage, price, rate, tab, toll
cost nothing	= free, gratis
costume	= dress, garb, outfit, style
cosy	= secure, snug, warm
cot	= cabin, bed, crib, hut, shack
coterie	= circle, clique, set
cottage	= cabin, chalet, cot, lodge
cotton	= agree, cloth, see, thread, yarn, understand
couch	= bed, cot, express, phrase, sofa, veil
could	= might
counsel	= advice, advise, caution, exhort, help, lawyer [see]
count	= add, census, charge, rate, rely, tally, tell, tot(al), trust
countenance	= brook, face, look, mien, visage

counter	=	bar, meet, oppose, opposite, resist, reverse, parry, table
counterfeit	=	dud, fake, forge, imitate
country	=	land, nation, rural, state; name of [brazil, burma, canada, chile, china, eire, france, greece, india, iran, israel, italy, japan, mexico, norway, peru, poland, russia, siam, spain, sweden, taiwan, tibet, turkey], (uk)
(flat) country	=	pampas, plain, prairie, steppe
(open) country	=	field, grassland [see], lea, meadow
countryman	=	farmer, hayseed, peasant, rustic, swain, yokel
(cross-)country runner	=	harrier
county	=	shire; name of [avon, devon, dorset, essex, kent, oxon, salop, york], (co)
(Irish) county	=	name of [cavan, clare, cork, galway, kerry, louth, mayo, meath, sligo]
(N Ireland) county	=	name of [antrim, armagh, down, tyrone]
(Scottish) county	=	name of [argyll, ayr, bute, elgin, fife, forfar, moray, nairn, perth, ross]
(Welsh) county	=	name of [brecon, flint, gwent, radnor]
coup	=	deed, exploit, feat, stroke, stunt
coupe	=	car, carriage, dessert
couple	=	articulate, both, brace, duo, hitch, join, pair, span, twain, two(some), wed, (pr)
coupling	=	marriage
courage	=	bottle, grit, guts, heart, nerve, pluck
course	=	flow, line, orbit, path, pursue, route, run, track, way, name of [dessert, entree, fish, soup]
(golf) course	=	links
(off) course	=	adrift, astray, lost, wrong
court	=	date, woo, (ct)
(go, take to) court	=	sue
cove	=	anchorage, bay, firth, harbour, inlet
cover	=	bury, conceal, hide, insurance, patch, protect, screen, top
cover(ing)	=	awning, canopy, cap, coat, flap, fur, hat, lid, mat, roof, rug, skin, wig
covered entrance	=	colonnade, porch, portico
covert	=	hidden, privy, secret, shelter
covet	=	crave, desire, want, wish
cow	=	daunt, flinch, lower, heifer, neat, quail
cower	=	cringe, crouch, fawn, grovel, quail, shrink
coy	=	backward, demure, modest, shy, timid
crack	=	break, chap, champion, chink, chip, crevice, expert, gag, gap, go, joke, quip, rift, split, try
crackpot	=	crank, eccentric, nut, weirdo
craft	=	art, guile, knack, skill, trade; name of [boat, plane, ship, vessel], (ss)
craftsman	=	artisan, wright

crafty	=	artful, foxy, sly, wily
cram	=	crowd, learn, lie, press, study, stuff
cramp	=	cramp, fasten, restraint, restrict, shackle, stint, thwart
crane	=	davit, derrick, gantry, hoist, steeve
crash	=	accident, collapse, collision, failure, fall, prang, smash
crate	=	box, case, chest, pack
crater	=	bowl, dip, hole, hollow
crawl	=	creep, drag, fawn, grovel, inch
crawler	=	insect, toady; name of snake [see]
crayon	=	chalk, pastel, pencil, sketch
craze	=	fad, mania, rage, thing, trend, vogue
crazy	=	bats, cuckoo, daft, gaga, loco, mad, nut(s), odd, weird
cream	=	best, elite, pick, prime, top
create	=	build, coin, found, invent, make, produce, sire, spawn
created	=	built, made
creature	=	animal [see], body, human, insect [see], person, soul
(bovine) creature(s)	=	cow(s), kine, neat, ox(en)
(poisonous) creature	=	name of [adder, asp, mamba, scorpion, viper]
(stubborn) creature	=	mule
(water) creature	=	name of [beaver, eft, frog, newt, otter, seal, sealion, terrapin, toad, turtle, walrus]
credit	=	belief, believe, loan, tick, trust, (cr)
creed	=	belief, canon, dogma, tenet, (ism)
creep	=	crawl, skulk, slide, slink, sneak, steal
creeper	=	insect, toady; name of snake [see]
crescendo	=	acme, apex, climax, crest, crown, swell
crest	=	apex, comb, crown, mane, pinnacle, plume, ridge
crevice	=	chap, chink, crack, fissure, split
crew	=	band, company, eight, gang, hands, squad, team
crib	=	bed, copy, cot, manger, pirate, stall
cricketer	=	bat, bowler, cover, fielder, point, slip
cricket side	=	leg, off, on
(town) crier	=	bellman
crime	=	fault, felony, offence, sin, vice, wrong; name of [arson, bigamy, blackmail, fraud, larceny, perjury, murder, rape, theft, treason]
criminal	=	bent, con, crook, fence, felon
crimson	=	blush, red(den), rose, rosy
cringe	=	cower, fawn, grovel
cripple	=	disable, hobble, impair, lame, maim
crisis	=	crunch, emergency, exigency
criticise	=	carp, censure, fault, knock, nag, pan, rate, reprove, review, roast, slam

criticism	= brickbat, censure, critique, reproach, review
crocodile	= cayman, gavial, saurian
crony	= ally, chum, friend, mate, pal
crook	= bend, bow, curve, felon, hook, rogue, staff, twist(er)
crooked	= bent, bowed, corrupt, twisted
crop	= clip, cut, lop, harvest, mow, produce, prune, yield; name of [corn, rice, rye, maize, wheat]
cross	= angry, crucifix, hybrid, irate, kiss, mad, mongrel, thwart, trial, vexed; name of [ankh, celtic, fitche, forme, greek, lorraine, maltese, papal, rood, saltire], (x)
(Greek) cross	= chi [x]
cross-country runner	= harrier
cross island	= malta
crossbar	= beam, brace, strut, transom
crossing	= ford, passage
crow	= boast, brag, exult, gloat, name of [carrion]
crowd	= army, crew, gate, host, lot, mass, mob, spectators
crown	= apex, cap, coronet, crest, diadem, head, invest, king, pate, queen, reward, sovereign, tiara, top, wreath
crude	= blunt, coarse, raw, uncouth, vulgar
crumb	= atom, bit, morsel, scrap
crumbs	= blimey, cor, gosh
crumble	= break, decay, fall, fragment
crusade	= cause, expedition, war, (me)
crush	= defeat, jam, press, quash, quell, rout, squash, trample
cry	= ah, bawl, complain(t), greet, keen, sob, wail, weep, whoop, yell, yelp
(animal) cry	= bleat, low, moo
cry of pain	= ouch, ow
cube	= die
cubes	= dice
cuckoo	= foolish, insane, silly
cue	= clue, hint, notion, pigtail, signal
cuff	= blow, box, hit, slap, smack, spank
cultivate	= nurse, plant, plough, raise, tend, till
culture	= breeding, civilisation, manners, polish
cunning	= arch, foxy, guile, shrewd, sly, wily
cunning move	= gambit
cup	= beaker, bleed, chalice, drink, fate, trophy, (a, b, c, d, dd)
cupboard	= cabinet, closet, locker, press
cupholder	= bra
cur	= cad, dog, louse, rat, toad, tyke
curate	= clergy [see]

curdle	= congeal, ferment, sour, turn
curdled food	= yog(h)urt
cure	= dry, ease, heal, mend, panacea, pickle, remedy, salt, smoke
curiosity	= concern, interest, regard, oddity
curious	= bizarre, nosy, odd, strange, weird
(be) curious	= inquire, nose, probe, pry, snoop
(were) curious	= nosed, pried
curl	= bend, coil, lock, ringlet, tress, twist
currency	= bill, note; name of money [see], (c, dr, ecu, fr, l, mk, p, sh)
(foreign) currency	= name of (foreign) money [see]
current	= amp(ere)s, electricity, flow, river, tide, (ac, dc)
(measure of) current	= amp, volt, watt, (v, w)
current fault	= fuse, short
current plan	= circuit
currently charged	= electric
curse	= anathema, blast, cuss, damn, jinx, malison, oath, plague, scourge, swear
curt	= blunt, brief, rude, short, tart, terse
curtain	= drape, screen, portiere, shroud, tableau, valence, veil
curtain fitting	= flounce, pelmet, rail, rod
curtsey	= bob, bow
curve	= arc(h), bend, bow, ogee, spiral, twist, wind
cushy job	= sinecure
custom	= convention, habit, rite, trade, usage, use, way, wont
customs charge	= duty
cut	= bob, chop, dock, gash, hew, joint, lop, mow, pare, reduce, saw, sawn, sever, share, shear, shred, slash, snub, trim, wound
cut down	= chop, fell, hew
cut grass	= mow, scythe
cut off	= crop, dock, halt, lop, shear, sever
cut short	= abort, abridge, dock, lop
cute	= chic, smart
cutter	= axe, knife, saw, ship
cutting	= acid, chill, clip, keen, raw, sharp, tart
cutting remark	= barb, dig, gibe, insult
cycle	= (a)eon, age, era, phase, series, tandem

D

dad	= father, pa, pop
daily	= char, cleaner, maid, (news)paper; name of [mail, mirror, standard, sun, telegraph, times], (ft)
dais	= platform, pulpit, rostrum, stage
dam	= barrage, barrier, block, check, choke, mother

damage	= cost, harm, hurt, impair, mar, rip, ruin, spoil
damp	= dank, dew, drizzle, humid, moist, wet
damsel	= gal, girl, lass, maid(en), miss, wench
dance	= ball, ballet, caper, frolic, hop, social, step; name of [bolero, cha-cha, foxtrot, gavotte, jive, mambo, polka, quickstep, rumba, samba, tango, twist, valse, waltz]
(folk) dance	= fling, hornpipe, jig, reel
dancer	= ballerina
dancing-girl	= alma(h), bayadere, geisha
dancing shoe	= pump
dandy	= buck, dude, fop, great, swell, toff
danger	= hazard, menace, peril, red, risk, threat
dangerous	= parlous, risky, unsafe
dank	= chilly, damp, moist, wet
dare	= brave, gamble, hazard, risk, venture
dark	= dim, gloomy, murky, sombre
dark(ness)	= black, dusk, gloom, murk, night, shade
dash	= brio, drop, elan, flair, fly, gusto, hint, panache, run, rush, scuttle, tear, zest
dashed	= bally, flew, ran, sped, tore
date	= court, escort, ides, nones, see, time, tryst
daunt	= cow, deter, flinch, quail, shake
dawn	= aurora, birth, break, genesis, light, onset, rise, sunrise
(present) day	= anniversary, birthday, christmas, now, xmas, (ad)
day before	= eve
daydream	= fantasy, reverie
day of the month	= name of [ides, nones]
days gone by	= ago, once, past
(olden) days	= ago, once, past
daze	= fog, numb, shock, stun, stupor
dead	= deceased, flat, gone, late, numb
dead centre	= cemetery, graveyard, necropolis
dead language	= latin
deadlock	= draw, halt, impasse, stop, tie
deadly	= fatal, lethal, mortal
deal	= bargain, barter, compact, cope, pact, sell, timber, trade, wood
(great) deal	= host, lot, sight
dealing with	= about, anent, apropos, on, over, (re)
dean	= clergy [see]
dear departed	= dead, late, (rip)
dearth	= lack, scarcity, want
death	= demise, end, exit, loss, quietus
debate	= argue, contest, discuss, dispute, fight, moot, talk
debt	= bill, due, hock, red, score, (iou)
(be in) debt	= owe

(in) debt	=	owed, owes, (r . . . ed)
debtor	=	ower
deceased	=	dead, late, (rip)
deceive	=	cheat, chicane, fraud, hoax, lie, trick
deception	=	deceit, fraud, hoax, lie, sham, trick
deceptive	=	false, illusory, specious
decide	=	choose, conclude, judge, opt, resolve, settle
decision	=	choice, judgment, resolve
deck	=	adorn, dress, grace, pack, trim
(ship's) deck	=	name of [focsle, orlop, poop]
declaim	=	mouth, orate, rail, rant, spiel
declare	=	affirm, assert, aver, avow, say, state, tell
decline	=	dip, ebb, fade, flag, forgo, refuse, rot, sink, wane
decoct	=	boil
decorate	=	adorn, (be)deck, garnish, inlay, trim
decoration	=	award, badge, gong, medal, (mbe, obe, om)
(wall) decoration	=	arras, cornice, frieze
decorations	=	insignia, regalia
decorative	=	adorned, ornamental, ornate
decorum	=	breeding, dignity, propriety, protocol
decrease	=	abate, decline, drop, lessen, lower
decree	=	act, arret, edict, fiat, law, ordain, order, ordinance, rule; name of [absolute, nisi]
decrepit	=	aged, feeble, frail, infirm, weak
deduce	=	derive, draw, glean, infer, reason
deed	=	act, exploit, feat, gest, title
deem	=	believe, consider, count, judge, reckon
deep	=	bass, briny, main, ocean, profound, sea, thick, vivid
deep valley	=	defile, gorge, gulch, gully, ravine
deer	=	name of [buck, caribou, doe, elk, roe, stag, wapiti]
defeat	=	annul, best, dish, down, eclipse, loss, rout, subdue, surpass, trounce, worst
defeated	=	loser
defect	=	desert, failing, failure, fault, flaw, lack, rat, turn, vice
defence	=	abat(t)is, aegis, armour, bailey, barbican, barricade, bastion, battlement, bulwark, castle, guard, mail, moat, mole, rampart, redoubt, shield
defend	=	guard, justify, protect, screen, shield, uphold
defer	=	accede, adjourn, bow, comply, delay, postpone, shelve
deference	=	esteem, homage, regard, respect
deficiency	=	lack, need, shortage, want
deficient	=	lacking, needing, scarce, short, shy
deficit	=	lack, loss, shortage
degrade	=	debase, disgrace, humble, lower, sink

degraded	= base, corrupt, low, seamy, vile
dejected	= blue, down, glum, low, sad
delay	= defer, lag, loiter, retard, stall, stay, tarry, wait
delayed	= late, tardy
delegate	= agent, emissary, envoy, legate, vicar
delete	= annul, cancel, efface, erase, remove, strike
deliberate	= mull, muse, ponder, think, wary, weigh
delicate	= dainty, deft, ethereal, flimsy, fragile frail, slight, soft, subtle, tender
delight	= exult, glory, joy, please, thrill
deliver	= bear, bring, hand, send, yield
dell	= dale, hollow, vale, valley
demand	= ask, claim, exact, need, require, want
demand money	= blackmail, extort, ransom
demean	= debase, humble, lower, stoop
demolish	= fell, raze, ruin, shatter, smash, wreck
demon	= devil, fiend, ghoul, satan
(little) demon	= imp
demonstrate	= evince, manifest, prove, show
demur	= balk, jib, object
demure	= coy, grave, modest, shy, sober, timid
den	= cave, haunt, hole, home, lair, room, study
denial	= no, negation, refusal, veto
denote	= imply, mark, mean, show, signify
dent	= chip, depression, dint, nick, notch
denude	= bare, expose, strip, uncover
deny	= disown, forbid, gainsay, impugn, negate, refuse, veto
denying	= negative
depart	= exit, go, leave, quit, stray, veer
(dear) departed	= dead, late, (rip)
departure	= exit, exodus, shift
depend	= dangle, hang, hinge, rely, rest, suspend
dependable	= loyal, tried, true, trusted
depict	= describe, draw, paint, portray
deposit	= ash, bank, dregs, lay, lees, lode, lodge, place, put, silt
depressed	= blue, down, glum, low, sad
depression	= blues, bowl, col, crater, dent, sag, vale, valley
depth	= abyss, drop, insight, midst, wisdom
depth of earth	= spit
deputy	= acting, agent, proxy, vice
deride	= mock, ridicule, scorn
descant	= comment, discourse, melody, song
describe	= depict, detail, draw, name, recite, relate, tell
desert	= abandon, defect, ditch, leave, quit, rat, sand, waste; name of [gobi, kalahari, mojave, namib, negev, sahara, thar]

deserted	=	derelict, deslate, left, quit
deserter	=	rat, traitor, truant
deserve	=	earn, merit, rate, warrant
design	=	draft, draw, etch, fashion, model, pattern, plan, sketch
designer	=	draughtsman, planner, plotter; name of [cardin, dior, quant]
desire	=	choose, covet, crave, list, long(ing), lust, wish, yearn, yen
desist	=	cease, forbear, halt, quit, stop
desolate	=	barren, bleak, dreary, forlorn, waste
despatch	=	dispatch [see]
despicable	=	base, low, mean, vile
despicable person	=	bounder, cad, cur, hound, rat, rotter, sneak
despise	=	contemn, disdain, scoff, scorn
despite	=	injury, malice, notwithstanding, outrage
despot	=	dictator, duce, franco, hitler, tyrant
dessert	=	entrements, pudding, sweet; name of [bombe, cassata, compote, coupe, crepe, fool, frappe, halva, ice, junket, parfait, pavlova, sorbet, strudel, sundae]
destiny	=	doom, fate, kismet, lot, nemesis
destitute person	=	beggar, mendicant, pauper
destruction	=	havoc, holocaust, mayhem, sabotage
detail	=	describe, item, nicety, point, relate, specific, tell
detain	=	arrest, confine, imprison, intern
detect	=	catch, find, locate, spot, trace
detective	=	cop, ferret, shamus, spotter, tracer, (cid, di, pi)
detective HQ	=	yard [Scotland Yard]
(British) detectives	=	yard, (cid)
deter	=	frighten, hinder, intimidate, prevent
determination	=	intent, purpose, resolve
determine	=	decide, end, limit, prove, resolve, rule, settle, show
determined	=	bent, firm, fixed, out, set
detest	=	abhor, hate, loathe
detonator	=	banger, cap
detriment	=	damage, harm, hurt, injury
deuce	=	devil, mischief, plague, two
develop	=	grow, evolve, mature, occur, ripen
devil	=	belial, deuce, demon, fiend, lucifer, satan, scratch
(little) devil	=	imp
devotee	=	addict, fan(atic), votary, zealot
devout	=	earnest, godly, holy, pi(ous)
dewlap	=	jowl
dexterity	=	finesse, knack, skill, sleight
dexterous	=	adroit, clever, deft, handy, righthanded
di	=	double, twice, two

dial	= face, ring, (o)
dialect	= brogue, idiom, language, lingo, speech, tongue, vernacular; name of [doric]
diamond	= coal, lozenge, rhomb, rock; name of [brilliant, rose, rough, table]
diamonds	= ice, suit
diary	= journal, log, record
diarist	= name of [pepys, evelyn]
dice	= chequer, cube, gamble
Dickens	= boz [pen name of Charles Dickens]
dicker	= bargain, chaffer, haggle
dictator	= despot, tyrant; name of [duce, franco, hitler, lenin, marcos, noriega, peron, stalin]
dictionary	= glossary, lexicon, (oed)
die	= cube, decease, demise, depart, expire, perish, wither
diet	= fare, fast, food, regimen, slim
differ	= disagree, quarrel, row, vary
difference	= change, contrast, dispute, nuance, odds, row
different	= other, varied, various
difficult	= contrary, grim, hard, knotty, rigid, tough
difficulty	= fix, jam, labour, pain, strain, trouble
diffident	= bashful, coy, demure, modest, shy
dig	= burrow, dredge, excavate, jab, nudge, poke, site; name of [ur]
digs	= flat, lodgings, pad, room
digger	= dredger, mole, shovel, spade, worm
digit	= finger, figure, integer, number, numeral, thumb, toe
dignified	= august, grave, noble
dilemma	= fix, jam, mess, pickle, plight, problem, spot
diligent	= busy, dutiful, industrious, studious
dim	= dark, dense, dull, faint, grey, slow
dimension	= breadth, height, length, size, width
din	= babel, noise, racket, row, uproar
dine	= eat, feast, lunch, sup
dined	= ate
dining area, room	= canteen, mess
dip	= basin, drop, fall, hollow, sag, swim
diplomats	= mission, (cd)
direct	= aim, control, guide, pilot, run, steer, straight, train
directed at	= for, to, towards
direction	= angle, slant, trend, (e, n, s, w)
directions	= map, plan
directors	= board
dirt	= earth, filth, gossip, ground, muck, mud, soil
dirty	= foul, obscene, soiled, sordid, unclean
disable	= cripple, hinder, hobble, lame, maim

disadvantage	= flaw, handicap, harm, loss, minus, snag
disagree	= differ, dissent, vary
disagreement	= clash, conflict, dispute, fight, scrap
disappear	= clear, evanesce, fade, vanish
disapprove	= boo, frown, hiss, object, spurn, veto
discard	= ditch, drop, dump, reject, scrap, shed
discharge	= axe, conge, emit, fire, free, ooze, oust, pardon, sack, void
disc	= record, (ep, lp, o)
discharge	= acquit, cashier, emit, fire, free, pay, perform, release, settle, shoot, unload
disciple	= learner [see], (l)
discipline	= chastise, control, drill, order, train
disclaim	= deny, disown, renounce
disconcert	= abash, confuse, faze, rattle, upset
discord	= clash, conflict, jar, quarrel, strife
discourage	= abash, cow, daunt, deter, dismay
discourse	= sermon, speak, speech, talk, treatise
discrete	= abstract, cautious, prudent, separate
discretion	= care, caution, prudence, tact
discrimination	= choice, judgment, taste
discuss	= argue, confer, debate
discussion	= debate, exchange, review, word
disdain	= contempt, despise, reject, scorn, spurn
disease	= ague, ailment, complaint, fever, illness, sickness; name of [asthma, bronchitis, cancer, catarrh, cold, dysentery, flu(e), gout, hepatitis, influenza, jaundice, leukaemia, measles, pneumonia, scurvy, thrush]
(tropical) disease	= name of [cholera, leprosy, malaria, typhoid]
disfigure	= deface, maim, mar, scar
disgrace	= infamy, odium, shame, sully, stigma, taint
disgust	= aversion, pah, nausea, repel, ugh
dish	= aerial, bowl, circumvent, defeat, food, frustrate, outwit, plate, platter, ruin, salver, serve, treen, tureen; name of food [see]
dislike	= aversion, detest, hate, hatred, resent
disloyal	= faithless, false, unfaithful, untrue
dismal	= bleak, dark, gloomy, glum, sad, sombre
dismay	= appal, daunt, horrify, shake
dismiss	= axe, cashier, fire, oust, reject, sack, spurn
dismissal	= boot, chop, conge, notice, push, sack
dismissed	= out
disorder	= ailment, chaos, complaint, confusion, disease, mess, riot, tumult
disown	= deny, disclaim, renounce, repudiate
dispatch	= haste, kill, message, remit, send, slaughter, slay, speed

dispatched	= sent, slew
displace	= banish, exile, expel, fire, oust, shift
display	= air, exhibit, flash, open, show, vaunt
display item	= exhibit, model
displeasure	= anger, aversion, dislike, wrath
dispose (of)	= dump, end, rid, scrap, sell, settle
disprove	= confound, rebut, refute
dispute	= argue, debate, doubt, moot, question
disreputable	= dingy, scaly, seedy, shabby, shady
disseminate	= broadcast, publish, radiate, scatter, sow, spread
dissertation	= essay, paper, thesis
dissipate	= dispel, disperse, dissolve, fritter, squander, waste
dissipated	= dissolute, raffish, wasted
dissolve	= divorce, end, fade, melt, thaw, vanish
distance	= gap, length, range, way
distant	= afar, aloof, cool, faint, far, remote
distaste	= disgust, horror, pah, ugh
distinction	= fame, merit, name, note, rank
distinguish	= classify, discern, judge, mark
distinguished	= eminent, famed, famous, notable, noted
distrain	= compel, detain, seize
distraint	= distress, seizure
distress	= grieve, hurt, pain, trouble, upset, worry
distribute	= allot, deal, dole, sell, share, spread
district	= area, quarter, region, sector, ward, zone
disturb	= bother, disrupt, shift, trouble, upset
disturbance	= affray, stir, tumult, uproar
ditch	= drain, drop, dyke, moat, rut, trench
ditto	= copy, duplicate, same, (do)
diverge	= branch, digress, fork, part, stray
diversion	= feint, game, hobby, pastime, recreation, sport
divert	= amuse, avert, deter, veer
divest	= bare, deprive, rid, strip, unclothe
divide	= chasm, dole, part, sever, share, split
divine	= clergy [see], guess, holy, hot, sacred, see, swell, (dd)
(water) diviner	= dowser
divorce	= annul, dissolve, part, sever, split
divorcee	= ex
dizzy	= faint, giddy
(feel) dizzy	= reel, swim, totter, wobble
do	= act, cheat, con, ditto, enact, fare, make, perform, serve, suit
dock	= bob, cut, harbour, jetty, lop, pier, quay, wharf
docks	= harbour, port, waterfront
doctor	= alter, fix, mend, rig, spike, treat; name of [locum, medic(o), physician, surgeon, vet], (doc, dr, gp, mb, md, mo)

(hospital) doctor	= intern
(Jewish) doctor of law	= rabbi
doctrine	= canon, dogma, ism, practice, principle, tenet, theory
document	= cite, deed, file, paper, record, (ms)
(legal) document	= deed, summons, writ
document copier	= roneo, scribe, xerox
dodge	= avoid, duck, evade, fence, hedge, ruse
dog	= bitch, canine, cur, follow, hound, mutt, shadow, trail, tyke; name of [afghan, alsatian, basset, beagle, borzoi, boxer, bulldog, collie, greyhound, husky, mastiff, pek(ines)e, pom(eranian), pug, retriever, ridgeback, rottweiler, setter, spaniel, terrier, whippet]
(poacher's) dog	= lurcher
(young) dog	= pup
doll	= girl, puppet, toy, woman
dollar	= buck
dolt	= dope, dunce, idiot, moron, oaf
domestic	= char, daily, help, maid, pet, tame
domestic animal, pet	= name of [cat, dog, hamster]
domineering	= bossy, imperious
donate	= bestow, give, present
donation	= alms, boon, gift, grant, present
done	= over, ready, spent
donkey	= ass, burro, moke, ned
doom	= condemn, damn, death, fate, lot, ruin
doomed	= destined, fated, fay, fey
door	= egress, entry, exit, gate
(part of) door	= hinge, jamb, lintel, muntin, panel
door-keeper, doorman	= bouncer, concierge, porter, usher
dope	= ass, dolt, drug [see], dunce, fool, idiot, moron, mug, oaf
dormant	= asleep, inert, latent, sleeping
dose	= draught, medicine, physic
dossier	= file, folder, portfolio
dot	= dowry, mark, period, point, speck, spot
dotage	= anility, senility
doting	= fond, loving, senile, silly, stupid
double	= clone, dual, fold, image, run, twice, twin, two(fold), (di)
doubled	= ran
doubt	= dispute, query, question, suspect
doubtless	= clearly, sure(ly), truly
dough	= flour, money, paste
doughty	= brave, stout, strong, valiant
dove	= pacifist, pigeon; kind of [cushat, ground, ring, rock, stock, turtle, wood]

down	=	best, blue, drink, eider, fell, glum, hill, low, nap, pile, sad
downcast	=	blue, glum, low, sad, unhappy
downfall	=	collapse, descent, ruin, deluge
downgrade	=	demote, lower
downhearted	=	downcast [see]
downpour	=	deluge, flood, rain, torrent
downright	=	absolute, clear, explicit, plain, total, utter
dowry	=	dot, dower, gift, talent
doze	=	drowse, kip, nap, siesta, sleep, snooze
drab	=	dreary, dull, flat, gloomy, grey, sombre, vapid
drabness	=	dark, gloom, murk
draft	=	conscript, cheque, copy, enlist, enrol, sketch
drag	=	haul, lug, pain, pull, tow, trail, tug, yank
dragoon	=	bully, cavalryman, compel, force, press
drama	=	crisis, play, scene, show
drastic	=	active, extreme, harsh, radical, severe, violent
draught	=	beer, current, dose, drink, outline, plan, sketch
draw	=	attract, depict, describe, lure, paint, pull, sketch, stalemate, suck, tie, tow, trace, (x)
draw forth, out	=	educe, elicit, evoke
drawback	=	fault, flaw, hitch, snag
drawer	=	artist, crayon, pencil, till
drawing	=	cartoon, sketch, traction
drawn	=	closed, haggard, strained, tense
dray	=	cart, horse
dread	=	awe, fear, fright, horror, quail
dreadful	=	awful, dire, macabre, tragic
dream	=	fancy, fantasy, imagine, reverie, vision
(bad) dream	=	nightmare
dreary	=	bleak, dismal, drab, dull, gloomy, sombre
dredge(r)	=	dig(ger)
dress	=	adorn, bind, clean, clothes [see], deck, drape, garnish, gird
(indian) dress	=	sari
(Japanese) dress	=	kimono
(short) dress	=	mini
dressed	=	bound, clad, girt
dressmaker	=	couturier, modiste, seamstress, tailor
drill	=	bore, exercise, furrow, practice, row, train, (pe, pt)
drink	=	alcohol, aperitif, beverage, bib, booze, bottle, cocktail, cup, down, draught, glass, lap, liquor, nip, peg, pint, short, sip, sling, snort, spirit(s), sup, swig, tipple, toot, tope, tot; name of [ale, badminton, beer, cider, cocoa, coffee, cola, eggnog, lager, liqueur, port, porter, mead, milk, sherry, soda, spirit [see], squash, stout, tea, tonic, water]

(Italian) drink	=	name of [asti, chianti, frascati]
(Japanese) drink	=	name of [sake]
(soft) drink	=	cola, mineral, pop
(Spanish) drink	=	name of [sangria, sherry]
drink noisily	=	slurp
drink of the gods	=	nectar
drinker	=	bibber, drunk, lush, soak, sot, tippler, toper, wino
(not) drinking	=	dry, sober, (aa, tt)
drinking bout	=	bender, binge, spree, toot
drinking spree	=	bender, binge, bout, toot
drip	=	bore, dribble, fall, nerd, trickle
dripping	=	fat, lard, suet, wet
drive	=	goad, herd, impel, jaunt, push, ram, ride, run, spin, spur, trip, urge, zip
drivel	=	blah, bosh, bunk, gas, rot, waffle
driver	=	chauffeur, iron, tee, wood
droll	=	comic(al), funny, jester, joker, odd
droop	=	flag, loll, sag, sink, wilt
drop	=	bead, cut, dab, ebb, fall, fumble, nip, pearl, shed, tear
dropper	=	pipette, syringe
drops	=	rain, shower
dross	=	refuse, rubbish, scum, slag
drove	=	crowd, flock, herd, ran, rode, thrust
drudge	=	hack, menial, plod, scrub, skivvy, toil
drug(s)	=	dope, narcotic(s), opiate(s); name of [acid, bhang, cannabis, cocaine, crack, grass, hash(ish), hemp, heroin, mandrax, marijuana, morphine, opium, pot, snow, speed, steroid]
drunk	=	legless, stocious, tight, tipsy
drunk(ard)	=	lush, soak, sot, toper, tosspot, wino
drunken sound	=	hic
dry	=	arid, barren, droll, sec, (aa, tt)
dual	=	binary, double, duplex, twin, twofold
duck	=	bob, bow, nil, nothing, wet, zero; name of [eider, mallard, teal, wigeon], (o)
duct	=	canal, channel, pipe, tube
due	=	charge, fee, just, owed, owing, right
due to	=	over, through
duet	=	brace, couple, duo, dyad, pair
dull	=	blunt, dense, dim, drab, dreary, flat, gray, grey, mat(t), overcast, stupid
dumb	=	dense, dim, mum, mute, silent, thick
dump	=	ditch, drop, hole, hovel, slum, tip
dunderhead	=	dope, moron, muggins, mutt, simpleton
duo	=	brace, couple, duet, dyad, pair
dupe	=	butt, cats-paw, fool, gull, sap, tool

duration	= age, time
dusk	= dim, evening, gloom, shade, sunset, twilight
dust	= ash, beat, con, drub, dupe, fool, lick, pollen, powder, rout, whip
dust up	= brawl, fight, fracas, row
duty	= chore, impost, job, levy, onus, roster, service, tariff, task, tax, toll
dwarf	= midge(t), pygmy, runt, stunt, tiny
dwell	= abide, live, remain, reside
dyad	= brace, couple, duet, duo, pair
dye	= colour, pigment, stain, tinge, tint; name of [archil, eosin, henna, ochre]
dyke-builder	= offa
dynasty	= empire, house, line, rule, sway; name of [aviz, bourbon, chou, han, ming, mogul, orange, ottoman, savoy, shang, stuart, sung, tang, tudor, valois, windsor, york, yuan, zand]

E

each	= apiece, every, per, (ea)
eager	= agog, avid, hot, keen
eagre	= bore, flood, tide, wave
ear	= attention, head, notice, spike
(part of) ear	= auricle, cochlea, concha, (ear)drum, helix, lobe, pinna, tragus
early	= betimes, forward, soon, young
earlier	= former, prior, sooner
earn	= deserve, gain, get, gross, make, merit, net, rate, win
earnest	= close, firm, grave, intent, serious, staid, steady, urgent, zealous
earth	= bury, clay, dirt, globe, ground, land, soil, (e)
(depth of) earth	= spit
ease	= allay, calm, lax, relax, rest, slack(en)
east(ern)	= orient(al), (e)
eastern poet	= omar
eastern potentate, ruler	= aga, ameer, amir, emir, shah, sultan
easy	= clear, mild, simple, soft
easy target	= sitter
eat	= chew, devour, dine, feed, ingest, scoff
eat nothing	= fast
eat out	= barbecue, picnic
eater	= fruit; name of fruit [see]
ebb	= abate, drop, fall, lull, recede, reflux, wane
eccentric	= bizarre, outre, odd, queer, rum, weird
eccentric (chap)	= card, case, character, crackpot, nut, oddity, quiz, weirdo
echo	= imitate, repeat, resound

economical	=	frugal, saving, sparing, thrifty
ecstasy	=	bliss, heaven, joy, rapture
eddy	=	maelstrom, vortex, whirl, whirlpool, whirlwind
edge	=	border, brink, flange, hem, kerb, limit, lip, rim, shoulder, side, trim, verge
(give, put on an) edge	=	hone, sharpen, strop, whet
edict	=	canon, decree, fiat, law, order, ukase
edit	=	adapt, censor, check, correct, emend, redact, revise, rewrite
edition	=	copy, issue, number, print, version, volume
educate	=	foster, nurture, school, teach, train, tutor
educated	=	erudite, learned, literate, taught
Edward	=	ed, ned, ted
eel	=	name of [conger, lamprey, moray]
eerie	=	strange, timid, timorous, weird
effective	=	actual, fit, powerful, striking, telling
effete	=	barren, done, epicene, feeble, spent
effort	=	go, shot, stab, strain, try
effrontery	=	brass, cheek, face, gall, nerve
egg	=	goad, nit, spur, urge, (o)
eggs	=	clutch, ova, roe, (oo)
egg-shaped	=	oval, ovate, ovoid
eider	=	down, duck
eight	=	crew
eightsome	=	reel
elaborate	=	complex, intricate, minute, precise
elan	=	dash, esprit, gusto, spirit, verve, vim
elapse	=	go, lapse, pass
elate	=	exalt, excite, inspire, raise
elated	=	exultant, proud
elation	=	euphoria, joy, pride
elderly	=	aged, ancient, grey, old(en)
elderly relative	=	gran, nan, nanna
elect	=	choose, chosen, coopt, elite, opt, pick, wish
elected	=	chose(n), in
elector	=	chooser, constituent, voter
electric flex	=	cord, lead, wire
electrician	=	spark
electricity	=	amp(ere)s, current, volts, watts, (ac, dc, elec)
electrocute	=	execute, fry, kill
elegance	=	dignity, grace, style
element	=	basis, factor, feature, part, rudiment; name of [air, earth, fire, water]
elements	=	weather
elevate	=	exalt, lift, raise, uplift
elevated	=	drunk, grand, high, lofty, noble, tipsy
eleven	=	legs [bingo], side, team, (xi)
elf	=	spirit [see]

elicit	= draw, educe, evince, evoke, extract
elite	= best, cream, elect, pick, prime, top
elude	= avoid, evade, dodge, duck
embargo	= ban, bar, block, check, stop
embark	= board, engage, enter
embarrassed	= red, shy
embassy	= legation, mission
embellish	= adorn, (be)deck, decorate, garnish, trim
embrace	= adopt, clasp, clinch, cuddle, entwine, hold, hug, include, kiss
emergency	= crisis, crunch, exigency, (sos)
eminent	= exalted, famed, famous, great, notable
emit	= discharge, exude, issue, utter, vent
emotion	= ardour, feeling, fervour, passion, warmth; name of [anger, hate, love, rage]
emperor	= king, ruler; name of [julian, nero, otho, titus], (emp)
emphasis	= accent, importance, stress, vigour
emphasise	= stress, underline, underscore
empire	= name of [ottoman, roman]
employ	= apply, engage, hire, use, utilise
employee	= hand, worker
employees	= staff
employer	= boss, owner, user
employment	= job, line, trade, use, work
empty	= bare, blank, clear, vacant, void
emulate	= compete, imitate, rival
enact	= decree, do, ordain, pass, play
enamour	= bewitch, charm, enchant, endear
enchant	= beguile, bewitch, charm, delight
enchantment	= charm, hex, magic, sorcery, spell, voodoo
enchantress	= fairy, siren, witch; name of [circe, lorelei]
enclose	= bound, fence, hold, pen, wrap
enclosure	= fence, pen, sty, wall, wrapper, (encl)
encounter	= clash, confront, contest, face, meet
encountered	= met
encourage	= cheer, egg, hearten, spur, urge
encouragement	= boost, cheer, heart, help, spur
encumber	= burden, hamper, impede, saddle
end	= aim, ambition, cease, close, final(e), finish, goal, kill, last, omega, stop, tail, term, tip
ended	= done, gone, over, past
ending	= close, end, final(e), finish
endearing	= charming, engaging, winning, winsome
endorse	= approve, back, confirm, ok(ay), sign
endure	= abide, bear, brook, last, persist, stand
enemy	= foe, rival
energy	= beans, brio, elan, erg, force, go, pep, power, vigour, (e)

enervate	=	tire, wane, weaken, weary
engage	=	book, enrol, hire, lease, rent
engaged	=	betrothed, busy
engagement	=	betrothal, bond, date, oath, troth, tryst
(military) engagement	=	action, battle, combat, sortie
England	=	blighty
(old) England	=	albion
English money	=	name of [crown, fiver, pence, penny, pony, pound, quid, shilling, tenner]
engrave	=	carve, chase, etch, impress, imprint
engross	=	absorb, interest, occupy, write
enigma	=	conundrum, mystery, puzzle, riddle
enjoy	=	have, hold, like, relish, savour
enjoyment	=	delight, gusto, pleasure
enlarge	=	dilate, expand, grow, increase, swell, wax, widen
enlist	=	enrol(l), enter, join, muster, sign
enliven	=	animate, brighten, cheer, quicken
enmity	=	hate, malice, spite, venom
enormous	=	gross, huge, titanic, vast
enough	=	adequate, ample, plenty, sufficient
enrage	=	anger, incense, ire, madden
enrol(l)	=	book, (en)list, enter, record, register
ensign	=	banner, flag, jack, pennant, standard
ensue	=	arise, flow, follow, result, stem
enter	=	begin, insert, join, pierce, record
entertain	=	amuse, charm, divert, fete, foster, please, regale, sing, treat
entertainer	=	host; name of [clown, comedian, juggler, magician, organist, pianist, singer]
entertainment	=	cheer, fun, play, revue, show, treat
enthral	=	captivate, charm, enchant, enslave
enthusiasm	=	ardour, fervour, gusto, spirit, vigour, zeal
enthusiast	=	buff, devotee, fan(atic), fiend, freak, zealot
entice	=	lure, tempt
entire	=	complete, full, intact, total, whole
entitle	=	call, dub, name, qualify, style
entourage	=	following, retinue, suite, train
entrance	=	adit, charm, door, egress, gate
(covered) entrance	=	colonnade, porch, portico
entreat	=	ask, beg, implore, plead
entreaty	=	appeal, petition, plea, prayer
entry	=	access, door, gate, log, passage, record
entwine	=	coil, curl, embrace, twist, wind
envious	=	green, jealous
environment	=	climate, context, domain, locale
environmentalist	=	green
envoy	=	bearer, courier, emissary, messenger

envy	= begrudge, covet, grudge, jealousy
ephemera	= handbills, pamphlets, periodicals
epicene	= effete, neuter, sexless
epicure	= gourmet
episode	= event, incident, occurrence, passage
epistle	= letter, message, missive, note
epoch	= age, date, era, period, time
equal	= alike, even, like, peer, same, uniform
equality	= balance, par(ity)
equestrian	= horseman, rider
equilibrium	= balance, calm, poise, rest
equip	= arm, gear, fit, furnish, provide, rig
equipment	= gear, kit, outfit, rig, stuff, tool(s)
(farm) equipment	= cart, harrow, plough, tractor
(kitchen) equipment	= cooker, freezer, fridge, hob, mixer, oven, sink, stove
equitable	= fair, just
era	= age, cycle, date, epoch, period, time
erase	= annul, cancel, delete, efface, expunge, remove
eraser	= rubber
erect	= build, firm, form, raise, rigid, stiff, straight
erection	= building, edifice, pile, structure
ergo	= hence, so, then, therefore, thus
ermine	= fur, stoat
error	= boob, fallacy, fault, flaw, lapse, miss mistake, slip, typo
escape	= avoid, bolt, elude, flee, flight, fly, getaway, leak, seep, slip
escaped	= fled, flew, ran
eschew	= avoid, duck, evade, forgo, shun
escort	= chaperon, date, guide, outrider, taker
esoteric	= abstruse, arcane, recondite, secret
essay	= attempt, go, paper, test, try
essential	= basic, key, main, must, vital
establish	= base, create, fix, found, lay, put, set
establishment	= business, company, concern, firm, house
estate	= car, class, land, order, property
estimate	= assess, figure, guess, judge, reckon
estuary	= delta, mouth
etch	= carve, cut, engrave, impress, stamp
eternal city	= rome
ethereal	= aerial, airy, delicate, heavenly, light
ethic	= ethical [see], ethos, morality
ethical	= correct, decent, honest, just, moral
ethos	= culture, ethic, spirit
European	= name of [briton, czech, dane, dutch, finn, french, german, greek, irish, lapp, lett, pole, scot, slav, swede, swiss, welsh], (eur)
evade	= avoid, dodge, duck, shirk, shun, shy

evanesce	= clear, disappear, fade, vanish
even	= flat, just, level, plain, plumb, quits, smooth, stable, still, uniform, yet, (een)
(not) even	= bumpy, odd, rough
evening	= dusk, sunset, twilight, (een, evg)
evening star	= venus
event	= bout, end, episode, fact, game, incident, issue, matter, result, upshot
(horse) event	= trial; name of [badminton]
ever	= always, (eer)
(for) every	= per
every body	= all, each, lot, (u)
everyone	= all, each, lot, (u)
everything	= all, each, lot, (u)
every year	= annual, (pa)
evidence	= mark, proof, sign, testimony, token
(give) evidence	= depose, swear, testify, witness
evident	= clear, obvious, patent, plain
evil	= bad, base, curse, immoral, satanic, sin, vile, wrong
ex	= divorcee, former, once, without
exact	= correct, demand, extort, precise, proper
exaggerate	= colour, magnify, pad, stretch
exaggeration	= hyperbole
exalt	= dignify, ennoble, extol, praise, raise
exaltation	= ecstasy, elation, euphoria, glory, joy
exalted	= grand, high, lofty, sublime
examine	= assay, check, inspect, scan, test, vet, view
examination	= audit, autopsy, biopsy, oral, test
example	= case, instance, model, sample, specimen, standard
(for) example	= as, say, (eg)
excavation	= dig, mine, pit, quarry; name of [ur]
exceedingly	= greatly, highly, hugely, very
excel	= beat, cap, outdo, pass, shine, top
excellent	= banner, fine, great, prime, top, (ai)
except	= bar, but, omit, save
excess	= glut, plethora, surfeit
exchange	= barter, repartee, swap, swop, switch, trade (stock) exchange bourse, (lse, se)
exclude	= ban, bar, debar, except, forbid, omit
exclusive	= scoop, select, single, sole, (excl)
excursion	= jaunt, outing, sally, tour, trip
excuse	= alibi, apology, forgive, pardon, plea, pretext, reason
exercise	= drill, lesson, practice, sport(s), stretch, study, use, (pe, pt)
exhausted	= done, spent, tired
(be) exhausted	= fade, pall, tire

exhibit	=	air, display, model, reveal, show
exist	=	are, be, live, occur, survive
exists	=	is
exit	=	door, egress, gate, outlet, vent
exodus	=	departure, escape, flight
exorbitant charge	=	earth
expand	=	dilate, enlarge, grow, spread, swell
expect	=	await, predict, reckon, think, trust
expected	=	due
expecting	=	antenatal, pregnant
expedition	=	haste, quest, speed, travel, trek, trip
(military) expedition	=	crusade, incursion, invasion, (me)
expel	=	ban, belch, eject, evict, oust, spew
expense	=	charge, cost, outlay, price, toll, use
(constant) expense	=	drain
expensive	=	dear, lavish, rich, steep, stiff
experience	=	feel, savour, taste, test, try, undergo
experienced	=	felt, had, skilled, versed, veteran
experiment	=	assay, proof, test, trial, try
expert	=	able, ace, adept, boffin, dabhand, deft, fundi, master, pro, pundit
(team of) experts	=	panel
expire	=	cease, die, end, exhale, perish
expired	=	dead, died, ended, over
explanation	=	account, meaning, reason, sense, theory
explode	=	blow, burst, erupt, pop, shatter
exploit	=	adventure, capitalise, deed, feat, stunt, use, utilize
explorer	=	navigator, probe, scout; name of [cabot, columbus, drake, scott]
explosive	=	amatol, dynamite, semtec, (he, tnt)
exposure	=	display, print, snap
exposures	=	pix
express	=	air, exact, say, speak, state, tell, train, utter, voice
expression	=	look, phrase, sign, token, word
ex-pupil	=	alumnus, (ob)
extend	=	offer, open, pose, spread, stretch
extensive	=	big, broad, huge, large, major, wide
extent	=	orbit, radius, range, scope, size
external	=	alien, exterior, out(er), outside, (ext)
extinct bird	=	dodo, moa, roc
extinguished	=	out
extol	=	exalt, hail, laud, praise
extra	=	added, bye, increase, more, wide, spare, super, surplus
extract	=	draw, juice, passage, pull, quote, select
extravagant	=	lavish, ornate, outre, profuse, steep, wild
extreme	=	drastic, last, limit, radical, stringent, utmost

extremity	=	acme, apex, brink, edge, end, limit, tail, toe, verge
exuberance	=	animation, cheer, elation, zest
eye	=	hole, look, observer, ogle, optic, orb, see, watch
(black) eye	=	mouse, shiner
eyelet	=	hole, loophole, peephole
eye-opener	=	lid
eyesore	=	blot, mess, mote, sight, stye

F

fable	=	fiction, figment, myth, story, tale
fabric	=	building, cloth, edifice, frame, material, rep, texture, tissue; name of cloth [see]
fabulous	=	fab, legendary, mythical, splendid
fabulous horseman	=	centaur
face	=	clock, confront, dial, mug, visage
facing	=	against, opposite, toward
fact	=	detail, event, reality, true, truth
facts	=	data, gen, info
faction	=	bloc, cabal, camp, clique, junta
(political) faction	=	party
factor	=	agent, deputy, element, item, steward, (rh)
factory	=	mill, plant, tannery, works
fade	=	decline, dim, ebb, evanesce, flag, vanish, wane, wilt, wither
faded	=	dim, dingy, pale, passe, shabby, worn
fag	=	gasper, smoke, tire
fail	=	fade, flag, founder, lose, miss, wane
failed	=	abortive, flopped, manque
failing	=	defect, fault, flaw, foible, lapse, sin, vice
failure	=	defect, fault, fiasco, flop, lemon, loser, neglect
faint	=	dim, dull, low, muted, swoon, thin, vague
fair	=	bazaar, blond(e), expo, fete, even, equal, gala, just, light, show
fairness	=	beauty, equity, justice
fairy	=	elf, fay, gnome, hob, peri, pixie, spirit [see], sprite
fairy king	=	name of [oberon]
faith	=	belief, creed, cult, dogma, fidelity, reliance, trust
faithful	=	devoted, loyal, staunch, true
fake	=	counterfeit, ersatz, false, feign, forge(ry), hoax, mock, phoney, pseudo, sham
fall	=	collapse, crash, drop, rain, sink, subside, trip, tumble
falls	=	cascade, cataract; name of [angel, niagara, victoria]

false	= bogus, fake, forged, lying, phoney, sham, untrue, wrong
false accusation	= calumny, libel, slander
false teeth	= bridge, crown, denture
false witness	= liar, perjurer
falsehood	= deceit, fib, fiction, lie, perjury
falsify	= cook, distort, forge, pervert
fame	= eclat, glory, kudos, lustre, prestige, renown, repute
familiar	= close, common, intimate, spirit, stock, thick, up, versed
familiar place	= hangout, haunt, resort
family	= blood, brood, clan, dynasty, kin(dred), kinsmen, line, strain
(Italian) family	= name of [medici]
(royal) family	= name of [stuart, tudor, windsor, york]
family tree	= genealogy, lineage, pedigree
famous	= august, eminent, famed, great, notable, noted, signal
fan	= arouse, cooler, fuel, stir
(Indian) fan	= punka(h)
fan(atic)	= addict, bigot, buff, devotee, extremist, fiend, freak, votary, zealot
fancy	= caprice, conceit, freak, idea, imagine, vagary, whim
(wild) fancy	= bog(e)y, chimera
fang	= claw, prong, spike, talon, tooth
far	= distant, long, miles, remote
(not) far	= close, near
farce	= comedy, joke, parody, satire, sham
farm	= croft, grange, ranch, station, till
(cattle, stock) farm	= ranch
(Jewish) farm	= kibbutz
farm building	= barn, byre, cote, shed, silo, stable, sty
farm equipment	= cart, harrow, plough, tractor
fashion	= craze, design, fad, make, mode, rage, style, tone, vogue
fashionable	= in, chic, hip, (u)
fast	= apace, diet, firm, fleet, quick, secure, starve, swift; name of [lent, ramadan]
fasten	= fix, bolt, lace, leash, rivet, secure, tie
fastener	= bolt, catch, clip, glue, knot, nail, nut, pin, screw, staple, stud, tack
fastness	= fortress, rapidity, security, stronghold
fat	= dripping, flab, gross, lard, obese, stout, suet
fat cats	= rich, wealthy
fatal	= deadly, lethal, mortal, terminal
fate	= chance, destiny, doom, karma, kismet, lot, nemesis

fated	=	doomed, fay, fey
father	=	abba, clergy [see], da, dad, pa, papa, pater, pop, sire, (fr)
fatuous	=	idiotic, inane, inept, silly
fault	=	boob, defect, error, flaw, glitch, lapse, slip
(current) fault	=	fuse, short
favour	=	back, bias, boon, gift, goodwill, grace, help, rosette
(in) favour	=	for, pro
(not in) favour	=	anti
favoured	=	in
favouring	=	for, pro
favourite	=	choice, idol, pet, pick
fear	=	alarm, awe, dread, fright, panic
fearful	=	afraid, awful, dire, grim, scared
fearless	=	bold, brave, gallant, stout, valiant
feast	=	beano, banquet, fete, gorge, spread
feat	=	deed, exploit, stunt, trick, venture
feather	=	fettle, plume
feathers	=	down
feature	=	facet, mark, star, trait, virtue; name of [chin, mouth, nose]
(IOW) feature	=	needles
fee	=	account, bill, charge, due, hire, pay, tariff, toll
feeble	=	decrepit, faint, frail, infirm, lame, puny, thin, weak
feel	=	aura, be, deem, grope, know, mood, paw, probe, sense, touch
feel better	=	improve, rally, recover, revive
feel dizzy	=	reel, swim, totter, wobble
feel pain	=	hurt, smart, sting
feeling	=	aura, emotion, hunch, idea, mood, nose, passion, sense, touch, view
feelings	=	ego
feign	=	fake, forge, invent, pretend, simulate
feign illness	=	malinger
fell	=	axe, cut, fierce, flatten, hew, hide, hill, lethal, level, moor, mount(ain), pelt, raze, sew, skin
felling	=	needlework
fellow	=	chap, he, gent, guy, man, sport; name of [al, des, don, ed, bill, les, mark, pete, ray, ron, stan, ted, tom], (f, fba)
(humble) fellow	=	heep [Uriah Heep]
(learned) fellow	=	don, sage, (ba, ma)
(slippery) fellow	=	eel
(tiny) fellow	=	tim [Tiny Tim]
female	=	dam, doe, girl [see], (f, fem)
fen	=	bog, marsh, morass, quagmire, swamp
fence	=	barrier, bulwark, evade, hedge, parry, railing, receiver, screen, wall

feral	= brutal, savage, vicious, wild
ferment	= boil, brew, froth, leaven, rise, seethe stir, tumult
fermented liquor	= cider, port, sherry, wine
fermenting agent	= yeast
ferocious	= cruel, fell, fierce, savage, wild
ferret	= detective, hunt, rummage, search(er)
fertiliser	= nitrate
festival	= carnival, feast, fete, gala, holiday; name of [easter, noel, xmas]
festive song	= carol
festivity	= fiesta, gaiety, mirth, revel
fetch	= bring, carry, earn, elicit, get, make
fete	= bazaar, fair, festival, gala, treat
feudal lord	= suzerain
fever	= ague, frenzy, heat, passion
feverish	= frantic, hectic, hot, pyretic
few	= little, meagre, rare, scant, some, thin
fewer	= less
fey	= doomed, fated
fiasco	= failure, flop
fibre	= bran, hemp, oakum, pile, sisal, thread
fiddle	= con, graft, fidget, toy, trifle, viol
fidget	= fiddle, play, trifle
fidgety	= jumpy, nervous, restive
field	= ambit, croft, domain, grassland [see], orbit, preserve, region, sphere
field officer	= colonel, major, (col, fo)
fielder, fieldsman	= cover, gully, point, slip
fiesta	= carnival, festival, fete, holiday
Figaro character	= barber
fight	= bout, box, brawl, crusade, dispute, duel, fray, joust, melee, scrap, spar, struggle, tilt, tussle
fight(ing)	= action, battle, combat, conflict, war(fare)
(scene of) fighting	= front, theatre
fighter	= boxer, bruiser, pugilist
figure	= cipher, digit, form, number, numeral, reckon, shape, statue, symbol; name of [one, two, ten, etc]; type of [decagon, heptagon, hexagon, nonagon, octagon, pentagon, triangle]
file	= case, dossier, folder, line, rasp, record, row
film	= coat, gauze, haze, mist, reel, screen, veil
(big) film	= epic
(show) film	= project
film follower	= sequel
film location	= set
film set	= location
(stop) filming	= cut

filthy	=	black, crude, dirty, foul, rank, sordid
final	=	end, last, latest, omega, terminal
final check	=	mate
finale	=	climax, close, end, epilogue, finis
finance centre	=	city
find	=	catch, detect, locate, strike, trace, unearth
(tried to) find	=	sought
(try to) find	=	hunt, seek
fine	=	amerce, capital, clear, fair, forfeit, good, mulct, narrow, nice, penalty, rare, slender, (f, ok)
finesse	=	craft, feint, skill, polish, tact, wile
finger	=	digit, identify, pilfer, touch, toy
finish	=	cease, close, complete, die, end, halt, perfect, polish, (fin)
finish game	=	mate
finished	=	done, final, gone, over, shut, spent
finite	=	limited, narrow, precise, set
fire	=	arson, barrage, boot, burn, flame, light, sack, shoot
(catch) fire	=	burn, ignite, light
(on) fire	=	ablaze, aflame, alight, flambe
firing line	=	front
firearm	=	name of [gun, revolver, rifle, pistol]
fireman	=	stoker
fireplace, fireside	=	grate, hearth, hob, ingle, range
firework	=	banger, maroon, rocket, sparkler, squib
firm	=	business, company, concern, fast, fix(ed), hard, house, set, solid, sound, stable, staunch, steady, strict, tight, (co)
first	=	alpha, initial, maiden, opening, premier, prime, top, (ist, noi)
(played, was) first	=	led
first batsman	=	opener [cricket]
first-class	=	capital, crack, excellent, prime, (a, ai)
first hand	=	new
first killer, murderer	=	cain [Biblical]
first lady, mate	=	eve [Biblical]
first man	=	adam [Biblical]
first performance	=	premiere
first place	=	head, lead, van
first-rate	=	capital, crack, excellent, prime, (a, ai)
firth	=	bay, bight, cove, creek, inlet, sound
fish	=	angle, bob, dap, school, sprat, troll, trawl; type of [flat, flying, gold, jelly, shell, sun, sword]; name of [anchovy, bar, barracuda, bass, bib, blenny, bonito, brisling, chad, cod, dorado, dory, eel, gar, hake, herring, ling, mullet, orfe, shad, shark, sturgeon, tuna, tunny]
(flat-)fish	=	name of [brill, dab, flounder, fluke, halibut, plaice, ray, skate, sole, turbot]

(freshwater) fish	= name of [ablen, ablet, barbel, bass, bleak, bitterling, bream, burbot, carp, char, dace, minnow, perch, pike, roach, rudd, ruff(e), salmon, tench, trout]
(jelly-)fish	= name of [blubber, medusa]
(shell)fish	= mollusc; name of [abalone, clam, cockle, crab, gaper, lobster, mussel, oyster, prawn, scallop, shrimp, winkle]
(smoked) fish	= name of [bloater, finnan, kipper]
(tin) fish	= torpedo
(young) fish	= name of [elver, parr, sprat, tiddler]
fishing tackle	= bait, float, fly, gaff, jig, line, lure, reel, rod, sinker, spinner, spoon
fissure	= break, chap, chink, cleft, crevice, fault, rent, rift
fit	= able, apt, hale, meet, proper, rig, right, spasm, suit(able), well
fitter	= engineer, mechanic, tailor
fitting	= apt, due, meet, proper, right, suitable
(curtain) fitting	= flounce, pelmet, rail, rod
fix	= clamp, jam, mend, mess, nail, patch, peg, pin, repair, set
flabbergast	= abash, amaze, astound, daze, stun
flag	= iris, pave, sag, tire; kind of [banderol(e), banner, burgee, colours, ensign, jack, pennant, pennon, standard, streamer]
flags	= bunting
flair	= ability, aptitude, gift, knack, talent
flake	= chip, film, layer, snow
flake out	= collapse, faint
flame	= blaze, beau, burn, fire, glow, lover, passion
(old) flame	= ex
flank	= haunch, hip, loin, side, thigh, wing
flap	= beat, brim, cover, fluster, flutter, lid, panic, wave
flare	= blaze, flame, flash, light, signal, very
flat	= even, level, maisonette, plane, prone
flat country	= pampas, plain, prairie, steppe
flat-fish	= name of fish [see]
flatter	= blandish, court, fawn, overpraise
flavour	= aroma, odour, relish, smell, tang, taste, zest; name of [anise, chilli, clove, garlic, ginger, herb [see], nutmeg, vanilla]
flee	= abscond, bolt, run, scarper, split
fleece	= bleed, rook, shear, soak, sting, wool
fleet	= armada, fast, quick, rapid, swift, (rn)
flex	= angle, bend, crook, curve, tighten
(electric) flex	= cord, lead, wire
flier	= bee, bird, glider, kite, pilot, plane

(night) flier	= bat, moth, owl
(straight) flier	= crow
flight	= bunk, escape, exodus, stair(s), steps, wing
(short) flight	= hop
flightless bird	= bustard, cassowary, emu, kiwi, ostrich, rhea
flinch	= baulk, cow, daunt, quail, shirk, wince
fling	= affair, hurl, go, shot, stab, throw, toss, try, whirl
flirt	= coquet, philander, tease, vamp
float	= cork, drift, hover, launch, raft, waft
floating zoo	= ark
flock	= crowd, drove, herd, host, sheep
flog	= beat, birch, cane, lash, sell, whip
flood	= bore, deluge, eagre, spate, tide, torrent
floor	= down, drop, fell, ground, stor(e)y; name of [attic, ground, mezzanine]
flounder	= blunder, lurch, stumble, wallow
flourish	= b(o)urgeon, grow, prosper, thrive, wave
flow	= glide, gush, pour, purl, run, teem
flower	= bloom, blossom; name of river [see] name of [anemone, arum, aster, begonia, celandine, crocus, daffodil, dahlia, daisy freesia, fuchsia, iris, lilac, lily, lobelia, lupin, narcissus, orchid, oxeye, pansy, peony, petunia, phlox, poppy, rose, stock, tulip, viola, violet, zinnia]
(bunch, cluster of) flowers	= bouquet, corsage, nosegay, posy, spray
flowing	= cursive, fluent, smooth
flummery	= bunk, hokum, humbug, nonsense
flutter	= bat [eyelids], bet, flap, flit, hover
fluid	= flowing, liquid, mobile, pliable, (fl)
fly	= aviate, bolt, clever, cunning, flee, pilot, smart, soar, wing
foam	= froth, head, lather, spray, spume, surf
fodder	= alfalfa, hay, lucerne, silage, straw
foe	= enemy, rival
fog	= brume, cloud, daze, haze, gloom, mist
foible	= failing, fault, frailty, penchant, vice
fold	= corral, crash, crease, lap, pen, pleat, tuck
folk	= clan, family, nation, people, race, tribe
folk dance	= fling, hornpipe, jig, reel
follow	= chase, dog, ensue, hunt, shadow, stalk, tag, tail, track, trail
follower	= adherent, cohort, disciple, fan, supporter
(film) follower	= sequel
following	= after, later, next, retinue, train, (ff)
folly	= idiocy, inanity, lunacy
fondle	= caress, cuddle, hug, pet, stroke

food	=	chow, fare, grub, meal, repast, tack, tuck, viand;
		name of [bread, cereal, egg, fish, meat [see], pate, salad, soup, stew, tart]
(curdled) food	=	yog(h)urt
(heavenly) food	=	ambrosia, manna
(hen-)food	=	egg
(Indian) food	=	curry
(Italian) food	=	pasta;
		name of [gnocchi, lasagne, ravioli, spaghetti]
(Japanese) food	=	name of [sukiyaki, sushi, tempura, teriyaki]
(sea-)food	=	scampi; name of fish [see]
food of the gods	=	ambrosia
fool	=	ass, bumpkin, clown, dolt, dope, goose, idiot, kid, moron, mug, muggins, nana, nit, oaf, sap, simpleton
foolish	=	crazy, daft, inane, mad, silly, simple, stupid
foot	=	base, bottom, pay, rear, step, (f, ft)
footballer	=	back, forward, striker, sweeper, wing, winger
footle	=	folly, loiter, trifle, twaddle
footwear	=	name of [boot, brogue, clog, gaiter, lace, mule, pump, sandal, shoe, slipper, sock, spat]
for	=	as, pro, (pp)
(one) for war	=	hawk, jingoist
(those) for	=	ayes, pros
for every	=	per
for example, instance	=	as, say, (eg)
forage	=	food, grub, rummage, scour, vetch
forbear	=	abstain, ancestor, avoid, eschew, forgo
forbid	=	ban, bar, outlaw, veto
forbidden	=	taboo
force	=	army, coerce, constrain, dragoon, impetus, make, militia, posse, press, prise, thrust, vis, (g)
(join) forces	=	enlist, unite
foreboding	=	omen, portent, presage
forecast	=	augur, call, plan, predict, presage
forecaster	=	augur, prophet, seer
forefront	=	centre, head, lead, van
foreign(er)	=	alien, outside(r), strange(r)
foreign currency, money	=	name of (foreign) money [see]
foreign friend	=	ami
foreign office	=	bureau, (fo)
foreman	=	boss, gaffer, ganger
foremost	=	arch, chief, first, head, leading, top
forerunner	=	harbinger, herald, precursor
forest	=	wood; name of [black, dean, sherwood]
(Shakespearean) forest	=	arden
forest officer	=	ranger
forfeit	=	drop, fine, lose, loss, mulct, penalty

forge	=	fake, form, make, mould, shape, smithy
forger	=	blacksmith
forgery	=	counterfeit, fake
forget	=	fail, neglect, omit, slight
forgetfulness	=	amnesia, lethe, oblivion
form	=	bench, class, figure, forge, make, mould, pew, shape
formal	=	aloof, correct, legal, prim, set, stiff
former	=	earlier, ex, late, old, once, past, prior
former pupil, student	=	alumnus, (ob)
former spouse	=	ex
formerly	=	already, before, ex, once, pre
fort	=	bastion, bastille, castle, citadel, fastness, keep, redoubt, stronghold
forte	=	loud, strong, (f)
(call, draw) forth	=	educe, elicit, evoke
(set) forth	=	deliver, depart, go, leave, present
forthcoming	=	free, future, next, open, ready
forthright	=	blunt, candid, direct, frank, open
fortress	=	fort [see]
fortune	=	bomb, chance, mint, pile, wealth
(good) fortune	=	luck
forty winks	=	kip, nap, sleep
forward	=	bold, brash, fore, on(ward), pert
forwards	=	ahead, forth, on(ward)
foster	=	cherish, feed, nurse, raise, serve
foul	=	evil, putrid, rank, soil, sordid, vile
found	=	base, create, endow, establish, rely, start
foundation	=	base, basis, fund, root, seat
fountain	=	jet, source, spring, well, spout
fourth	=	quarter, quartile
fowl	=	bantam, bird, chicken, cock, hen, rooster
fox	=	baffle, bewilder, deceive, puzzle, trick
fraction	=	decimal, half, proper, quarter, vulgar
fragment	=	bit, chip, morsel, part, scrap, sliver
fragrance	=	aroma, balm, nose, scent, smell
(of) France	=	French [see]
(south of) France	=	midi, sud
frank	=	blunt, candid, direct, open, plain
frantic	=	berserk, fraught, furious, mad, wild
fraternity	=	guild, league, order, society, union
fraud	=	cheat, fake, gyp, hoax, sham, swindle
fray	=	brawl, conflict, fight, fracas, melee
freak	=	caprice, fanatic, fancy, vagary, whim
free	=	buckshee, clear, gratis, lax, loose, release, rid, sans, untie
freedom	=	ease, facility, liberty, licence
freeze-up	=	ice
freight	=	bulk, cargo, goods, haul, lading, load

French city	= name of [aix, arras, calais, dieppe, dijon, lille, lyon(s), nancy, nice, nimes, paris, rheims, rouen, tour]
French friend	= ami
Frenchman	= breton, gaul, norman; name of [alain, henri, jean, louis, pierre, rene], (m)
French money	= name of [franc, sou]
French resort	= name of [cannes, nice, riviera]
French railway	= metro
French river	= name of (French) river [see]
French wine	= vin; name of [beaune, burgundy, chablis, champagne, claret, graves, macon, medoc, muscat(el), sauternes]
frenzied	= amok, amuck, frantic, furious, wild
frenzy	= craze, folly, fury, mania
frequent	= common, haunt, resort
frequent visitor	= habitue
frequently	= much, oft, often
fresh	= airy, bold, green, new, novel, pure
(not) fresh	= off, stale
freshwater fish	= name of fish [see]
fret	= fuss, goad, pine, stew, vex, worry
friend	= ally, chum, crony, mate, pal, quaker
(Australian) friend	= cobber
(foreign, French) friend	= ami
(Spanish) friend	= amigo
friendly	= amiable, benign, close, fond, genial
friendly power	= ally
friendship	= amity
fright	= alarm, awe, fear, scare, shock, terror
frighten	= alarm, appal, awe, cow, daunt, scare, shock, startle
frightening	= awful, hairy, scary, spooky
frigid	= aloof, cold, cool, icy, stiff
frill	= cuff, edge, fringe, ruche, ruff
frills	= airs, extras, finery, fuss, jazz
fringe	= bang, border, edge, frill, hem, rim, verge
frisk	= caper, frolic, gambol, romp, search, skip
frivolous	= futile, paltry, silly, trifling, trivial
frolic	= caper, frisk, gambol, revel, romp, sport, spree
from	= ex
from birth	= natal
front	= cover, face, fore, lead, show, van
(ship's) front	= bow, prow, stem
frontier	= border, boundary, limit
froth	= barm, bubbles, foam, lather, scum, spume, suds
frown	= glower, lower, scowl, wrinkle

frozen water	=	ice
fruit	=	name of [apple, apricot, avocado, aubergine, banana, date, fig, grape, guava, hip, jack, kiwi, lemon, lime, litchi, lychee, mango, melon, nut, orange, peach, pear, plum, raisin]
(pureed) fruit	=	fool
fruit supplier	=	orchard
frustrate	=	baffle, dash, defeat, dish, ruin, thwart
fry	=	burn, cook, scorch, young
fuel	=	fan, feed, food, inflame; name of [coal, coke, diesel, gas(oline), oil, peat, petrol, spirit, wood]
fugitive	=	emigre, fleeting, refugee, runaway
full	=	all, entire, replete, sated, whole
fun	=	cheer, game, jest, joke, lark, play, rag, sport
(make) fun	=	deride, mock, rag, rib
funny	=	amusing, comic(al), droll, odd, strange
function	=	do, duty, job, purpose, role, use
funeral	=	burial, wake
funeral carriage	=	bier, hearse
fungus	=	name of [mould, mushroom, toadstool]
fur	=	con(e)y, ermine, mink, pelt, sable
furnace	=	kiln, oast, oven
furnish	=	arm, equip, fit, gear, outfit, rig, supply, yield
furniture	=	suite; name of [bed, chair, chest, dresser, table]
further	=	also, extra, foster, other, promote
fury	=	anger, ire, rage, wrath
fuss	=	ado, bother, flap, row, stir, worry
(make a) fuss	=	create, perform
futile	=	useless, vain
future	=	coming, later, unborn

G

gabble	=	blab, chatter, drivel, prattle, spout
Gaelic	=	celt, erse
gaffe	=	blunder, boob, howler, slip
gag	=	balk, choke, crack, demur, hoax, jest, jib, joke, quip, retch
gaga	=	crazy, doting, nuts, senile
gain	=	acquire, bag, earn, profit, reach, reap
gainsay	=	deny, dispute, impugn, negate
gait	=	bearing, mien, pace, step, walk
gaiter	=	spat
gala	=	fete, gay, merry, party
gale	=	blast, cyclone, hurricane, snorter, squall, storm, tempest, tornado, typhoon, wind
gall	=	brass, cheek, irk, nerve, rile, vex
gallant	=	beau, blade, bold, brave, game, noble

gallery	= balcony, gods, loggia, museum; name of [louvre, tate]
galley	= warship; name of [bireme, trireme]
gallop	= bolt, hie, race, run, sprint, tear
gallows	= gibbet, scaffold
galore	= heaps, lots, plenty
gamble	= back, bet, chance, dice, flutter, hazard, punt, risk, stake, wager
gambler	= backer, better, dicer, punter
(small) gambling	= spec[ulation]
gambol	= caper, cavort, frisk, frolic, romp
game	= fun, keen, lame, match, sport; name of [badminton, billiards, bingo, bowls, croquet, fives, football, hockey, hurling, lacrosse, lotto, polo, pool, racquets, rugby, snooker, soccer, squash, tennis]; name of animal [boar, buck, deer, hare, hog, impala, kudu, rabbit, stag]
(board) game	= name of [backgammon, chess, draughts, halma, ludo, monopoly, scrabble]
(card) game	= name of [baccarat, basset, bezique, blackjack, brag, bridge, canasta, cribbage, ecarte, euchre, faro, gin, loo, nap, patience, poker, pontoon, ruff, rummy, snap, solitaire, solo, whist]
(finish) game	= mate
(wall) game	= name of [fives, pelota, racquets, squash]
game park	= reserve
(number of) games	= rubber, set
gang	= band, crew, horde, mob, pack, squad
gangster	= al [Al Capone]
gaol	= bridewell, brig, cooler, jail, nick, prison, stir
gaolbird	= con(vict), lag
gaoler	= guard, screw, warden, warder
gaol sentence	= life, stretch, time
gap	= breach, break, chasm, cleft, crack, hiatus, hole, lacuna, schism, vent, void
gape	= crack, gawk, look, ogle, stare, yawn
garb	= clothes [see]
garbage	= junk, litter, offal, refuse, swill
garden	= bed, eden, kew, lea, plot
gardener	= name of tool [hoe, rake, spade]
garland	= adorn, deck, festoon, lei, sash
garment	= clothes [see]
(under)garment	= name of [bodice, bra, chemise, hose, shift, singlet, slip, vest]
garner	= amass, hoard, gather, save, store, stow
garnish	= adorn, (be)deck, decorate, dress
garret	= attic, loft

gas	= boast, humbug, petrol, talk; name of [ammonia, argon, butane, ether, helium, krypton, marsh, methane, mustard, neon, niton, ozone, propane, radon, xenon]
(marsh-)gas	= methane
(mixture of) gases	= air
gash	= cut, gouge, slit, tear, wound
gasp	= blow, gulp, pant, puff
gate	= crowd, door, egress, entrance, exit, port(al), spectators
gatehouse	= lodge
gather	= amass, collect, fold, garner, harvest, hoard, muster, pleat, pluck, reap, see, tuck, twig, understand
gathering	= assembly, crowd, function, meeting, rally
(riotous) gathering	= mob
(social) gathering	= concert, function, party, soiree
gaudy	= bright, gay, gimcrack, florid, loud, showy, tawdry, vulgar
gazette	= journal, (news)paper, (gaz)
gear	= cog, dress, garb, habit, kit, rig, tackle
gel	= clot, congeal, jelly, set
gem	= gemstone [see], jewel, stone
gemstone	= name of [agate, alexandrite, amber, amethyst, aquamarine, beryl, citrine, diamond, emerald, garnet, jade, jasper, lapis lazuli, onyx, opal, pearl, peridot, ruby, sapphire, tiger's eye, topaz, turquoise, zircon]
gen	= data, dope, facts, info, news, word
gender	= sex; name of [common, feminine, masculine, natural, neuter], (g)
general	= broad, catholic, common, global, normal, officer, public, universal, usual, vague; name of [butler, custer, dayan, foch, gordon, grant, haig, junot, lee, ney, patton, rommel, slim, smuts, wolfe]
general infantryman	= joe, serviceman, soldier, (gi)
generate	= beget, breed, produce, sire, spawn
generator	= dynamo, magneto
generation	= age, epoch, era, period, time(s)
generosity	= bounty, charity, largess(e)
generous	= ample, free, full, handsome, lavish, liberal, prodigal, profuse
(not) generous	= close, mean, stingy, tight
genre	= class, kind, species, style, type, variety
gent	= chap, fellow, guy, male, man
gentle	= clement, kind, lenient, mild, soft, tender, (p)
gentleman	= cavalier, sir

gentlemanly	= civil, noble, polite, suave, urbane
genuine	= actual, dinkum, echt, real, right, sincere, true
germ	= bud, bug, seed, spore, virus
germs	= bacteria
German	= aryan, nazi, teutonic
German boy	= name of [dieter, gunter, hans, heinz, helmut, karl, ulrich]
German soldier	= boche, hun, jerry
German city	= name of [bonn, berlin, bremen, cologne, dresden, essen, hamburg, hanover, kiel, leipzig, munich, rostock]
German man	= herr; name of German boy [see]
German money	= name of [krone, mark]
German river	= name of (German) river [see]
German road	= autobahn
German wine	= name of [hock, mosel, rhine, riesling]
German woman	= frau
germane	= akin, apposite, apropos, apt, relevant
get	= acquire, become, catch, earn, gain, grow, obtain, procure, reach, win
get away	= escape, flee, run, start
getaway	= break, escape, flight
get off	= alight, land, light
get on	= age, agree, board
get over	= cross, ford, mend
get up	= arise, dress, rise
get-up	= clothes [see]
geyser	= heater, spring
ghost	= spirit [see]
giant	= gog, huge, ogre, titan(ic), vast
gibe	= jeer, jest, scoff, taunt, tease, twit
gift	= boon, favour, flair, genius, grant, largess, present, talent
gifted	= able, clever, talented
gin	= snare, trap
girdle	= band, belt, sash
girl	= bimbo, bird, chick, damsel, gal, her, lass, maid(en), miss, she, wench; name of [ada, amy, ann(e), di, doris, ena, eve, maria, nan, olive, sal, val, vi]
(big) girl	= bertha
(clinging) girl	= ivy
(dancing-)girl	= alma(h), bayadere, geisha
(Irish) girl	= colleen
(old) girl	= dam(osel), dutch, ma, mother, wife, woman
(pretty) girl	= belle
(stage) girl	= name of [bluebell, tiller]
(US) girl	= gal
(old) girlfriend	= ex

girth	= band, bulk, size, width
give	= afford, bestow, confer, donate, grant, present, yield
give an account	= relate, tell
give an edge	= hone, sharpen, strop, whet
give away	= betray, leak, reveal, tell
give evidence	= depose, swear, testify, witness
give up	= cease, cede, quit, stop
giver	= donor
glace	= ice, iced
glad	= gay, happy, merry, pleased
gladden	= cheer, delight, elate, please, rejoice
glamour	= allure, charm, it, (sa)
glance	= graze, look, peek, scan, shave, skim
glare	= blaze, frown, glower, scowl
glass	= barometer, drink, lens, mirror, pane, tumbler, window
glaze	= coat, enamel, gloss, lacquer, shine
glee	= delight, laughter, merriment, mirth
glen	= dale, dell, strath, vale, valley
glider	= flier, plane, serpent, snake
globe	= ball, earth, orb, round, sphere, (o)
gloom	= blues, cloud, dark, fog, haze, mist
gloomy	= dark, dim, dismal, drab, sombre
glorify	= exalt, extol, honour, laud, praise
glory	= exult, rejoice, renown
gloss	= glaze, lustre, sheen, varnish, veneer
glove	= gauntlet, mitt(en), sheath
glower	= frown, lower, scowl, stare
glum	= dismal, dour, down, morose, sullen
glut	= cloy, excess, gorge, indulge, surfeit
glutton	= gourmand, pig
gnome	= dwarf, elf, goblin, maxim
go	= attempt, exit, fling, hie, leave, move, oomph, pep, run, shot, stab, travel, try, turn, vigour, whirl, work
go away	= avaunt, begone, depart, leave, scram
go back	= return, reverse, revert
go bad	= addle, rot, spoil
go down	= decline, descend, drop, fall, set
go in	= enter
go off	= addle, explode, repair, rot, quit, spoil
go out	= ebb, exit
go quickly	= haste, hurry, run, rush
go red	= blush, flush
go steady	= court, date
go to court	= sue
go wrong	= boob, err, fail
goad	= drive, egg, spur, urge

goal	=	aim, ambition, end, object, target
goat	=	billy, kid
God	=	name of [allah, apollo, ares, baal, bacchus, dis, cupid, eros, hades, hermes, jove, manes, mars, neptune, odin, pan, pluto, poseidon, ra, sol, thor, vulcan, zeus]
(drink of the) gods	=	nectar
(food of the) gods	=	ambrosia
Goddess	=	name of [athena, ceres, diana, hera, iris, isis, irene, juno, rhea, venus]
godfather, parent	=	angel, backer, patron, sponsor
going (off)	=	fusty, high, off, rancid, sour, stale
(not) going	=	inert, static, still
going down	=	descent
goings-on	=	acts, behaviour, conduct
going up	=	ascent, climb
gold	=	aurum, (au, or)
golf club	=	name of [baffy, brassie, iron, driver, niblick, putter, spoon, wedge, wood]
golf course	=	links
(bad) golf shot	=	hook, shank, slice
golfer	=	club, golf club [see]
gone	=	ago, blown, dead, left, lost, over, past, wasted
(days) gone by	=	ago, once, past
gone off	=	absent, away, out, sour, (awol)
gong	=	award, medal, (bem, mc, mm)
good	=	fine, fit, healthy, meet, proper, pure, sound
(make) good	=	fix, mend, repair
(no) good	=	useless, (nbg, ng, us)
(very) good	=	capital, pi, pious
good book	=	bible, (nt, ot)
good buy	=	bargain, snip
good condition	=	mint
good fortune	=	luck
good thing	=	boon, godsend, windfall
goodwill	=	amity, comity, favour, zeal
(shabby) goods	=	tat
goody-goody	=	prig, prude
goose	=	fool, prod
gore	=	blood, pierce, stab
gory	=	bloody, red, sanguine
gossip	=	chat, news, rumour, talk, tattle(r)
got a load of	=	saw
gourd	=	melon
gourmet	=	epicure
govern	=	check, control, curb, master, reign, rule, sway
government	=	oligarchy, province, ruling, state, (gov, govt)
government control	=	authority, law, order, rule
governor	=	beg, bey, dey, pasha, regent, satrap, (gov)

grace	= adorn, dignity, elegance, favour, mercy
gracious	= affable, gallant, genial, handsome, liberal, merciful
graduate	= bachelor, master, pass, (ba, ma)
grain	= cereal, colour, dye, granule, seed; name of [barley, corn, maize, millet, oat(s), rice, rye, wheat]
(beard of) grain	= arista, awn
grand	= fine, great, noble, piano, regal, super
grasp	= clutch, fathom, grip, hold, see, sense, take
grass	= green, hay, inform(er), lawn, nark, pasture, pot, reed, turf; name of [bamboo, bent, buffalo, esparto, kikuyu, millet, panic, sedge]
(cut) grass	= mow, scythe
(marsh) grass	= reed
grassland	= lea, ley, mead, meadow, pampas, pasture, plain, prairie, savanna(h), steppe
gratify	= delight, gladden, indulge, please
gratitude	= ta
gratuity	= largess, tip
grave	= carve, crypt, etch, fell, pit, serious, solemn, sombre, tomb
grave-mound	= barrow, tumulus
graveyard	= cemetery, necropolis
gray	= grey [see]
grease	= bribe, fat, oil, soil
great	= big, fab, famous, fat, large, noted, (gt)
great actor	= star
great deal	= host, lot, sight
great man	= giant, hercules, ogre, titan
great many	= heaps, host, lots, oodles, piles
Greek character, letter	= name of (Greek) letter [see]
Greek cross	= chi [x]
green	= envious, fresh, go, grassy, jealous, raw; shade of [lime, olive, sage, vert]
greet	= hail, meet, salute, wave, welcome
greeting	= hello, hi, hullo
(Jewish) greeting	= shalom
gremlin	= goblin, jinx, spirit, sprite
grey	= ashen, drab, dull, horse, pale, wan
grief	= distress, regret, sorrow, woe
grim	= bleak, cruel, dour, harsh, stern
grin	= beam, smile
grind	= chore, crush, file, grate, mill, sand
grip	= clasp, clutch, grasp, hold, seize
groom	= comb, ostler, preen, primp, sice, syce
groove	= channel, furrow, hollow, rut, track
ground	= acre, arena, dirt, earth, land, patch, soil, terrain

(open) ground	=	field, grassland [see], lea, meadow
(swampy) ground	=	bog, fen, marsh, mire, morass, quagmire
grounds	=	basis, dregs, lees, rationale, reason
groundwork	=	base, basis, footing
group	=	batch, bevy, bloc, cluster, crowd, number, pack, sect, set, team; name of number [two, ten, twenty, etc], (gr)
(bird) group	=	aviary, colony, flock, gaggle, rookery
(political) group	=	party
group of stars	=	constellation, nebula; name of [bull, crab, orion, plough]
grouse	=	complain(t), grumble [see]
grove	=	coppice, copse, spinney, wood
grow	=	arise, become, breed, develop, increase, pass, produce, raise, sprout
grow old(er)	=	age, mature
grow weary	=	cloy, fade, jade, pall, tire
growth	=	crop, lump, rise, stye, tumour, wart
grub	=	eats, food, larva, maggot, nosh
grumble	=	beef, bitch, crab, gripe, moan, nark, nag
grunter	=	boar, hog, pig, sow
guarantee	=	bond, pledge, surety, vouch, word
guard	=	defend, lookout, protect, sentinel, sentry, shield, ward, watch(man)
guardian	=	curator, keeper, minder, trustee, tutor, ward, warden, warder
(tower) guardian	=	beefeater, yeoman
guerrilla leader	=	che
guess	=	estimate, opine, opinion, stab, think
guide	=	direct, escort, lead, pilot, steer, usher; name of [helm, rudder, tiller, wheel], (g)
guinea-pig	=	cavy, rodent
guise	=	attire, dress, facade, front, garb, mask, veil
gulch	=	gorge, gully, ravine
gull-like bird	=	skua, tern
gulp	=	bolt, gobble, guzzle, swallow, wolf
gum	=	affix, glue, paste, resin, stick
gumption	=	acumen, nous, savvy, sense, wit(s)
gun	=	arm, firearm, revolver, rifle; name of [bazooka, bofors, bren, browning, colt, derringer, gat(ling), machine, magnum, luger, sten, tommy, uzi]
gunmen	=	artillery, (ra)
gunpowder	=	nitre
gush	=	babble, flood, flow, pour, spout, surge
gust	=	blast, blow, gale, puff, rush, squall, storm
gusto	=	brio, dash, elan, zest
gut	=	channel, passage, sound, strait
gutter	=	channel, ditch, drain, duct, sluice

guy	= bloke, chap, fellow, lad, man, youth
gyp	= bilk, cheat, con, do, fake, hoax, pain
gypsy	= gipsy, nomad, romany, rover
gyrate	= rotate, spiral, turn

H

habit	= bent, clothes [see], custom, routine, usage, use, wont
(retiring) habit	= neglige, nightcap, nightdress, pyjamas
hack	= cut, drudge, horse, jade, mangle, notch
had	= got, held, kept, owned, conned
haemorrhage	= bleed
haemorrhaged	= bled
hag	= beldam, crone, shrew, vixen, witch
haggard	= drawn, lean, pinched, untamed, worn
haggle	= bargain, barter, cavil, dicker, huckster
hail	= cheer, exalt, greet, salute, welcome
hair	= bristle, lock, mane, mop, shock, tress
haircut	= name of [shingle, tonsure]
hair-piece	= toupee, wig
hair style	= coiffure; name of [afro, bangs, beehive, bob, bun, chignon, pageboy, pigtail, plait, pouffe]
hair tint	= dye, henna, ochre
hairy	= barbate, hirsute, risky
hale	= drag, healthy, hearty, robust, strong
half	= demi, semi
half asleep	= comatose
halo	= aureola, circle, disc, nimbus, ring
halt	= arrest, cease, close, end, game, lame, limp, stem, stop
hamlet	= village
hammer	= beat, gavel, mallet, pound, rap, sledge
hand	= help, pass, paw, sailor [see], (l, r)
(clenched) hand	= fist
(first) hand	= new
(lend a) hand	= abet, aid, assist, help, second
(second-)hand	= old, used
hands	= care, control, crew, power, workmen
handcart	= barrow
handle	= grip, haft, hilt, knob, lever, name, stock, title, touch, treat
handout	= alms, charity, dole, issue, leaflet
(press) handout	= release
handsome	= fair, generous, liberal, plentiful, stately
handwriting	= fist, hand, scrawl, script
handy	= adroit, deft, dexterous
hang	= bow, dangle, drape, droop, loll, sag, suspend, swing

hang around	=	dally, haunt, hover, loiter, tarry
hang on	=	bide, cling, hinge
hanger	=	necklace, pendant, pendulum, tassel
hanger-on	=	leech, minion, parasite, sponger, sycophant
hanging	=	beetle, curtain, drape, loose, pendent
hangar	=	shed, shelter
happen	=	arise, befall, ensue, occur, pass
happening	=	affair, case, chance, event, scene
happy	=	blest, blithe, bright, gay, glad, jolly, merry, up
harbinger	=	forerunner, herald, precursor
harbour	=	basin, dock, haven, hide, marina, port, refuge, shelter, shield
hard	=	adamant, brittle, difficult, firm, rigid, set, solid, stiff, tough, (h)
hard work	=	grind, labour, slog, sweat, toil, travail
hardly	=	barely, just, scarce(ly)
hardship	=	difficulty, rigour, privation
harm	=	damage, hurt, impair, mar, ruin, spoil
harmony	=	accord, concert, rapport, tune, unity
harness	=	gear, hitch, saddle, tack(le), yoke
harridan	=	hag, shrew, virago, vixen
harry	=	badger, fret, hassle, nag, pester, vex
harsh	=	bitter, cruel, drastic, dry, grim, rough, severe, strident
harvest	=	crop, garner, mow, pick, reap, yield
has to	=	must
hash	=	chop, medley, mess, mince, muddle, stew
haste	=	hie, hurry, hustle, run, rush, speed, urgency
hasty	=	hurried, quick, rash, speedy, urgent
hat	=	lid, headgear [see], tile, top
hatch	=	breed, concoct, contrive, lay, spawn
hatter	=	milliner
hate	=	abhor, detest, enmity, loathe, odium
hateful	=	foul, heinous, odious, vile
haul	=	booty, cargo, drag, load, loot, lug, pull, spoil(s), swag, tow, tug
haulm	=	stalk, straw
haunch	=	hance, hip, loin
haunt	=	badger, den, frequent, lair, pursue, resort
have	=	gain, get, hold, keep, own
hawk	=	bark, cry, peddle, sell, tout, vend
(untamed) hawk	=	haggard
hawker	=	dealer, duffer, huckster, monger, pedlar, trader, vendor
(make) hay	=	ted
hazard	=	chance, danger, jeopardy, peril, risk, wager
haze	=	cloud, film, fog, mist, obscure, spray
hazel	=	filbert, nut

head	= bean, brain, chief, foam, froth, lead, leader, master, ness, nut, pate, poll, skull, teacher, top
(part of) head	= corona, crown, inion, occiput, pate, poll, sinciput, temple, tonsure, vertex
(shave(n)) head	= tonsure
head office	= base, (ho)
heads	= obverse
headdress	= name of [crown, diadem, tiara]
headgear	= bonnet, cap, hat, hood, scarf, top; name of hat [balmoral, beret, biretta, boater, bowler, busby, coif, cloche, derby, fedora, fez, homburg, panama, pork-pie, stetson, tam, topper, toque, tricorn, trilby]
headland	= bluff, cape, ness, point
headquarters	= base, depot, (ho, hq)
headshrinker	= analyst, freud
health resort	= hydro, spa
healthy	= fit, good, hale, robust, sound, well
heap	= banger, boneshaker, lot, jalopy, mass, mound, pile, stack
hear	= catch, hark, heed, judge, listen, try
hearing	= ear, inquiry, review, sound, trial
hearsay	= buzz, gossip, report, rumour, talk
heart	= centre, core, guts, pluck, soul, ticker
hearth	= fireplace, fireside, grate, hob, ingle
heat	= fever, fury, rut, warm
heath	= fell, moor(land), muir
heather	= erica, ling
heave	= hurl, lift, pitch, push, roll, shove, toss
heaven	= bliss, ecstasy, nirvana, utopia, zion
heavenly body	= asteroid, comet, meteor, planet, star
heavenly food	= ambrosia, manna
heavy	= bulky, gross, massive, stodgy, weighty
heavyweight	= ton
Hebrew	= israelite, jew, semite; name of [abraham, issac, jacob], (heb)
hedge	= barrier, bound(ary), fence, row, screen, stall
heel	= bounder, cad, incline, lean, list, tilt; name of [high, platform, stiletto, wedge]
heir	= inheritor, scion, successor
helix	= bend, spiral, volute
helm	= guide, steer, tiller, wheel
helmet	= name of [pith, topee, topi]
help	= abet, aid, assist, back, hand, second, (sos)
helper	= abettor, aide, ally, backer, second
helpmate, helpmeet	= husband, partner, spouse, wife
hem	= border, edge, fringe, margin, skirt
hen	= capon, chicken, fowl, layer
hen-food	= egg

Henry	= hal, (h)
herald	= forerunner, harbinger, precursor, usher
herb	= name of [basil, chive, dill, fennel, mint, oregano, orpin, parsley, rosemary, sage, simple, sorrel, tansy, thyme]
herd	= crowd, drive, drove, flock, run, tend
here	= in, present
(not) here	= absent, away, gone, out, there
heritage	= bequest, estate, legacy, lot, share
hermit	= anchorite, eremite, monk, recluse
hermitage	= ashram, retreat
hero worshipper	= leander
heroic story	= epic, saga
hesitate	= delay, dither, hem, pause, stammer, waver
hessian	= boot, fly, hemp, jute, sacking
hew	= axe, carve, chop, cut, fell, lop
Hibernian	= irish
hidden	= buried, covert, doggo, privy, secret
hide	= bury, cache, conceal, cover, fleece, fur, leather, mask, morocco, pelt, skin, tan
hide-out	= den, lair, shelter
hie	= dash, hurry, run, rush, speed
hierarchy	= grading, ladder, ranking
hi-fi	= stereo
high	= fetid, noble, off, smelling, stale, tall, up
highs	= ups
highball	= lob
high up	= above, aloft, atop
highwayman	= foodpad, robber; name of [turpin]
hike	= hitch, hoof, leg, lift, ramble, tramp, trek, walk
hill	= brae, butte, down, fell, heap, knoll, mound, mount, tor
hilltop	= brow, crest, crown, ridge, summit
hinder	= let, deter, hamper, impede, retard, stymie, thwart, trammel
hinge	= depend, joint, pivot, rest, turn
hint	= clue, cue, dash, help, infer, tip, touch, trace, wrinkle
hip	= blues, fruit, joint
hire	= cost, fee, lease, let, rent(al)
hirsute	= hairy
history	= annals, past
hit	= beat, lam, punch, rap, smash, strike, success, swat, tap, whack
hitch	= couple, harness, jerk, knot, lift, marry, noose, snag, thumb, wed; name of [blackwall, clove, cow, half, rolling, swab, timber]
hoard	= amass, gather, husband, stash, stock, store

hoax	= bam, deceive, dupe, fool, gull, joke
hob	= cooker, elf, goblin, oven, peg, pin
hock	= pawn, pledge
hoist	= crane, elevate, jack, lift, raise, tackle, winch
hokum	= bunk, flummery, humbug, nonsense
hold	= clasp, clutch, grasp, grip, have, keep, maintain, own
hold back	= check, curb, dam, hesitate, stem, stop
hold up	= delay, heist, jam, rob, snag, theft, wait, waylay
holdall	= bag, basket, grip
holder	= bag, grip, incumbent, owner
(canvas) holder	= easel
hole	= aperture, cavity, eye, fix, gap, hovel, orifice, pit, scrape, vent, void, (o)
(big) hole	= abyss, chasm, crater
holiday	= break, leave, package, recess, vacation
(on) holiday	= off, away
holiday home	= camp(er), caravan, tent
hollow	= corrie, cwm, dent, dimple, dip, empty, groove, pit, vacant, void
holy man	= clergy [see], prophet, saint, (st)
home	= abode, base, den, house, in, nest, pad
(at) home	= in
(indian) home	= tepee, teepee, wigwam
homeless boy, child	= arab, waif
honest	= artless, frank, just, true, upright
honey	= mel, nectar
honorary	= brevet, nominal
honour	= award, badge, glory, homage, kudos, pay, respect, (mbe, obe, om)
honour (card)	= name of [ace, jack, king, knave, queen]
(international) honour	= cap
honourable	= honest, just, noble, upright, worthy, (hon)
honours	= bays, laurels
hood	= bonnet, cowl, gangster, mobster, robin
hoodwink	= baffle, cheat, con, dupe, fool, hoax
hooligan	= rough, rowdy, thug, tough, yob(bo)
hoop	= band, circle, ring, (o)
hoot	= boo, cry, hiss, jeer, laugh, yell
hooter	= horn, owl, nose, siren
hop	= ball, bound, dance, jump, leap, lope, skip, spring
hope	= aspire, belief, bob [Hope], faith, rely, trust
horn	= antler, butt, gore, hooter, peak, warner
horrify	= appal, awe, dismay, frighten, scare
horror	= awe, dread, fear, fright, terror
hors d'ouvre	= starter

horse	= bronco, charger, colt, filly, gelding, hack, hunter, jade, mare, mule, mount, mustang, nag, pony, ride, runner, steed, stud; name of [arab, barb, bay, cob, dray, gray, grey, palomino, piebald, pinto, roan, shire, sorrel], (gg)
(spirited) horse	= arab
(war-)horse	= charger, steed, trooper
(wild) horse	= bronco, mustang
horse-drawn carriage	= name of (horse-drawn) vehicle [see]
horse-drawn vehicle	= name of (horse-drawn) vehicle [see]
horse event	= trial; name of [badminton]
horseman	= cossack, equestrian, hussar, rider
(fabulous) horseman	= centaur
horsemen	= cavalry
hospital doctor	= intern
host	= army, entertainer, horde, lot, many, treat, (mc)
hostage	= captive, prisoner
hostel(ry)	= inn, lodge, tavern
hostile	= adverse, alien, anti, bellicose, warlike
hostilities	= conflict, fighting, war, warfare
hot	= angry, ardent, fiery, keen, warm, torrid, (h)
hotel	= hostel, inn, lodge, motel, tavern, (h)
hotel servant	= bellboy, boots, concierge, housekeeper, maid, page, porter, valet
hotelier	= name of [forte, hilton, hyatt]
hothead	= daredevil, madcap, tearaway
hound	= badger, chase, harass, harry, urge, worry
hounds	= pack
hour	= time
house	= bungalow, chalet, firm, home, lodge, manor, semi, villa; name of [commons, lords, lower, upper], (hc, hl, ho)
(slaughter-)house	= abattoir, butchery, shambles
household	= family, home, menage
hover	= drift, float, hang, poise, waver
how	= method, way
however	= but, except, only, save, yet
huckster	= bargain, haggle, hawker [see], mercenary
hue	= colour, dye, shade, tinge, tint
huff	= blow, gasp, miff, pant, pique, sulk
hug	= clasp, clinch, embrace, enfold
huge	= colossal, gigantic, jumbo, titanic, (os)
human	= being, body, mortal, person, soul
humane	= benevolent, kind, merciful, tender
humble	= abase, low(er), meek, modest, poor
humble fellow	= heep [Uriah Heep]

humbug	= bunk(um), cheat, deceit, gyp, flummery, fraud, hoax, hokum, nonsense, sham, sweet
humdrum	= boring, dreary, dull, routine
humiliate	= abase, demean, humble, shame
humour	= caprice, comedy, fun, mood, whim, wit
humourist	= comic, droll, joker, wag, wit
humourous	= comic, droll, funny, gilbertian, witty
hundred	= ton, (c)
hunger	= long, pine, starve, thirst, yearn, yen
(morbid) hunger	= bulimia, bulimy
hunk	= adonis, beau, dandy, hunch
hunks	= miser
hunt	= chase, ferret, hound, quest, run, search, seek, track
hunter	= horse, orion [constellation], steed
hurl	= cast, chuck, fling, pitch, throw, toss
hurly-burly	= bedlam, chaos, furore, hubbub, turmoil, uproar
hurrah	= hooray, yippie
hurricane	= cyclone, gale, storm, tempest, typhoon
hurried	= brief, cursory, hectic, quick, ran, swift
hurry	= dash, haste, hie, race, run, rush, speed, urge
hurst	= hillock, sandbank, wood
hurt	= bruise, damage, harm, injure, mar, smart, spoil, sting, throb
hurtful	= cruel, cutting, mean, nasty, unkind
husband	= budget, hoard, mate, save, spouse, store
husbandry	= economy, thrift
hush	= quiet(en), silence, soothe, still
hush-hush	= confidential, secret
husk	= case, hull, pod, shell, shuck, skin
husks	= chaff
hustle	= crowd, elbow, hurry, rush, shove, solicit
hut	= cabin, chalet, cot, hovel, shack, shed; name of [nissen]
hybrid	= cross, mongrel, sterile
hydro	= hotel, resort, spa
hygienic	= clean, pure, sanitary
hymn	= aria, chorale, lay, psalm, song
hypnotised	= spellbound, under
hypocrisy	= cant, deceit
hypothesis	= premise, theory, thesis

I

I object	= me
iceberg	= floe, growler
ice-cream	= cone, slider, wafer
icy	= arctic, bitter, cold, frigid
idea	= brainwave, concept, fancy, notion, plan, thought, view, whim

ideal	= model, paragon, perfect, standard
idealist	= romantic, utopian, visionary
idem	= same, (id)
identical	= alike, clone, equal, like, ringer, same, twin
identity	= name, (id, ka)
idiom	= jargon, language, phrase, style, usage
idiot	= ass, cretin, dolt, dope, fool, moron, nana, oaf, sap, twit
idiotic	= asinine, crazy, daft, dumb, inane, mad, nuts, silly, stupid
idle	= futile, inert, lax, lazy, loaf, vain
idol	= deity, god, hero, icon, image, star
ignoble	= base, low, mean, vile
ignorant	= green, naive, rude, unaware, unread
ignore	= bypass, cut, discount, neglect, omit, pass
ill	= ailing, bad, sick
(become, get) ill	= ail, sicken
ill-behaved child	= imp
ill-mannered	= coarse, impolite, rude, uncouth
ill-tempered	= cross, curt, grumpy, sharp, testy
ill will	= acrimony, animosity, animus, grudge, hostility, rancour, spite, strife
illness	= ailment, disease, disorder, malady
(feign) illness	= malinger
illegal	= banned, bootleg, illicit, lawless
illicit whiskey	= moonshine
illuminated	= lit
illumination	= beam, insight, lamp, light, ray
illusion	= chimera, fallacy, mirage, phantasm, spectre
illustrate	= draw, show, sketch
illustration	= case, diagram, example, picture, sketch, (ill)
image	= double, icon, idol, motif, spit, topos
imagination	= fancy, insight, notion, vision, whimsy
imagine	= assume, believe, dream, fancy, surmise, think
imbecile	= cretin, fool, idiot, moron
imitate	= ape, copy, echo, mimic, mock, parody
imitation	= copy, ersatz, fake, mock(ery), sham, parody, spoof, spurious
immature	= adolescent, green, jejune, juvenile, puerile, raw, young
immaturity	= nonage, rawness, youth
immoderate	= extreme, steep, stiff, undue
immoral	= corrupt, dissolute, evil, libertine, obscene, wanton
imp	= demon, gamin, graft, rascal, scamp, scion, shoot, urchin
impair	= damage, harm, hurt, mar, ruin, spoil
impart	= convey, relate, state, tell
impasse	= deadlock, stalemate, standoff

impede	= bar, block, brake, check, hinder
impediment	= bar, block, check, lisp, snag, stutter
imperial measure	= feet, foot, furlong, inch, mile, yard
impetus	= force, impulse, incentive, momentum, spur
implement	= tool, name of tool [see]
implore	= appeal, beg, crave, plead, pray
import	= intent, meaning, purport, sense, weight
importance	= moment, value, weight, worth
important	= big, pompous, urgent, weighty
important person	= bigwig, nabob, nob, pot, (vip)
imposing	= august, grand, majestic, noble
impost	= duty, levy, tariff, tax
impostor	= charlatan, cheat, fraud, phoney, quack
impound	= confine, confiscate, restrain
impress	= engrave, etch, inscribe, stamp
impression	= idea, notion, print, stamp, sway
impressive	= grand, lavish, powerful
improve	= better, mend, rally, recover
improvise	= ad-lib, coin, concoct, devise, vamp
impudence	= cheek, face, gall, lip, neck, nerve
impudent	= bold, cheeky, forward, pert, rude, saucy
impugn	= deny, dispute, gainsay, negate
impulse	= drive, force, goad, push, urge, spur
impute	= ascribe, censure, charge
in	= amid, chic, elected, favoured, home, smart
inane	= banal, empty, foolish, silly, stupid, void
inappropriate	= alien, inapt, unfit(ted), unsuitable
inapt	= awkward, clumsy, gauche, unskilful
incantation	= charm, rune, spell
incense	= anger, aroma, balm, enrage, ire, madden, perfume, spice
inch	= crawl, creep, edge, (in)
incident	= episode, event, occurrence
incite	= egg, goad, provoke, rouse, urge
incitement	= goad, push, spur, stimulus
inclination	= bent, bias, cant, grade, penchant, ramp, slope
incline	= bend, cant, dip, lean, list, ramp, slope, stoop, tend, tilt
inclined	= bent, fain, leant, likely, prone, willing
include	= add, contain, count, cover, embrace, involve
income	= earnings, money, pay, revenue, salary, stipend, wage(s), (inc)
incomplete	= broken, part, partial, short
in connection with	= about, anent, apropos, on, over, (re)
inconvenience	= bother, trouble
increase	= add, boost, enlarge, extra, grow, more, rise, up, wax, (inc)
(sudden) increase	= spurt, surge
incubate	= brood, hatch

in debt	= owed, owes, (r . . . ed)
indecent	= blue, coarse, crude, dirty, foul, lewd
indentation	= crater, dent, nick, notch
independent	= autonomous, free, separate, sovereign, (ind)
indian	= asian, brave, hindu; name of [apache, aztec, cree, crow, gandhi, inca, nehru, mohawk, navaho, pawnee, sikh, sioux, tupi], (ind)
(young) indian	= papoose
indian dress	= sari
Indian fan	= punka(h)
Indian food	= curry
indian home, tent	= tepee, teepee, wigwam
Indian language	= name of [gujarati, hindi, tamil, urdu]
Indian money	= name of [anna, rupee]
Indian peasant	= ryot
Indian river	= name of [ganges, indus]
indian sign	= totem
Indian veil	= name of [purdah, yashmak]
indian woman	= squaw
indicate	= denote, hint, imply, point, show
indication	= clue, cue, hint, omen, sign, token
indication of rank	= crown, pip, stripe
indict	= accuse, charge
indigenous	= endemic, innate, native, natural
indigent	= broke, needy, poor
indistinct	= dim, dull, faint, hazy, vague
individual	= being, entity, one, single, special, (i)
indoctrinate	= drill, imbue, instil, school, train
indolent	= lazy, slothful
industry	= effort, labour, trade, zeal, (ind)
ineffective	= futile, useless, vain, weak
inept	= absurd, fatuous, futile, silly, unfit
inert	= dead, dull, idle, lax, static, still
inexpensive	= budget, cheap, modest
inexperienced	= callow, fresh, green, raw
infant	= baby, bairn, child
infantryman	= joe, serviceman, soldier, (gi)
in favour of	= for, pro
infection	= cold, flu, poison, virus
infer	= conclude, deduce, derive, gather
inferior	= less(er), lower, minor, under, worse, (b, inf)
infirm	= feeble, frail, lame, puny, weak
inflame	= anger, arouse, fire, heat, provoke
inflexible	= rigid, stiff
inflict	= deal, deliver, strike, wreak
influence	= affect, bias, clout, power, pull, sway
influential	= important, potent, powerful
inform	= advise, instruct, sing, squeal, teach, tell

informed	= sang, taught, told
informal	= casual, irregular
info(rmation)	= data, dope, facts, gen, news, word, (inf)
informer	= grass, nark, rat, snitch
ingenious	= adroit, clever, natty, skilful
ingenuous	= artless, frank, naive, natural, simple
inhabit	= dwell, live, occupy, people, tenant
initial	= early, first, letter, opening, primary
initiate	= begin, arouse, ignite, kindle, open, start
injection	= jab, shot
injury	= damage, harm, hurt, mischief, wrong
inlet	= bay, bight, cove, creek, firth, sound
inn	= auberge, hostel(ry), hotel, lodge, pub, tavern
innate	= inborn, natural
inner	= bull, central, middle, secret
insane	= crazy, daft, loco, mad, mental, nuts, (sa . . . ne)
inscription	= epitaph, (rip)
insect(s)	= bug, grub, imago, larva, pest, pupa; name of [ant, aphid, bee, beetle, cleg, cicada, cricket, dor, flea, fly, gnat, grig, hornet, lice, locust, louse, mawk, maggot, mantis, moth, midge, midget, moth, nit, spider, tick, wasp, weevil]
(tiny) insect	= mite
inside	= in, inner, (si . . . de)
insincere	= affected, faked, false, feigned
insipid	= banal, bland, flat, limp, vapid, weak
(be) insipid	= bore, pall
insolent	= arrogant, impudent, insulting, rude
inspect	= examine, review, study, survey, view
inspiration	= arousal, genius, muse, spur, stimulus
install	= fit, fix, lodge, settle
instance	= case, cite, example, mention, name, suit
(for) instance	= as, say, (eg)
instant	= flash, moment, second, trice, urgent
instinct	= gift, gut, id, impulse, knack, talent
institution	= college, convent, custom, law, museum, ritual, rule, school, society
instruct	= bid, inform, order, school, teach, tell, train
instruction	= course, lesson, order, teaching, training
instrument	= device, gadget, tool [see], utensil
(musical) instrument	= name of [accordion, balalaika, banjo, bassoon, bugle, cittern, clarinet, concertina, cornet, cymbal, fife, flute, guitar, harmonica, harp, horn, lute, lyre, mandolin, oboe, organ, piano, piccolo, recorder, sackbut, sax(ophone), sitar, trombone, trumpet, tuba, ukulele, viol(a), zither]
insult	= abuse, affront, offend, slight, snub

insurance	= cover, indemnity, security, warranty
integer	= digit, figure, number, whole
integral	= complete, entire, full, sum, total, whole
intellect	= brain, genius, mind, nous, reason, sense, wit
intellectual person	= academic, brahmin, don, professor
intelligence	= acumen, brains, gen, news, nous, sense, wit, (mi)
(provide) intelligence	= advise, inform
intelligent	= bright, clever, sharp, shrewd, smart
intend	= aim, design, mean, plan
intended	= aimed, fiancee, meant
intense	= ardent, eager, extreme, fierce, violent, severe
intensity	= compass, range, scope, sweep
intent	= aim, bent, eager, import, rapt, sense
inter	= bury, entomb, inurn
interbreed	= cross, mix
interbred	= cross, hybrid, mongrel
interest	= bias, concern, engross, hobby, profit, return, share, stake, (i, int)
(stimulate) interest	= arouse, hold, whet
(not) interested	= bored
interfere	= conflict, meddle, tamper
interference	= static
interim	= caretaker, meantime, meanwhile, stopgap
international	= global, universal, worldwide, (i, int)
international (honour)	= cap
international (match)	= test
intersperse	= diversify, mix, scatter
interval	= break, lull, pause, space, (int)
in the majority	= adult
in the red	= owing
in thing	= craze, fad, fashion, rage, trend, vogue
intimidate	= browbeat, bully, cow, daunt, deter
intrigue	= affair, plot, rivet, ruse, scheme
introduce	= insert, launch, open, preface, present
introduction	= foreword, preamble, preface, prologue
(musical) introduction	= overture, prelude
introductory	= initial, nascent, opening, prefatory
introductory book	= primer
intuition	= hunch, insight, instinct
invalid	= false, null, untrue, void
invective	= abuse, abusive, railing, sarcasm
invent	= coin, create, devise, feign, patent
inventor	= author, creator, father, founder, maker, originator, patentee; name of [baird, bell, boyle, brunel, davy, edison, ford, galileo, marconi, watt]
inventory	= catalogue, list, stock
inverse	= contrary, converse, opposite, reverse

investment	=	ante, asset, bond, share, stake, stock
investor	=	angel, patron, sponsor, stag
IOW feature	=	needles
irate	=	angry, cross, enraged, mad, peeved
Ireland	=	eire, erin
iris	=	flag, rainbow
Irish boy	=	name of (Irish) boy [see]
Irish county	=	name of (Irish) county [see]
Irish girl	=	colleen
Irishman	=	name of Irish boy [see]
Irish money	=	name of [punt]
Irish parliament	=	dail
Irish robber	=	tory
irk	=	annoy, irritate [see], vex
iron	=	club, press, smooth, (fe)
irony	=	mockery, sarcasm, travesty
irresolute	=	fickle, infirm, timid, weak
irritable	=	cross, hot, sore, tense, testy
irritate	=	anger, annoy, badger, gall, grate, harass, hector, madden, needle, nettle, peeve, rile
irritating chap, person	=	blighter, nuisance, pain, pest
irritation	=	anger, itch, pain, pest
island	=	ait, atoll, inch, isle; name of [arran, bali, capri, corfu, cos, crete, cuba, delos, elba, ellis, haiti, hawaii, iona, malta, man, rhode, rhodes, sark, scilly, skye, tahiti, wight], (i, is)
(cross) island	=	malta
(small) island	=	ait, inch, isle
isle	=	ait, inch, man [Isle of], (i, iom, iow)
ism	=	canon, doctrine, dogma, practice, theory
issue	=	arise, birth, child(ren), edition, emit, offspring, outflow, scion, seed, son, spring
(without) issue	=	childless, (sp)
Italian	=	latin, roman, (i, it)
Italian city	=	name of [bari, florence, genoa, milan, naples, parma, pisa, rome, trieste, turin, venice, verona]
Italian drink, wine	=	name of [asti, chianti, frascati]
Italian family	=	name of [medici]
Italian food	=	pasta; name of [gnocchi, lasagne, ravioli, spaghetti]
Italian man	=	signor, (s)
Italian money	=	name of [lira, lire]
Italian river	=	name of [arno, po, tiber]
itch	=	ache, crawl, long, lust, pine, tingle, yen
item	=	a, also, an, article, it, likewise, object, thing, too, unit
(auction) item	=	lot

(display) item	= exhibit, model
(sports) item	= event, heat, race
ivory	= cream, key, tusk, white

J

jab	= dig, injection, poke, prod, shot, stab, thrust
jack	= card, hoist, knave, lift, raise, sailor seaman, salt, tar, (j)
jacket	= case, folder, skin; name of [anorak, blazer, coat, matinee, reefer]
jackpot	= kitty, pool, pot, prize
Jacob	= israel [Biblical]
jade	= green, nag, shrew, slut, vixen
jaded	= sated, spent, tired, weary
jagged	= cleft, rough, uneven
jagged point	= barb, hook, spike
jail	= brig, clink, cooler, gaol, jug, nick, prison, quod, stir
jail sentence	= life, stretch, time
jailbird	= con, convict, felon, lag
jailer	= guard, screw, warden, warder
jalopy	= banger, boneshaker, heap
jam	= bind, cram, fix, hole, pickle, preserve, spot
jamboree	= carnival, fete, party, spree
Japanese dancing-girl	= geisha
Japanese dress	= kimono
Japanese drink	= name of [sake]
Japanese food	= name of [sukiyaki, sushi, tempura, teriyaki]
Japanese money	= name of [sen, yen]
Japanese tree	= bonsai
jar	= crock, grate, jolt, jug, pot, urn, vase
jargon	= argot, cant, idiom, lingo, patois, slang
Jason's ship	= argo
jaunt	= airing, stroll, tour, trip
jaw	= babble, chat, gossip, natter, scold
jealous	= envious, green, rival
jealousy	= envy, spite
jeer	= boo, gibe, hiss, mock, scoff, sneer
jelly	= aspic, gel
jelly-fish	= name of [blubber, medusa]
jeopardy	= danger, hazard, peril, risk
jerk	= lurch, pull, tic, twist, twitch, yank
jerry	= boche, can, hun
jest	= crack, fun, gag, hoax, joke, quip
jester	= clown, comic, joker, wag, wit
jet	= black, fountain, spirt, spout, spurt; name of [comet, harrier, jumbo, mig, mirage]
jetty	= dock, mole, pier, quay, slipway, wharf

jewel	=	bijou, gem(stone), rock, sparkler, trinket; name of gemstone [see]
jewellery	=	bangle, chain, choker, ring, snide
Jewish doctor of law	=	rabbi
Jewish farm	=	kibbutz
Jewish greeting	=	shalom
Jewish language	=	name of [hebrew, yiddish]
Jewish priest	=	rabbi
(not) Jewish	=	gentile, goy
jib	=	balk, refuse, shrink
jig	=	bob, caper, dance, skip, wobble
jingle	=	air, chime, ditty, ring, song, tune
(advertising) jingle	=	slogan
jinx	=	bewitch, curse, gremlin, hex, voodoo
Joan of Arc	=	maid [of Orleans]
job	=	chore, con, dupe, duty, line, office, post, task, work
(cushy) job	=	sinecure
jockey	=	cheat, con, hoax, rider, trick
jocularity	=	badinage, banter, glee, mirth
joe	=	sweetheart, (gi)
jog	=	jar, jolt, prod, push, run, stir, trot
join	=	add, bond, couple, enlist, knit, link, marry, seam, sew, tie, unite
joined	=	sewn, tied, wed
join forces	=	enlist, unite
join together	=	cement, fuse, glue, unite, wed, weld
join union	=	marry, wed
joint	=	cut, dive, hinge, knot, seam, shared; name of [ankle, elbow, hip, knee, knuckle, patella, wrist], (jt)
joke	=	fun, gag, jest, pun, quip, tease
joker	=	card, clown, comic, jester, wag, wit
jollity	=	fun, humour, mirth
jolly	=	blithe, gay, happy, merry
journal	=	diary, gazette, log, record
journalist	=	editor, hack, scribe, (ed)
journalists	=	press
journey	=	fly, go, jaunt, passage, run, trek, trip, voyage
jowl	=	cheek, dewlap, jaw
joy	=	bliss, ecstasy, gem, glee, mirth, treat
judge	=	arbiter, assess, critic, expert, rate, reckon, reckoner, ref(eree), settler, trier, try, umpire; name of [beak, deemster, dempster, justice, magistrate, recorder], (ja, jag)
judges	=	bench
judg(e)ment	=	decision, doom, fate, sense, verdict, wisdom
jug	=	cooler, ewer, gaol, jail, mug, stir, toby, urn
juggle	=	alter, doctor, fix

juice	= fluid, liquid, sap, serum, squash
jumble	= chaos, medlay, mess, mix, muddle
jumbo	= giant, huge, jet, plane
jump	= bound, hop, leap, omit, skip, start, vault
jumper	= flea, frog, horse, sweater
junction	= angle, joint, seam, union, (t)
junior	= lesser, lower, minor, subordinate, under, younger, (jnr, jr, jun)
just	= apt, barely, but, due, even, fair, fit, good, hardly, honest, meet, mere, moral, only, right(eous), scarce(ly), true
just after	= on
justice	= fairness, judge [see], law, right, (jp)
justification	= defence, grounds, rationale, reason
justify	= defend, excuse, sanction, uphold
juvenile	= boy, child, girl, immature, infant, minor, youth, young, (juv)

K

keel	= faint, swoon, topple, upset
keen	= agog, ardent, avid, cry, eager, fervid, sharp, hot, weep, zealous
keenness	= acumen, ardour, edge, fervour, wit, zeal, zest
keep	= board, castle, citadel, food, fort, fortress, have, hold, mind, preserve, retain, run, save, stock, store
keep back	= deny, hide, refuse, retard, stifle
keeper	= curator, custodian, gaoler, guardian, jailer
(door-)keeper	= bouncer, concierge, doorman, porter, usher
keg	= barrel, breaker, cask, drum, firkin, tun, vat
Kelly	= ned
kept	= had, held, ran
kerb	= edge, fender, stone
kernel	= core, germ, gist, nub, pith, seed
kettle	= drum
kettledrum	= timbal
key	= answer, basic, chief, ivory, main, (a, b, c, d, e, g)
keys	= piano
keynote	= centre, core, gist, heart, kernel, pith, theme
kibbutz	= commune, farm
kick	= boot, gripe, punch, punt, quit, rebel, stop, thrill
kicker	= crab, crank, grump, grouse, horse
kick off	= begin, launch, open, start
kid	= baby, bairn, chaff, child, con, dupe, fool, goat, hoax, infant, rag, rib, tot
kidnap	= abduct, nobble, seize, shanghai
kill	= cull, end, lynch, murder, scotch, scrag, shoot, slay, stifle, waste

killed	= dead, shot, slain, slew
killer	= assassin, butcher, murderer, slayer; name of weapon [dagger, gun, knife, rifle]
(first) killer	= cain [Biblical]
(lady-)killer	= cassanova, libertine, lothario, rake, romeo, roue, wolf, womanizer
killing	= carnage, execution, homicide, massacre, murder, slaughter
kiln	= furnace, oast, oven
kin, kindred	= blood, family, kith, relation, stock
kind	= amiable, benevolent, benign, class, genial, genre, ilk, mellow, mild, sort, tender, type
kindle	= fire, ignite, light, stir, whet
kindling	= punk, tinder, touchwood
king	= emperor, monarch, rex, ruler, (hm, k, r)
(biblical) king	= name of [herod]
(fairy) king	= name of [oberon]
(old) king	= name of [arthur, canute, cole, lear], (gr)
kingdom	= monarchy, nation, realm, reign, state
kink	= bend, crimp, flaw, hitch, knot, quirk, vagary, whim
kiss	= buss, caress, neck, peck, smooch, (x)
(two) kisses	= double-cross, (xx)
kit	= clobber, clothes [see], gear, rig, tackle
kitchen equipment	= cooker, freezer, fridge, hob, mixer, oven, sink, stove
(ship's) kitchen	= caboose, galley
kitty	= cat, fund, pool, pot, tom
knack	= bent, flair, forte, gift, skill, talent
knave	= bounder, cheat, jack, rogue, scamp, varlet, villain
knell	= chime, peal, ring, toll
knife	= blade, cut(ter), slash, stab, woun; name of [bayonet, bowie, cleaver, dagger, dirk, flick, kris, lancet, machete, palette, panga, stiletto]
(surgeon's) knife	= name of [bistoury, scalpel]
knight	= banneret, paladin, sir, (ch, k, kb, kt)
knight errant	= champion, paladin, peer
knit	= bind, furrow, heal, mend, weave
knob	= boss, bump, knurl, lump, node, nodule, nub, stud, umbo
knock	= blame, blow, buffet, bump, criticise, hit, pan, rap, slap, tap
knock off	= kill, murder, nick, rob, steal
knock out	= kayo, stun, (ko)
knockout	= hit, smash, stunner
knoll	= butte, hill, mound, peal, ring, toll

knot	=	bend, bond, hitch, link, lump, maze, node, nodule, tangle, tie, web; name of [bowline, cats-paw, figure-of-eight, granny, reef, overhand, seizing, sheepshank, slip, stevedore's, surgeon's, thumb, true lover's, turk's head]; name of bend [carrick, common, fisherman's, sheet]; name of hitch [blackwall, clove, cow, half, rolling, swab, timber], (kn)
(ancestral) knot	=	granny
knotty	=	complex, difficult, hard, knobbed, nodose, sticky
knout	=	scourge, whip
know	=	feel, grasp, have, see, wist
(Scots) know	=	ken
knowhow	=	ability, flair, knack, skill, talent
knowing	=	alert, astute, aware, clever, expert, sage, smart, wise
knowledge	=	gen, info(rmation), lore, ology, wisdom
knowledgeable	=	erudite, learned, sage, smart, wise
known	=	felt, had, kent, seen, (a, b)
(also) known as	=	alias, (aka)
(make) known	=	air, broadcast
(well) known	=	famous, notable, noted
knowing	=	alert, aware, bright, clever, sharp
knuckle under	=	submit, yield
kudos	=	eclat, fame, prestige, renown

L

label	=	brand, call, docket, name, tab, tag, ticket, trademark
laborious	=	onerous, tedious
labour	=	effort, grind, job, left, pains, sweat, toil, travail, work, (lab)
labourer	=	drudge, hand, navvy, worker
labyrinth	=	coil, jungle, maze
lace	=	beat, braid, fasten, lash, spike, tie, twine
lacerate	=	cut, gash, rend, rip, tear, wound
lachrymose	=	sad, tearful
lack	=	absence, dearth, miss, need, require, want
lacking	=	flawed, minus, sans, without
lackadaisical	=	dull, idle, languid, lazy, limp
lackey	=	flunky, menial, pawn, toady, valet
lacklustre	=	drab, dull, flat, sombre
laconic	=	brief, curt, short, terse
lacquer	=	japan, shellac
lad	=	boy, chap, fellow, guy, master, son, stripling, youth; name of [al, des, don, ed, bill, les, mark, pete, ray, ron, stan, ted, tom]

ladder	= etrier, run [stocking], steps
lady	= dame, madam, wife; name of [ada, amy, ann(e), di, doris, ena, eve, maria, olive, sal, val, vi]
(first) lady	= eve [Biblical]
(old) lady	= dam(osel), dutch, gran, ma, mother, wife, (oap)
(young) lady	= deb, girl, miss
ladybird	= beetle, clavicorn
lady-killer	= cassanova, libertine, lothario, rake, romeo, roue, wolf, womanizer
lady's-maid	= abigail
lag	= con(vict), ebb, idle, jailbird, loaf, straggle, tarry, trail, wane
laggard	= idler, loafer, slowcoach, snail
lager	= ale, beer, chaser
lair	= burrow, den, hole, nest
lake	= loch, lough, mere, pond, tarn, water; name of [albert, como, erie, geneva, huron, kariba, lucerne, lugano, malawi, michigan, nasser, nyasa, onega, ontario, placid, rudolf, superior, utah, victoria], (l)
lam	= batter, beat, drub, hit, paste, strike
lame	= feeble, flimsy, game, halt, poor, thin
lament	= complaint, dirge, elegy, monody, sob, threnody, wail
lamentable	= low, mean, pitiful, poor, tragic
lamentation	= dirge, grief, moan, plaint, sorrow
lamp	= lantern, light, meteor, planet, star; name of [standard, tilley]
lampoon	= mock, parody, satire, skit
lance	= impale, pierce, pike, spear, spike
land	= domain, earth, estate, light, plot, site, terrain, tract; measure of [acre, hectare, morgen, rood]
(barren) land	= desert
(building) land	= plot, site
(marsh)land	= bog, fen, morass, quagmire, swamp
landed	= berthed, docked, down, got, lit, won
landlord	= host, laird, owner, lessor, letter, rentier
landmark	= cairn, milestone, signpost, watershed
landowner	= laird, franklin
landscape	= panorama, prospect, scene, view, vista
lane	= passage, road, track, way
(turning) lane	= filter
language	= cant, lingo, tone, tongue, voice; name of [afrikaans, arabic, dutch, english, erse, flemish, french, gaelic, german, greek, gujarati, hebrew, hindi, italian, portuguese, urdu, russian, spanish, swahili, tamil, xhosa, zulu]
(dead) language	= latin

(Indian) language	=	name of [gujarati, hindi, tamil, urdu]
(Jewish) language	=	name of [hebrew, yiddish]
(plain) language	=	prose
(universal) language	=	name of [esperanto, ido]
lantern	=	case, lamp, light; name of [chinese, dark, magic]
(parish) lantern	=	moon
lap	=	circuit, coil, drink, flap, fold, lobe, round, wrap
lapse	=	break, end, error, fault, gap, slip
lapsed	=	fell, invalid, obsolete, sunk, void
larceny	=	theft
lard	=	fat, grease, suet
large	=	big, bulky, fat, great, major, (l, os)
(at) large	=	footloose, free, loose
(very) large	=	colossal, gigantic, huge, jumbo, titanic, (os)
large beast	=	behemoth, mammoth, mastodon, monster, ogre
large number	=	army, host, nation, (c, d, m)
large-scale	=	broad, global, vast, wide
large statue	=	colossus
larger number	=	extra, more
largess(e)	=	baksheesh, donation, generosity, tip
lark	=	antic, caper, fling, fun, prank, rag, spree
larva	=	grub, insect, name of [tadpole]
lash	=	beat, birch, hit, lam, swipe, whip
lass	=	damsel, gal, girl, maid(en), miss, wench
lassitude	=	fatigue, languor, lethargy, torpor
last	=	abide, end, final, omega, rear, survive, ultimate
last batsmen	=	tail [cricket]
last part	=	tail
last place	=	crypt, end, grave, rear, tomb, vault
last word	=	amen, finis
latch	=	bar, bolt, catch, hasp, snib
late	=	behind, dead, ex, former, long, past, recent, tardy
late batsmen	=	tail [cricket]
later	=	after, next, thereafter
latest	=	current, in, final, last, modern, now
latent	=	concealed, dormant, hidden
lateral	=	edgeways, side, sideways
lather	=	beat, flap, flog, foam, froth, fuss, stew, suds, whip
latitude	=	extent, play, range, room, scope, width, (lat)
latter	=	final, last, latest, modern, recent
laugh	=	guffaw, ha, ho, hoot, snigger, titter
laughter	=	glee, merriment, mirth
launch	=	cast, debut, fling, open, throw
launder	=	iron, press, wash
laundry	=	dhobi, washing

laurel	=	bay
laurels	=	credit, fame, glory, honour, kudos
law	=	act, axiom, canon, decree, edict, rule, measure, statute
lawful	=	just, legal, legit, licit, valid
lawn	=	grass, linen, turf
lawsuit	=	action, case, suit, trial
lawyer	=	advocate, attorney, barrister, counsel, solicitor, (da)
(Mohammedan) lawyer	=	mufti
lawyers	=	bar
lay	=	best, bet, deposit, hatch, place, posit, put, stake
layer	=	bed, film, hen, mantle, row, sheet, tier
layman	=	amateur, laic
laziness	=	indolence, sloth
lazy	=	idle, indolent, inert, remiss, slack, torpid
lea	=	field, ley, mead, meadow, pasture
lead	=	clue, conduct, flex, guide, head, pencil, top, van, (pb)
leader	=	article, boss, chief, guide, head, pilot
(guerrilla) leader	=	che
leading	=	ahead, arch, chief, first, foremost
leading actor	=	star
leaf	=	flap, needle [pine], petal, sheet
leafy place	=	arbour, bower
leaflet	=	bill, brochure, pamphlet, tract
league	=	band, club, guild, order, union
lean	=	cant, heel, list, tend, thin, tilt
leap	=	bound, hurdle, jump, spring, vault
learn	=	con, get, read, see, study, swot
learned	=	erudite, expert, literate, read, versed, wise
learned fellow, man	=	don, sage, (ba, ma)
learner	=	amateur, apprentice, beginner, disciple, novice, pupil, scholar, starter, student, tiro, trainee, (l)
learning	=	doctrine, erudition, knowledge, lore, science, study
lease	=	contract, hire, let, loan, rent
leash	=	chain, curb, fasten, fetter, strap, tie
least	=	lowest, minority, slightest, smallest
leather	=	beat, hide, morocco, pelt, skin, suede, tan
leave	=	abandon, allow, depart, exit, go, holiday, hols, let, part, permission, quit, resign, will
leave out	=	bar, except, exclude, omit
leaves	=	foliage, salad, tea, tobacco
leaven	=	imbue, infuse, ferment, steep
lecture	=	address, lesson, rate, reproof, sermon, speech, talk
lectures	=	course, syllabus
lecturer	=	don, reader

ledge	= lode, ridge, shelf, sill
ledger	= book, journal
lee	= shelter
leech	= healer, physician, sucker, worm
leer	= eye, gloat, jeer, ogle, peer, stare
left	= gone, labour, let, over, port, quit, red, sinistral, went, (l)
left-hand page	= verso
leg	= branch, hop, on, pole, prop, run, stage, support
leg bone	= name of [femur, fibula, tibia]
legs	= eleven [bingo]
legal	= lawful, legit(imate), licit, valid
legal action	= case, lawsuit, suit, trial
legal adviser	= lawyer [see]
legal document	= deed, summons, writ
legally prevent	= estop
legation	= mission, embassy
legend	= caption, fable, motto, myth, saga, tale
legitimate	= fair, lawful, legal, licit, valid
legless	= drunk, stocious, tight
Leicester	= sheep
lend	= advance, confer, grant, loan
lend a hand	= abet, aid, assist, help, second
(measure of) length	= name of [chain, cubit, ell, feet, foot, furlong, inch, league, metre, mile, pole, yard], (cm, f, ft, in, m, mm, yd)
lent	= fast
lentil	= dal, dahl, pod, pulse, seed
less	= little, minor, minus, under, without
let	= allow, hire, lease, leave, left, permit, rent, sanction
let out	= emit, free(d), leak, release
lethal	= deadly, fatal, mortal
letter	= billet, capital, character, epistle, initial, landlord, line, missive, note, serif, symbol; name of [aitch, bee, cee, dee, tee, vee, zed]
(Greek) letter	= name of [alpha, beta, chi, delta, gamma, khi, nu, omega, omicron, phi, pi, theta]
letters	= mail, post
lettuce	= cos
let-up	= break, interval, lull, pause
level	= aim, even, flat, flush, plane, raze, tier
lever	= bar, handle, prise, pry
levy	= duty, exact, excise, tax, tithe, toll
liable	= apt, bound, open, prone
liar	= ananias, fibber
liberal	= ample, broad, free, generous, handsome, (l, lib)
liberate	= free, release, rescue
libertine	= debauchee, rake, rip, roue, satyr

liberty	= freedom, licence
lice	= nits
licence, license	= leave, permit, right, sanction
licentious	= lawless, lax, lewd, wanton
licit	= allowed, lawful, legal, legit, valid
lid	= cap, cover, hat, top
lie	= cheat, deceit, fib, repose, rest, story
liege	= lord, sovereign
liegeman	= subject, vassal
lien	= right
life	= animation, elan, energy, esprit, span, spirit, verve, vita
lift	= boost, heave, hoist, jack, raise, soar, steal
light	= beacon, candle, dawn, fair, fire, lamp, land, minor, ray, spot, very
(night)light	= moon, star
light meal	= snack
lighter	= barge, lucifer, match
like	= akin, as, dig, enjoy, equal, relish, same, similar, twin
(look) like	= resemble
like this	= so, thus
likewise	= also, item, so, too
(well-)liked	= in, popular
lily	= name of [arum, caffre, day, easter, lent, lotus, may, orange, pond, tiger, water]
(water-)lily	= lotus
limb	= arm, bough, branch, leg, spur, wing
limber	= agile, lissom(e), pliant, supple
limit	= bound(ary), confine, edge, end, extreme, restrict, term
limited	= finite, narrow, precise, set
limp	= flaccid, halt, hitch, hobble, weak
line	= file, lineage [see], queue, rank, rope, route, row, string, tier, track, wire, wrinkle, (br, l, ry)
(firing) line	= front
line up	= align, dress, queue
line-up	= array, row, team
lines	= ode, poem, verse, (br, ll, ry)
lineage	= ancestry, descent, family, house, origin, race, tribe
linger	= idle, lag, loiter, stay, tarry
link	= bond, chain, join, knot, tie, yoke
lion	= cat, leo [Zodiac]
lip	= brim, cheek, edge, murmur, speaker
liqueur	= name of [absinth, anisette, arak, benedictine, cognac, cointreau, curacao, drambuie, kirsch, kummel]
liquid	= bright, clear, drink [see], fluid, juice, solvent, wet

(fermented) liquor	=	cider, port, sherry, wine
(malt) liquor	=	ale, beer, lager, porter, stout
(spirituous) liquor	=	name of spirit [see]
lissom(e)	=	agile, limber, lithe, nimble, supple
list	=	cant, catalogue, choose, desire, file, heel, lean, roll, rota, roster, table, tally, tip, tilt
listed	=	askew, aslant, athwart, leant
listen	=	attend, bug, hark, hear, heed
listener	=	ear
listeners	=	audience
lithe	=	agile, limber, lissom(e), nimble, supple
lithely	=	supply
litter	=	debris, farrow, junk, mess, refuse, stretcher, trash, waste
little	=	bit, dwarf, short, slim, small, tiny, trace, wee, whit
little animal, beast	=	calf, cub, foal, kid, kitten, lamb, pup
little chap	=	dwarf, midget, pygmy
little demon, devil	=	imp
little man	=	gent[leman]
little person	=	dwarf, elf, fairy, goblin, leprechaun, pixie, sprite
little thumb	=	tom [Tom Thumb]
little Tom	=	thumb [Tom Thumb]
live	=	abide, be, dwell, exist, inhabit, quick, reside
lively	=	active, agile, alert, busy, nimble, pert
lives	=	is
livid	=	angry, ashen, pale, purple, wan
Livingstone	=	ken, (dr)
lizard	=	name of [agama, basilisk, gecko, iguana, monitor]
load	=	bale, cargo, lading, onus, stack, worry
(got a) load of	=	saw
loaded	=	awash, flush, full, laden, rich
loaf	=	bannock, bap, block, bread, head, idle, laze, loll, oatcake, tin
loan	=	advance, allow, credit, lend, touch
loaned	=	lent
loath	=	reluctant, unwilling
loathe	=	abhor, detest, hate
lob	=	loft, throw, toss
local	=	home, inn, native, parochial, pub
location	=	locus, place, point, site, spot, venue
(film) location	=	set
(university) location	=	campus
loch	=	bay, lake, lough; name of [eil, leven, lomond, maree, neagh, ness, nevis, ryan, tay]
lock	=	bolt, curl, hair, mesh, mortise, quiff, ringlet, snib, tress, tuft

locker	=	gaoler, jailer, key
lockup	=	cage, cell, cooler, gaol, jail, jug
loco	=	bats, crazy, daft, insane, mad, nuts
lode	=	deposit, vein
lodge	=	bestow, board, billet, cabin, deposit, gatehouse, house, inn
lodger	=	boarder, roomer, tenant
log	=	diary, journal, record, stump, trunk, yule
loin	=	haunch
London park	=	hyde
(part of) London	=	bow, soho, (ec, sw, wc, wi)
long	=	ache, crave, desire, far, itch, late, pine, tall, yen
(before) long	=	anon, shortly, soon
(very) long	=	age(s), eons, moons
long-established	=	abiding, fixed, old
long time	=	aeon, age(s), eon
long-winded	=	prolix, verbose, wordy
(no) longer	=	ex, formerly, once
longing	=	ache, itch, urge, thirst, yen
loo	=	bog, head, john, privy, toilet
look	=	behold, eye, gape, gaze, glance, leer, lo, peek, peep, peer, see, stare, view
look for	=	hunt, pursue, seek
look like	=	resemble
look-out	=	prospect, sentinel, sentry, watch
looker	=	eye, gaper, gazer, peeper, seer, viewer
loom	=	appear, brew, emerge, impend, weaver
loop	=	circle, circuit, curve, ring, round, (o)
loophole	=	escape, eyelet, gap, pretext, slot
loot	=	booty, haul, rifle, rob, steal, spoil(s), swag
looting	=	pillage
lop	=	cut, dock, hang, hew, prune, slouch
lope	=	bound, hop, run, skip, spring
loquacious	=	chatty, garrulous, talkative
lord	=	baron, earl, laird, liege, noble, peer
(feudal) lord	=	suzerain
lore	=	doctrine, erudition, knowledge, learning
lose	=	drop, elude, evade, fail, mislay, misplace, miss, yield
loser	=	dud, failure, flop, lemon
loss	=	death, defeat, failure, waste
losses	=	dead, debt, deficit, toll
lost	=	adrift, astray, bygone, gone, mislaid, misspent, wayward
lot	=	all, amount, doom, fate, host, many, mass, much, plot, set, share, whole
lots	=	heaps, lumps, many, oodles, parts, piles, reams
lots of people	=	army, crowd, host, legion, swarm
lots of time	=	ages, eons, moons

loth	= loath [see]
lotion	= balm, cream, salve
lottery	= draw, raffle, sweep(stake), tombola
loud	= forte, noisy, rowdy, strident, (f)
lout	= boor, clod, dolt, oaf, thug, yob(bo)
louvre	= slat, turret
love	= adore, amour, nil, nought, zero, (o)
lover	= beau, doter, fiance, flame, mistress, suitor, swain, sweetheart
low	= base, coarse, crude, down, moo, sad, sordid, vile, vulgar
low-value	= cheap, shoddy
low-value coin	= cent, copper, dime, penny, sou
lower	= below, beneath, cow, cut, debase, demean, frown, nether, scowl, under
lowly	= mean, meek, mild, modest
loyal	= devoted, faithful, staunch, true
loyalist	= patriot
lozenge	= diamond, rhomb, sweet, tablet
lubricate(d)	= oil(ed)
lucent, lucid	= beaming, bright, clear, shining
lucifer	= devil, lighter, match, satan
lucre	= gain, money, profit, riches, wealth
lug	= drag, ear, haul, pull, tote, tow, tug
luggage	= bag(gage), (suit)case, grip, trunk
luminary	= celebrity, guru, sage, star
lump	= bear, heap, lout, mass, nub, oaf, pile, wad
lunge	= dive, plunge, rush, thrust
lure	= bait, carrot, decoy, draw, entice, pull, siren, tempt
lurid	= bloody, gory, grim, livid, vivid
lust	= greed, libido, passion, thirst
lustre	= glitter, gloss, sheen, shine
luxurious	= lavish, opulent, plush, rich

M

macabre	= eerie, grim, horrid, weird
mace	= club, staff
machine	= device, engine, robot, tool
machinery	= gear, plant, tackle
macho	= male, manly, potent, virile
mackintosh	= raincoat, (mac, mack)
mad	= angry, bats, berserk, crazy, daft, insane, irate, loco, nuts, rabid, wild
madcap	= brash, hasty, hothead, rash, reckless
madden	= anger, enrage, incense, irritate
madhouse	= asylum, bedlam
madman	= maniac, nut(ter), psycho, raver

madness	= anger, insanity, lunacy, rage
madam	= lady
made	= built, did, done, formed, named, netted, won
magazine	= armoury, arsenal, comic, journal, mag, rag
magic	= charm, mystic, sorcery, spell, wizardry
magistrate	= alcalde, archon, bailie, beak, doge, judge [see], justice
magistrates	= bench
maid	= damsel, girl, lass, miss, wench
(country) maid	= gal
(lady's-)maid	= abigail
(nurse)maid	= amah, ayah, bonne
maiden	= female, first, maid [see], untried, virgin
mail	= armour, letters, post, send
mailboat	= packet
maim	= cripple, disable, lame, mutilate
main	= chief, deep, major, might, ocean, sea, staple
maintain	= argue, assert, claim, hold, insist, keep, support, uphold
majestic	= august, grand, noble, regal, royal
major	= chief, grave, main, serious, star
majority	= bulk, mass, more, most
(in the) majority	= adult
make	= brand, build, construct, do, earn, erect, fashion, force, form, mould, name, net, win
make a fuss	= create, perform
make away	= flee, fly, run, scoot
make-believe	= charade, dream, fantasy, mock, sham
make fun	= deride, mock, rag, rib
make good	= fix, mend, repair
make hay	= ted
make known	= air, broadcast
make merry	= feast, frolic, revel
make off	= abscond, bolt, flee, fly, run
make up	= atone, compose, concoct, devise
malady	= ailment, disease, illness, sickness
male	= cock, gent, man, ram, stag, (m)
males	= men
malediction	= anathema, curse, slander
malefactor	= convict, crook, felon, outlaw, villain
malevolence	= hate, hatred, malice, rancour, spite
malevolent	= evil, malign, nasty, wicked
malignant	= cancerous, cavalier, harmful, royalist
(not) malignant	= benign
mall	= avenue, plaza, street, walk
malt liquor	= ale, beer, lager, porter, stout
(sea-)mammal	= name of [dolphin, dugong, morse, porpoise, seal, sealion, walrus, whale]

man .	=	chap, fellow, gent, he, isle, male; name of [al, des, don, ed, bill, les, mark, pete, ray, ron, stan, ted, tom], (iom)
(first) man	=	adam [Biblical]
(French)man	=	breton, gaul, norman; name of [alain, henri, jean, louis, pierre, rene], (m)
(German) man	=	herr; name of [dieter, gunter, hans, heinz, helmut, karl, ulrich]
(great) man	=	giant, hercules, ogre, titan
(holy) man	=	clergy [see], prophet, saint, (st)
(Irish)man	=	name of [connor, eamon, liam, mick, paddy, pat(rick), seamus, sean, spud]
(Italian) man	=	signor, (s)
(learned) man	=	don, sage, (ba, ma)
(little) man	=	gent[leman]
(married) man	=	groom
(medical) man	=	chemist, doctor, intern, pharmacist, surgeon, vet
(old) man	=	codger, father, geezer, husband, pa, (oap)
(patient) man	=	job [Biblical]
(Russian) man	=	name of [boris, igor, ivan, serge]
(Scots)man	=	mac, mon; name of [an(gus), ia(i)n, jock, rab(bie), sandy]
(skilled) man	=	artisan
(Spanish) man	=	caballero, don, grandee, hidalgo, senor
(top) man	=	name of [aga, ameer, amir, bey, emir, emperor, lord, king, monarch, president, ruler, shah, supremo, tsar]
(Welsh)man	=	name of [dai, emlyn, evan, owen, taffy]
(wise) man	=	guru, elder, magus, oracle, pundit, sage, savant; name of [nestor, solomon, solon]
manage	=	control, cope, oversee, run
manager	=	boss, head, runner, (mgr)
mandate	=	charge, decree, edict, fiat, order, rescript
manger	=	crib, pen, stall, trough
mania	=	craze, fetish, frenzy
maniac	=	fan, fiend, madman, nut(ter), psycho
manifest	=	cargo, clear, lading, obvious, prove
manipulate	=	guide, ply, steer, use
manner	=	air, mien, mode, tone, vein, way
manoeuvre	=	dodge, ploy, ruse, trick, wangle, (op)
manor	=	chateau, estate, house, mansion, villa
manservant	=	butler, valet
manual	=	book, guide, handbook, tutor
manufacture	=	build, create, erect, forge, make, (mfg, mfr)
manuscript	=	article, book, paper, (ms)
many	=	host, lot(s), (c, d, m)
(great) many	=	heaps, host, lots, oodles, piles

map	= atlas, chart, plan; kind of [contour, relief, survey]
mar	= damage, harm, hurt, impair, injure, spoil, taint
maraud	= foray, loot, pillage, raid, sack
marauder	= brigand, corsair, pirate, raider
march	= demo, file, parade, tramp, trek
Margaret	= meg, peg
margin	= border, edge, limit, rim, verge
marijuana	= dope, grass, hash(ish), hemp, pot, weed
marina	= basin, dock, harbour, port
mark	= line, note, scar, smear, spot, stain, standard, stroke, weal, (mk, x)
(punctuation) mark	= colon, comma, dash, dot, period, stop
(top) mark	= alpha
marks	= score
marksman	= potter, shootist, sniper, tell [William]
market	= mart, sell, (ec)
(meat) market	= abattoir, butchery, shambles
market official	= eurocrat [EC]
maroon	= firework, idle, rocket, slave, strand
marquee	= tent
marriage	= coupling, espousal, hand, link, match, merger, union, wedlock
marriage settlement	= dowry, portion
married	= wed, (m)
married man	= groom
married woman	= bride
marry	= espouse, join, splice, unite, wed
marsh(land)	= bog, fen, morass, quagmire, swamp
marsh-gas	= methane
marsh grass	= reed
marvellous	= grand, super, superb
mascot	= amulet, charm, luck, talisman
mask	= cloak, cover, hide, veil, visor, vizard
mass	= assemble, bulk, crowd, gather, lithurgy, lump, pile, service, volume
mast	= pole, spar
master	= control, digest, grasp, lad, learn, sir, sire, teacher, (ma, mba, msc)
(question) master	= catechist
master of ceremonies	= compere, host, (mc)
mastery	= command, control, power, skill, sway
mat	= carpet, dull, rug, tangle
(table) mat	= coaster
match	= bout, copy, equal, game, light(er), lucifer, marriage, marry, peer, tie, trial, vesta
(international) match	= test
matchmaker	= fir
mate	= ally, buddy, china, chum, crony, pal, spouse, twin, wed, wife

(first) mate	= eve
matelot	= sailor [see]
material	= cloth, fabric, key, rep, stuff, tapestry, vital, yarn; name of cloth [see]
matter	= concern, count, object, point, stuff, substance, thing, topic
mature	= adult, age, develop, due, grow, owing, ripe(n)
maxim	= adage, axiom, gnome, motto, rule, saw, saying
maximum	= greatest, highest, most, top, utmost, (max)
may	= can
maybe	= ablin(g)s, perchance, perhaps, possibly
meadow	= field, lea, ley, mead, pasture
meagre	= paltry, puny, scant(y), spare, sparse
meal	= fare, feed, food, repast; name of [breakfast, dinner, lunch, supper, tea]
(light) meal	= snack
mean	= aim, average, base, beggarly, close, connote, convey, denote, intend, low, medium, near, norm, par, poor, spell, tight
meaning	= import, intent, purport, sense, tenor
means	= agency, estate, funds, income, method, mode, money, way, wealth
means of transport	= vehicle [see]
meanwhile	= interim, interval
measure	= extent, gauge, law, mete, ration, scale, size, space, step
(imperial) measure	= feet, foot, furlong, inch, mile, yard
(printer's) measure	= em, en
measure of capacity	= bushel, gallon, gill, litre, noggin, peck, pint, quart(er), (cc, gal, l, pt, qu)
measure of current	= amp, volt, watt, (v, w)
measure of length	= chain, cubit, ell, feet, foot, furlong, inch, league, metre, mile, pole, yard, (cm, f, ft, in, m, mm, yd)
measure of weight	= drachm, dram, grain, gram, ounce, pound, quarter, quintal, scruple, stone, ton, tonne, (cwt, g, lb, oz, t)
measurement	= measure [see]
meat	= name of [bacon, baron, beef, brisket, gammon, ham, lamb, liver, kidney, mince, mutton, oxtail, pork, sausage, steak, tongue, tripe, veal, venison]
(piece of) meat	= chop, cutlet
meat market	= abattoir, butchery, shambles
mechanic	= fitter, machinist, turner, welder
medal	= award, badge, decoration, gong, (bem, gm, mm)
media	= means, press, radio, (tv)

medic(o)	=	doctor, (doc, dr, mo)
medical man	=	chemist, doctor, intern, pharmacist, surgeon, vet
medicine	=	cure, dosage, dose, draught, nostrum, pill, physic, specific
(quack) medicine	=	placebo
meditate	=	arbitrate, muse, ponder, reflect, think
meditation	=	musing, study, thought
medium	=	average, fair, mean, organ, psychic, vehicle, (m)
meet	=	apt, assemble, face, fill, gather, hunt, muster, right, sit
meeting	=	event, match, meet, rally, tryst, (agm)
meeting place	=	forum, venue
melancholy	=	blue(s), dismal, down, dumps, gloom, glum, sad, woe
melee	=	affray, brawl, clash, fight, fracas
mellow	=	dulcet, kind, rich, ripe(n), soft
melody	=	music [see]
melodic pipe	=	chanter
melon	=	gourd
member	=	arm, hand, leg, limb, man, (m, mep, mp)
(original) member	=	founder
memento	=	relic, reminder, souvenir, token
memo	=	note, record, summary
memoirs	=	diary, journal
memorial	=	cenotaph, epitaph, monument, tombstone, wreath
memorial service	=	obit
(newspaper) men	=	press
(wise) men	=	magi
(of) men's clothes	=	sartorial
menagerie	=	zoo
mend	=	cure, darn, fix, heal, repair, sew
mendacious	=	false, lying, untrue
mendicant	=	beggar, pauper
menial	=	base, low, mean, serf, servant, vile
mentality	=	mind, wit, (iq)
mentor	=	coach, guide, guru, tutor
mercenary	=	greedy, huckster, sordid, venal
merchandise	=	goods, stock, wares
merchant	=	broker, dealer, seller, trader, vendor
merciful	=	clement, humane, lenient, tolerant
mercy	=	blessing, clemency, leniency, pity
mere	=	bare, just, plain, pure, utter
merit	=	deserve, due, earn, rate, value, worth
merriment	=	fun, glee, laughter, mirth
merry	=	gay, glad, happy, jolly
(make) merry	=	feast, frolic, revel
mesh	=	knit, net, snare, tangle, web

mess	=	botch, bungle, chaos, dirt(y), disorder, foul, hash, litter, muddle, shambles, sight
message	=	dispatch, errand, letter, missive, note, word
messenger	=	courier, emissary, envoy, runner
metal	=	name of [aluminium, brass, bronze, copper, gold, iron, lead, nickel, pewter, silver, steel, tin, zinc]
(raw) metal	=	mineral, ore
mete	=	allot, boundary, measure, portion
method	=	form, manner, means, mode, way
methodical	=	neat, precise, tidy
meticulous	=	exact, fussy, precise, strict
metier	=	craft, forte, line, trade
metro	=	tube
midday	=	amend(s) [a.m. end(s)], noon
middle	=	core, inner, mean, mid, midst, waist
middle-of-the-road	=	moderate, (mor)
midget	=	dwarf, gnome, pygmy, runt, small, tiny
mien	=	air, bearing, look, manner
might	=	beef, clout, could, main, muscle, power, sway
migrant	=	drifter, gypsy, nomad, settler, vagrant
militant worker	=	striker
military body	=	army, battalion, brigade, division, legion, platoon, soldiers, troop(s), unit
military engagement	=	action, battle, combat, sortie
military expedition	=	crusade, incursion, invasion, (me)
milk	=	bleed, drain, fleece, rook, tap
milk-pan	=	trug
milk-producer	=	cow
milliner	=	hatter
mimic	=	ape, echo, mock, parody, parrot
minar(et)	=	lighthouse, tower, turret
mind	=	brain, care, memory, obey, opinion, psyche, reason, tend, watch, will, wit
minder	=	guardian, keeper, nurse
mine	=	charge, dig, fund, lode, pit, shaft, tunnel, vein, wealth
miner	=	collier, pitman
mineral	=	drink, jet, liquid, ore, pop, soda; name of [mica, olivine, spinel]
mingle	=	blend, join, merge, mix, unite
minim	=	note
minimal, minimum	=	base, least, lowest, smallest, (min)
minister	=	clergy [see], (dd, rev)
ministers	=	cabinet
ministry	=	service, (fo)
mink	=	fur, stole
minor	=	junior, lesser, petty, slight, ward
minor actor	=	extra

minster	= cathedral, church
minstrel	= bard, poet, musician, singer
minus	= deficit, less, loss, subtract
minute	= exact, fine, little, small, tiny, (m, min, mo)
mirage	= illusion, phantasm
mire	= bog, fen, marsh, mud, slime, swamp
mirror	= copy, glass, image, reflect, twin
mirth	= glee, laughter, merriment
mischief	= damage, deuce, harm, hurt, injury, strife
mischief-maker	= imp
mischievous character	= imp
miser	= niggard, scrooge, skinflint, tightwad
miserly	= close, mean, near, tight
misery	= agony, dolour, grief, hell, woe
misfortune	= blow, harm, ill, loss, mishap, tragedy
mislay	= lose, misplace, miss
mislead	= bluff, deceive, dupe, fool, hoodwink
misleading	= false, specious, tricky
misplace	= lose, mislay, miss
miss	= avoid, error, fail, girl [see], lass, omit, pass, skip, spinster
(American) miss	= gal
missile	= arrow, bolt, dart, javelin, rocket, weapon; name of [cruise, exocet, patriot, polaris, scud, tomahawk], (abm, sam)
mission	= aim, goal, embassy, legation, quest
mist	= brume, cloud, dew, film, fog, gloom, haze
mistake	= bloomer, err(or), flaw, error, gaffe, goof, slip
mistakes	= errata
mistress	= courtesan, doxy, lover, paramour
mitt	= hand, glove, mitten
mix	= blend, cross, fuse, mingle, stir, whisk
mixture	= alloy, amalgam, blend, cross, fusion
mixture of gases	= air
mix-up	= hash, mess, muddle, shambles, tangle
moan	= groan, lament, sigh, sob, wail, whine
mob	= crew, crowd, gang, lot, rabble, scum
mock	= ape, deride, fake, mimic, scoff, sham, taunt
mode	= fashion, style, ton, tone, vein, vogue, way, wise
model	= ideal, pose(r), sit(ter), (t)
(artist's) model	= poser, sitter
modern	= current, late(st), new, novel, recent
modern time(s)	= now, present, (ad)
modest	= coy, demure, diffident, humble, meek, shy
modify	= adapt, alter, amend, change, vary
Mohammed	= ali [Mohammed Ali]
Mohammedan lawyer	= mufti
moist	= damp, dank, humid, wet

mole	=	birthmark, blemish, breakwater, pier, pimple, spot
moment	=	flash, import(ance), instant, second, shake, tick, trice, weight, worth, (m, mo, sec)
monarch	=	king, rex, ruler, (k, r)
(old) monarch	=	name of [arthur, canute, cole, lear], (gr)
monarchy	=	kingdom, nation, realm, reign, state
monastery	=	abbey, cloister, convent, friary, house, nunnery, priory, retreat
money	=	brass, bread, capital, cash, coin, currency [see], dough, income, lucre, means, note(s), proceeds, purse, riches, tin, wealth, (ecu, l)
(ask for) money	=	beg, sponge
(borrow) money	=	touch
(demand) money	=	blackmail, extort, ransom
(English) money	=	name of [crown, fiver, pence, penny, pony, pound, quid, shilling, tenner]
(foreign) money	=	name of [anna, cent, dime, dinar, dollar, drachma, escudo, franc, guilder, krone, lira, lire, mark, nickle, peseta, peso, pistole, punt, quarter, rand, real, rial, rouble, rupee, sen, sou, yen]
(French) money	=	name of [franc, sou]
(German) money	=	name of [krone, mark]
(Indian) money	=	name of [anna, rupee]
(Irish) money	=	name of [punt]
(Italian) money	=	name of [lira, lire]
(Japanese) money	=	name of [sen, yen]
(more) money	=	increase, raise
(risk) money	=	ante, bet, gamble, punt, stake, wager
(Russian) money	=	name of [rouble]
(Scandinavian) money	=	name of [krone, ore]
(Spanish) money	=	name of [peseto, pistole, real]
(US) money	=	name of [cent, dime, dollar, nickel, quarter]
money-box	=	chest, coffer
money order	=	cheque, draft, (mo)
monitor	=	check, listen, screen, track, watch
monk	=	abbot, dom, friar, lama, prior
monkey	=	ass, imp, primate, simian; name of [ape, babacoote, baboon, chimp, chimpanzee, drill, gibbon, gorilla, lemur, marmoset, orang(-outang), vervet]
monolithic	=	colossal, giant, huge, massive
monotonous	=	boring, dull, flat, tedious
monster	=	abortion, giant, huge, mammoth, titan;lname of [centaur, cyclops, dragon, gorgon, griffin, hydra, minotaur, ogre, sphinx]
monstrous	=	giant, great, huge, titanic, vast
(day of the) month	=	name of [ides, nones]

months	= moons, (mos)
monument	= column, edifice, record, statue
mood	= aura, humour, temper, tenor, vein
moon	= month, mope, satellite;
	name of [blue, harvest, hunter's], (o)
moor	= anchor, berth, dock;
	name of [arab, berber]
moor(land)	= fell, heath
mop	= clean, sponge, swab, wash, wipe
moral	= chaste, decent, ethic(al), ethos, good, just,
	maxim, noble, pure, puritan
morale	= esprit, heart, mettle, spirit
morass	= bog, fen, marsh, mire, quagmire, swamp
morbid	= grim, macabre, morose, sad, sick
morbid hunger	= bulimia, bulimy
more	= added, also, extra, over, plus, too
more money	= increase, raise
more rum	= odder
morning	= dawn, daybreak, sunrise, (am)
moron	= ass, cretin, dolt, dope, dunce, fool, idiot,
	imbecile
morose	= dour, gloomy, sour, sullen, surly
morse	= code, walrus
morsel	= bit, bite, crumb, grain, scrap
mortal	= being, deadly, dire, fatal, grave, human,
	lethal
mortgage	= bond, hawk, pawn, pledge
moslem	= name of [ismaili, shiite]
most	= greatest, largest, mainly, majority
motet	= anthem
mother	= dam, ma, mater, mum, raise, rear
mother of pearl	= nacre
motion	= gesture, move(ment), sign(al), stir
motive	= cause, object, reason, spur
motor	= auto, car, drive, dynamo, turbine
motor car	= coupe, estate, limo(ousine), saloon, sedan;
	name of car [see], (gt, mg, rr, vw)
motorway	= road, (m, mi)
motto	= adage, maxim, saying, saw, slogan
mould	= cast, fungus, knead, mildew, pattern
moulding	= ogee
mound	= bank, butte, heap, hill(ock), knoll, pile, stack
(burial, grave-)mound	= barrow, tumulus
mount	= ascend, climb, horse, nag, raise, ride, rise,
	soar
mount(ain)	= alp, ben, fell, tor, (mt)
	name of [ararat, blanc, carmel, cook, eiger,
	etna, everest, fuji, kenya, ida, sinai, table]
mountain road	= col, pass

mountains	= massif, range; name of [alps, andes, atlas, balkans, mourne, pennine, rocky, taunus, ural]
mourn	= grieve, keen, sorrow, wail, weep, woe
mournful	= dole, sad, sombre
mournful song	= dirge, elegy, lament, requiem
mouse	= shrew, vole; name of [mickey]
mouser	= cat, owl
mouth	= cheek, delta, estuary, gob, maw, opening, orifice, os, rant, trap, utter, yap
mouths	= ora
move	= act, go, flit, march, pass, propose, rock, roll, shift, stir
(cunning) move	= gambit
(strategic) move	= tack, tactic
move sideways	= crab, edge, sidle
move slowly	= crawl, ease, edge
movement	= flow, motion, party, shift, stir, tic
(art) movement	= name of [baroque, cubism, dada, deco, noveau, op, pop, realism, rococo]
mow	= crop, cut, scythe, shear, trim
much	= ample, lot, oft, plenty, very
(too) much	= troppo
(very) much	= ultra
mud	= bog, clay, dirt, fen, mire, swamp
muddle	= bungle, confuse, jumble, mess, tangle
mug	= cup, dial, face, jug, mouth, rob, stein
mug(gins)	= dope, fool, idiot, muff, noodle, simpleton
multitude	= army, crowd, horde, host, legion
mum	= dumb, mother, mute, silent
murder	= execute, homicide, kill, slaughter, slay, spoil
(first) murderer	= cain [Biblical]
murder victim	= abel [Biblical]
muscle	= biceps, brawn, clout, flexor, might, sinew, strength, tendon
muse	= bard, brood, dream, mull, poet, ponder, speculate, think; name of [calliope, clio, erato, euterpe, melpomene, polyhymnia, terpsichore, thalia, urania]
museum	= gallery
music	= air, melody, opus, song [see], strain, tune; name of [bebop, blues, jazz, pop, reggae, rock, swing]
(rock) music	= lullaby
(write) music	= compose
musical	= name of [blitz, cats, evita, oliver]
musical ability	= ear
musical instrument	= name of [accordion, balalaika, banjo, bassoon,

<pre>
                              bugle, cittern, clarinet, concertina, cornet,
                              cymbal, fife, flute, guitar, harmonica, harp,
                              horn, lute, lyre, mandolin, oboe, organ, piano,
                              piccolo, recorder, sackbut, sax(ophone), sitar,
                              trombone, trumpet, tuba, ukulele, viol(a),
                              zither]
</pre>

musical introduction   = overture, prelude
musical note   = breve, flat, music, natural, pitch, sharp, tone;
                         musical note, scale do(h), ray, re, me, mi, fa(h),
                         so(h), la(h), te, ti, (a, b, c, d, e, f, g)
musical work   = opus, (op)
musician   = name of [bugler, busker, cellist, drummer,
                         flautist, minstrel, oboist, pianist, piper,
                         troubadour]
musicians   = band, concert, waits
(some) musicians   = brass, strings, wind
Mussolini   = duce
muster   = gather, marshal, meet, rally
mute   = dumb, lower, muffle, mum, silent
mutilate   = butcher, cripple, cut, maim, slash
mutiny   = rebel, revolt, riot, rise
my   = blimey, cor, wow
myself   = me
mystery   = enigma, puzzle, riddle, secret
mystic   = esoteric, magic(al), occult, spiritual;
                         name of [guru, parsee, prophet, seer]
mystify   = baffle, beat, puzzle, stump
myth   = fable, fancy, legend, saga, story, tale
mythology   = legend, lore

                              N

nab   = arrest, catch, seize, snatch
nadir   = base, bottom, depths, foot, zero
nag   = annoy, hack, henpeck, horse, mare, moan,
                         mount, shrew
nail   = brad, fix, hammer, peg, pin, tack
naive   = artless, innocent, jejune, juvenile, simple
naked   = bare, nude, starkers, unclad
(run) naked   = streak
name   = dub, call, label, term, title, (n)
(another, assumed) name = alias, nickname, pseudonym, sobriquet, (aka)
(noble) name   = title;
                         name of [baron, baroness, count, earl, lady,
                         lord, sir]
(other) name   = alias, moniker, nickname, pseudonym,
                         sobriguet
(writer's) name   = byline
nameless   = anon(ymous), obscure, unknown
nameplate   = plaque

namely	= viz
nanny	= amah, ayah
nap	= down, doze, drowse, pile, nod, siesta, sleep, snooze
nappy	= diaper
nark	= annoy, decoy, grass, grumble, inform(er), spy
narrate	= describe, recite, recount, relate, tell
narrow	= close, cramped, fine, mean, near, slim, taper, thin, tight
narrow valley	= defile, gorge, gulch, gully, ravine
narrow-minded	= biased, bigoted, insular, petty, sectarian
narrows	= channel, gulf, passage, sound, straits
nasty	= bad, cheap, crude, evil, foul, low, mean, vicious, vile
nasty person	= bounder, cad, cur, heel, rat, rotter
nation	= country, people, race, realm, state, tribe
national	= citizen, civic, civil, public, subject, (nat, natl)
native	= aboriginal, endemic, home, inborn, innate, local, oyster, (nat)
natty	= clever, dapper, spruce, ingenious
natural	= artless, common, frank, inborn, innate, native, normal, usual, (nat)
nature	= humour, mood, outlook, temper
naughty	= arch, bad, cheeky, impish, ribald, risque, roguish, vulgar
nauseate	= disgust, repel, repulse, revolt, sicken
navigate	= direct, fly, pilot, sail, steer
navigational aid	= compass, dogstar, radar, sextant, star
navigator	= explorer, navvy, pilot, sailor; name of [cabot, columbus, drake, scott]
navy	= armada, fleet, (mn, rn)
NCO	= name of [corporal, sergeant]
near	= akin, approach, by, close, handy, mean, miserly, nigh, stingy, tight, (nr)
nearly	= about, almost, (a)round, nigh, roughly
neat	= cow, deft, nice, ox, oxen, pure, smart, tidy, trim
neatness	= grace, nicety, order, style
nebulous	= cloudy, dim, hazy, obscure, vague
necessity	= fate, need, want
necklace	= chain, choker, pendant
neckpiece	= nape
need	= lack, miss, must, poverty, require, requisite, want
needle	= annoy, bait, goad, irk, irritate, leaf, nag, rile, rivalry, sew, stylus
needle-book (case)	= etui, housewife
needy	= broke, indigent, poor
negate	= annul, cancel, deny, gainsay, refute, repeal
negative	= contrary, denial, nay, no, not

neglect	=	default, fail(ure), forget, miss, omit
negligent	=	careless, lax, remiss, slack
negligible	=	minimal, minor, minute, petty, slender, slight, small, trivial
negotiate	=	arrange, bargain, confer, parley, settle, transact, treat
neighbourhood	=	environs, locale, locality, vicinity
neither	=	nor
nerve	=	bottle, courage, grit, guts, pluck, sinew, spunk, vein, will
nervous	=	anxious, edgy, fraught, neurotic, skittish, tense, timid, uptight
nervous response, twitch	=	spasm, tic
nervousness	=	anxiety, fluster, tension, worry
ness	=	cape, head, point
nest	=	aerie, den, eyrie, haunt, home, refuge
net	=	catch, clear, mesh, nab, web, trap
nether	=	below, beneath, lower, under
nettle	=	anger, annoy, fret, rile, sting, vex
network	=	grid, grill, maze, mesh, web, (lan)
nevertheless	=	but, still, yet
new	=	fresh, modern, novel, recent, virgin
(not) new	=	old, used
new soldier	=	recruit, rookie
newly-wed	=	bride, groom
news	=	bulletin, buzz, gossip, report, story, word
news story	=	bulletin, report
newspaper	=	gazette, journal, rag, tabloid
newspaper men	=	press
newspapers	=	press
niche	=	alcove, corner, nook, recess
nick	=	chip, cut, notch, prison, score, steal
nigh	=	about, almost, around, close, near
night	=	black, dark
night before	=	eve
night flier	=	bat, moth, owl
nightclub	=	casino, disco
nightfall	=	dusk, sunset
nightlight	=	moon, star
nil	=	love, nothing, nought, zero, (o)
nimble	=	active, adroit, agile, deft, fleet, lissome, lithe, swift
nip	=	bite, chill, cold, dram, drink, drop, pinch
nipper	=	baby, child, crab, infant, pincer, tot
(big) nipper	=	drunk(ard)
nippy	=	agile, fast, nimble, quick, spry
N Ireland county	=	name of [antrim, armagh, down, tyrone]
nit	=	egg, fool, idiot, larva
nits	=	lice

nitty-gritty	= basics, core, facts, gist
nitwit	= dummy, fool, idiot, ninny
no	= denial, negative, refusal
no good	= useless, (nbg, ng, us)
no longer	= ex, formerly, once
nob	= bigwig, nabob, pot, swell, toff
nobble	= bribe, disable, nick, pinch, steal
nobility	= class, elite, majesty, peerage, virtue
noble	= august, fine, gentle, grand, high
nobleman	= name of [baron, chevalier, count, earl, elector, graf, grandee, lord, knight, marquis, peer]
noble name	= title; name of [baron, baroness, count, earl, lady, lord, sir]
nobody	= cipher, menial, nonentity
nocturnal	= night(ly)
nod	= agree, bob, bow, dip, doze, drowse, duck, nap, salute, sign(al)
node	= knob, knot
nodose	= knobbed, knotty
nog	= beer, peg, pin, stump
noggin	= cup, dram, gill, mug, nip, tot
noise	= din, grunt, fracas, hubbub, racket, row, rumour, sound, tumult
(celebrate) noisily	= revel, roister
(drink) noisily	= slurp
noiseless	= mute, quiet, silent
noisy	= loud, strident
noisome	= foul, obscene, odious, offensive, nasty, repugnant, vile
nomad	= drifter, gipsy, gypsy, rover, wanderer
nomadic	= migrant, wandering
nom de plume	= alias, pseudonym
nominal	= brevet, formal, honorary, puppet, small, titular, token
nominate	= appoint, choose, elect, name, submit
nomination	= choice, election
nonaligned	= impartial, neutral
nonchalant	= blase, calm, casual, cool, offhand
non-clerical, clergy	= laic, laity, lay, secular
nonconformist	= maverick, radical, rebel
nondescript	= dull, mousey, ordinary
nonetheless	= yet
nonplus	= baffle, confuse, dismay, puzzle, stump
non-professional	= amateur, lay
nonsense	= bilge, boloney, bosh, bunk(um), flummery, greek, hokum, humbug, rot, tosh, tripe, twaddle
nonsensical	= absurd, crazy, foolish, inane, silly
noodle	= fool, head, mug, pasta, simpleton

nook	=	alcove, cavity, corner, cranny, recess
noon	=	amend(s) [a.m. end(s)], midday
noose	=	halter, lasso, loop, trap
norm	=	average, mean, model, pattern, rule
normal	=	common, natural, sane, stock, usual
North African	=	name of [arab, berber, moor]
northerner	=	finn, lapp, scot, swede
nose	=	beezer, boko, bouquet, proboscis, smell sniff, snoop, snout
not in time	=	late, tardy
(and) not	=	nor
notable	=	eminent, famed, famous, great, noted
notary	=	advocate, clerk, solicitor
notch	=	degree, dent, dint, nick, rung, step
note	=	heed, mark, memo, message, money, observe, see
(musical) note	=	breve, flat, minim, music, natural, pitch, sharp, tone; do(h), ray, re, me, mi, fa(h), so(h), la(h), te, ti, (a, b, c, d, e, f, g)
(take) note	=	heed, listen, obey
noted	=	famed, famous, great, saw, seen
notes	=	chord, money, scale
nothing	=	duck, free, love, nil, nix, nought, nowt, trifle, (o)
(eat) nothing	=	fast
(cost) nothing	=	free, gratis
nothing to do	=	idle
notice	=	banns, observe, poster, review, sack, see, sign, (ad)
notify	=	advise, apprise, inform, tell, warn
notion	=	caprice, clue, concept, fancy, idea, image, thought, whim
notwithstanding	=	although, despite, however, though, yet
nous	=	gumption, intellect, mind, sense
novel	=	book, fiction, fresh, new, rare, romance, story, tale; name of [she]
novice	=	learner [see], (l)
now	=	present, (ad)
nuclear	=	atomic
nude	=	bald, bare, exposed, naked, starkers
nudge	=	dig, elbow, jog, prod, push
nuisance	=	bore, bother, pest, plague
null	=	invalid, void
number	=	digit, ether, figure, integer, some; name of [one, two, ten, etc], (no)
(large) number	=	army, host, nation, (c, d, m)
(larger) number	=	extra, more
(small) number	=	few, (no)
(smaller) number	=	fewer

number of games	= rubber, set
nun	= abbess, novice, prioress, sister, (sh)
nunnery	= abbey, cloister, convent, priory
nurse	= foster, matron, sister, tend(er), treat
nurse(maid)	= amah, ayah, bonne
nut	= crank, fiend, kernel, lunatic, shell; name of [almond, areca, betel, brazil, cashew, filbert, hazel, pecan]
nuts	= crazy, daft, gaga, insane, mad
nymph	= dryad, houri, naiad, oread

O

oaf	= blockhead, clod, dimwit, dolt, dope, duffer, dunce, fool, idiot, moron
oafish	= dense, dim, dull, dumb, stupid, thick
oar	= blade, paddle, row, scull
oarsman	= paddler, rower, sculler, stroke
oast	= kiln, oven
oath	= bond, curse, expletive, pledge, profanity, vow, word
oats	= grain, grits, groats, porridge
obedient	= docile, dutiful, pliable
obeisance	= bow, curtsy, homage
obelisk	= column, needle, pillar
obese	= fat, gross, rotund, stout
obey	= comply, conform, heed, submit, yield
obfuscate	= bewilder, cloud, darken, fog, perplex
object	= aim, article, demur, end, goal, item, jib, point, thing
(I) object	= me
(we) object	= us
objection	= but, cavil, dissent, doubt, protest, quibble
obligation	= bond, debt, duty, liability, must, onus, tie, trust
oblige	= bind, coerse, compel, force, make
obliged	= beholden, bound, grateful, made, thankful
obliquely	= aslant, aslope
(walk) obliquely	= crab, edge, sidle
obliterate	= annul, cancel, delete, efface, erase
oblivion	= amnesty, forgetfulness, lethe
obscene	= blue, bawdry, coarse, evil, foul, horrid, vile
obscure	= blur, cloud, deep, dim, hide, opaque, vague
observable	= clear, open, overt, patent, visible
observant	= alert, mindful, quick, vigilant
observe	= detect, espy, eye, note, notice, regard, see, spot, view
observed	= saw, seen
observer	= eye, seer, spotter, witness
obsess	= bedevil, engross, grip, haunt, torment
obsessive	= compulsive, fixed

obsolete	=	archaic, bygone, dated, dead, ex, old, out, passe, (obs)
obstacle	=	bar, barrier, check, hitch, hurdle, snag
obstinate	=	dogged, firm, mulish, pigheaded, stubborn
obstruction	=	bar, block, check, jam, let, snag, stop
obtain	=	earn, gain, get, procure, secure, win
obtuse	=	blunt, dense, dull, stupid, thick
obverse	=	heads
obvious	=	clear, evident, patent, plain
occasion	=	cause, entail, event, reason, time
occident(al)	=	west(ern)
occupation	=	business, career, job, line, work, (occ)
occupier	=	lodger, owner, resident, tenant
occupy	=	busy, dwell, inhabit, people, tenant
occur	=	arise, befall, happen
occurence	=	affair, episode, event, incident
ocean	=	deep, main, sea, water; name of [antarctic, arctic, atlantic, indian, pacific], (o, oc)
octave	=	do(h), ray, re, me, mi, fa(h), so(h), la(h), te, ti; octet
odd	=	bizarre, outre, peculiar, quaint, queer, rare, rum
odious	=	foul, hateful, horrid, vile
odds	=	difference, remnants, scraps, variance, strife
off	=	bad, going, gone, out, sour, stale
off colour	=	ashen, ill, pale, wan
off course	=	adrift, astray, lost, wrong
offal	=	entrails, heart, kidney, liver, refuse
offence	=	crime, felony, insult, outrage, snub
offend	=	gall, insult, miff, repel, sin, snub
offensive	=	attack, foul, noisome, obscene, odious, onslaught, repugnant, vile
offer	=	bid, cite, essay, propose, proposal, tend(er)
offhand	=	aloof, brusque, casual, curt, glib
office	=	bureau, job, post, role
(bishop's) office	=	bishopric, diocese, see
(foreign) office	=	bureau, (fo)
(head) office	=	base, (ho)
offices	=	aegis, aid, favour, help
officer	=	capt(ain), col(onel), ensign, gen(eral) maj(or), ranker; name of [flag, petty, warrant], (co, nco, oc, od)
(field) officer	=	colonel, major, (col, fo)
(forest) officer	=	ranger
(Ottoman, Turkish) officer	=	bey
(police) officers	=	yard, (cid)
(prison) officer	=	gaoler, jailer, screw, warden, warder
(superior) officer	=	sir

official	=	agent, formal, notary, pooh-bah, proper, reeve, steward
(church) official	=	beadle, elder, verger, warden
(market) official	=	eurocrat [EC]
offshoot	=	adjunct, branch, limb, sprout
offspring	=	child, issue, progeny, scion, son
of us	=	our
ogee	=	bend, curve, talon
ogle	=	eye, leer, peer, stare
ogre	=	bogey, demon, giant, monster, spectre
oil	=	anoint, grease, lubricant, lubricate, smear; name of [attar, linseed]
oiler	=	oilcan, tanker
ointment	=	balm, cream, lotion, salve
okay	=	agree, approve, endorse, pass, ratify, (ok)
old	=	aged, ex, past, senile, stale, (o)
(the) old	=	ye
(very) old	=	aged, ancient, antique, elderly, (vo)
(you) old	=	thee, thou, ye
(your) old	=	thine, thy
old boy	=	alumnus, man, (ob)
old citizen	=	roman, trojan
old city	=	name of [pompeii, sparta, troy, tyre, ur]
old coin	=	name of [angel, crown, denarius, doubloon, ducat, farthing, florin, groat, pistole, sovereign, talent, tester]
old copper	=	denarius, (d)
old England	=	albion
old-fashioned	=	ancient, archaic, dated, out, passe, square
old flame, girlfriend	=	ex
old girl	=	dam(osel), dutch, ma, mother, wife, woman
old king	=	name of [arthur, canute, cole, lear], (gr)
old lady	=	dam(osel), dutch, gran, ma, mother, wife, (oap)
old man	=	codger, father, geezer, husband, pa, (oap)
old monarch	=	name of [arthur, canute, cole, lear], (gr)
old paper	=	papyrus
old penny	=	copper, denarius, (d)
old person	=	codger, geezer, pa, pensioner, (oap)
old robber	=	brigand, footpad, highwayman, pirate
old soldier	=	archer, dragoon, lancer, moth, redcoat, veteran
old theatre	=	vic
old vessel	=	ark; name of [argo, mayflower, victory]
old war	=	name of [boer, crimea(n), roses]
old way	=	via
old woman	=	beldam(e), crone, dutch, hag, ma, mother, virago, wife, witch
old-womanish	=	anile
old wood	=	hurst

old writer	= name of [aesop, cicero, dante, homer, ovid, plato, virgil]
olden days	= ago, once, past
older	= senior
(get, grow) old(er)	= age, mature
omen	= augur(y), bode, portent, presage, sign
omission	= default, failure, gap, lack, neglect
(sign of) omission	= caret
omit	= drop, fail, miss, neglect, skip
on	= about, atop, forward, live, over
on condition	= if
on fire	= ablaze, aflame, flambe
on holiday	= away, off
on stage	= acting
on strike	= out
once	= ex, former, late, old, past
one	= a, ace, an, any, single, some, unit, (i)
(Scottish) one	= yin
one against war	= dove
one for war	= hawk, jingoist
oneness	= singleness, unity
onerous	= grave, hard, heavy, weighty
one-time	= ex
one who tends	= nurse, sister
only	= barely, but, just, simply, sole, (o)
onset	= alpha, attack, birth, dawn, genesis, outbreak, start
onus	= burden, charge, load, task
ooze	= drip, emit, leak, mire, seep, slime
open	= ajar, candid, clear, frank, overt, plain, start, undo
open-air	= alfresco
open country, ground	= field, grassland [see], lea, meadow
opening	= adit, chink, crack, gap, hole, initial, mouth, orifice, os, pore, primary, rent, vent
opera	= name of [aida, carmen]
operatic character	= name of [figaro, igor, mimi]
operate	= act, cut, do, go, run, use, work
operating	= on
operation	= action, exercise, play, surgery, use, (op)
(series of) operations	= campaign
opinion	= appraisal, belief, idea, mind, tenet, view
opponent	= enemy, foe, rival
opportunity	= break, chance, shot
oppose	= confront, contest, counter, defy, face, fight, gainsay, resist
opposed	= against, anti, averse
opposing	= against, enemy, rival, versus, (v)
opposite	= adverse, antonym, contrary, converse, diverse, facing, inverse, reverse, (opp)

(stand) opposite	=	face
opposite page	=	verso
opposition	=	dissent, enemy, foe, opponent, rival
optimum	=	best, (opt)
opulent	=	lavish, profuse, rich, wealthy
oral	=	spoken, verbal, vocal
orate	=	mouth, preach, say, speak, tell
oration	=	address, homily, lecture, speech, spiel
orb	=	ball, eye, globe, round, sphere, world
orbit	=	circle, course, path, radius, range, reach, scope, sweep
orchestra	=	band
ordain	=	anoint, call, decree, enact, invest
ordeal	=	test, trial
order	=	bid, book, charge, class, command, decree, discipline, edict, instruction, row, sect, tell; name of [bath, garter, merit], (o, obe, om)
(money) order	=	cheque, draft, (mo)
ordered	=	bade, bidden, told
orderly	=	neat, regular, tidy, trim
ordinance	=	canon, decree, edict, law, rite, statute
ordinary	=	common, drear, dull, mediocre, normal, routine, usual
ordnance	=	artillery, cannon, guns, supplies
ornate	=	adorned, decorative, florid, flowery
ore	=	metal, mineral
organ	=	name of [ear, eye, heart, kidney, liver, lung, nose]
organisation	=	agency, business, concern, group, (org)
organize	=	form, frame, order, plan, run
orient(al)	=	east(ern)
original member	=	founder
ornament	=	adorn, beautify, (be)deck, figurine
osier	=	willow
other	=	added, extra, more, spare, variant
other name	=	alias, moniker, nickname, pseudonym, sobriquet
others	=	balance, remainder, rest
otherwise	=	besides, else, or
Ottoman officer	=	bey
ought	=	must, nothing, owed, should, zero, (o)
ounce	=	atom, crumb, drop, iota, scrap, shred
oust	=	banish, eject, exile, expel, remove
out	=	abroad, absent, asleep, away, gone
outbuilding	=	barn, hut, privy, shed
outcast	=	exile, leper, pariah
outcome	=	effect, issue, result, upshot
outcrop	=	ridge, spur
outdo	=	beat, cap, best, eclipse, top
outdoor	=	alfresco

outfit	=	crew, firm, garb, gear, kit, suit, togs
outflow	=	ebb, gush, issue, jet, spout
outhouse	=	barn, hut, privy, shed
outing	=	jaunt, spin, trip
outlaw	=	ban, bandit, bar, forbid, robber, thief
outlay	=	cost, disburse, expense, spend
(small) outlay	=	song
outlet	=	egress, exit, hole, shop, store, vent
outline	=	border, draft, draw, frame, plan, profile, sketch
outset	=	alpha, birth, dawn, genesis, start
outside	=	alfresco, alien, foreign, strange, without
outstanding	=	due, great, special, owing, (ai)
oval	=	ovate, ovoid, pitch
ovation	=	applause, reception, triumph
oven	=	furnace, kiln, oast, range, stone
over	=	about, above, across, anew, atop, left, more, oer, on, past, too
overact	=	ham
overawe	=	abash, alarm, cow, daunt, scare
overbalance	=	capsize, topple, upset
overcast	=	cloudy, dull, grey, murky, sunless
overcharge	=	clip, fleece, skin, soak, stick, (oc)
overcome	=	beat, best, crush, defeat, master
overdue	=	late, owing, tardy
overhaul	=	check, fix, mend, pass, service
overhead	=	above, aloft, hat, roof, sky, smash
overheated	=	hot
overpraise	=	flatter
overseas	=	abroad, away, out
overseer	=	boss, foreman, gaffer, super
overshadow	=	dwarf, excel, obscure, surpass, veil
overt	=	open, patent, plain, public, visible
overtake	=	catch, engulf, happen, outdo, pass
overthrow	=	defeat, depose, oust, topple, unseat
overtop	=	better, cap, excel, outdo, surpass
overturn	=	subvert, topple, upset
overweight	=	fat, gross, obese, plump, portly
owing	=	due, (iou)
own	=	admit, concede, have, hold, possess
owns	=	has
owner	=	holder, possessor, prop(rietor)
ownership	=	title
ox	=	name of [neat, yak, zebu]
Oxford river	=	name of [isis]
oyster	=	bivalve, mollusc, native

P

pace	=	gait, rate, speed, step, stride, tempo, trot
pacific	=	calm, gentle, mild, placid, still

pack	= bale, cram, deck, fold, group, kit, load, scrum
package	= bale, batch, box, carton, holiday, parcel, wrap
packet	= bundle, fortune, mailboat, mint, pile
packing	= lute, straw
pad	= cushion, digs, flat, foot, home, room, sole
pad(dy)	= temper
padre	= chaplain, clergy [see], father, priest
pagan	= atheist, heathen, infidel
page	= boy, folio, (fly)leaf, paper, sheet, (p)
(left-hand) page	= verso
(opposite) page	= verso
(right-hand) page	= recto
pain	= ache, agony, cramp, grief, gyp, hurt, pang, pest, sting
(cry of) pain	= ouch, ow
(feel) pain	= hurt, smart, sting
(was in) pain	= ached, hurt
paint-brush	= sable
painter	= chain, rope
painter, painting	= name of [cezanne, constable, dali, degas, holbein, manet, matisse, monet, picasso, renoir, titian, turner]
painting	= art, canvas, fresco, mural, picture
pair	= brace, couple, duet, duo, dyad, two(some), (oo, pr)
pal	= ally, buddy, chum, friend, mate
palace	= basilica, mansion; name of [blenheim, buckingham, elysee]
paladin	= champion, knight, peer
pale	= ashen, blanch, dim, dull, fade, faint, stake, wan, whiten
pall	= bore, cloud, cloy, jade, tire, weary
pallid	= anaemic, ashen, pale, wan
palm	= bribe, conceal, hand, hide, mitt, paw; name of [areca, coconut, date]
pamper	= coddle, cosset, pet, pimp, spoil
pamphlet	= brochure, folder, leaflet, tract
pan	= criticise, flay, knock, peter [Pan], pot, rap, slam, slate, trug
panache	= brio, dash, elan, flair, style, verve
pander	= cater, gratify, pimp
pane	= glass, window
panel	= board, jury
panic	= alarm, fear, flap, fluster, fright
pant	= blow, gasp, huff, puff
paper	= essay, exam, gazette, journal, page, rag, tabloid, test, (ms)
(old) paper	= papyrus
(quantity of) paper	= quire, ream

paper size	=	name of [atlas, crown, demy, elephant, foolscap, imperial, medium, quarto, royal]
papers	=	press, quire, ream
paperwork	=	editing, subbing
par	=	average, equal, mean, median, norm
parallel	=	akin, analogy, compare, like, match
parasite	=	cadger, sponge(r), vermin; name of [bot(t), bug, flea, fluke, ivy, leech, louse, tick]
parcel	=	box, lot, pack(age), part, piece, plot, portion, set, tract
pardon	=	amnesty, assoil, excuse, condone, forgive, remit, reprieve
pare	=	clip, crop, cut, peel, shave, trim
parent	=	da, dad, ma(ma), mum, pa(pa)
parish lantern	=	moon
parity	=	analogy, equality, quits, unity
park	=	common, deposit, estate, garden, grounds, leave
(game) park	=	reserve
(London) park	=	name of [hyde]
(Irish) parliament	=	dail
parody	=	farce, lampoon, satire, skit, spoof
parrot	=	echo, lory, macaw, mimic, repeat
parson	=	clergy [see]
part	=	bit, bite, element, piece, region, rend, role, section, sever, share, split
(last) part	=	tail
part actor	=	extra
part of church	=	altar, apse, chancel, nave, pew, pulpit reredos
part of door	=	hinge, jamb, lintel, muntin, panel
part of ear	=	auricle, cochlea, concha, (ear)drum, helix, lobe, pinna, tragus
part of head	=	corona, crown, inion, occiput, pate, poll, sinciput, temple, tonsure, vertex
part of London	=	bow, soho, (ec, sw, wc, wi)
part of plant	=	anther, calyx, leaf, petal, pistil, sepal, stalk, stamen, stem, style
part of river	=	reach, stretch
particle	=	atom, bit, crumb, grain, iota, jot, mite, mote, piece, scrap, shred, speck, whit
(charged) particle	=	ion
particular	=	exact, fact, fussy, minute, respect
partition	=	fence, screen, share, split, wall
partner	=	ally, colleague, helpmate, helpmeet, husband, mate, spouse, wife
(brave) partner	=	squaw
party	=	bash, beano, cabal, clique, do, faction, group, revel, sect, social, thrash, tory, (lab, lib)

pass	= cap, col, elapse, gap, go, gorge, hand, overtake, permit, skip, ticket, visa, warrant
passing show	= pageant, parade
passage	= adit, aisle, hall, journey, lane, path, route, transit, voyage
passe	= aged, dated, faded, obsolete, old
passion	= amour, anger, emotion, fire, flame, ire, love, lust, rage, zeal, zest
passive	= asleep, docile, idle, inert, quiet
past	= ago, by(gone), ex, gone, late, over, yore
paste	= dough, hit, lam, punch, strass, stick
pastel	= chalk, crayon, drawing, woad
pastime	= game, hobby, leisure, play, sport
pastor	= clergy [see]
pastoral	= bucolic, country, rural, rustic, simple
pastry	= bun, cake, crust, dough, pie, tart; name of [flaky, puff]
pasture	= field, grass, herbage, lea, meadow
pat	= caress, dab, pet, stroke, tap, touch
patch	= cover, fix, ground, mend, plot, repair
pate	= crown, head
patent	= clear, licence, open, plain
path	= course, road, route, track, trail, way
pathos	= pity, sadness
patient	= calm, invalid, mild, quiet
patient man	= job [Biblical]
patio	= stoep, terrace, veranda(h)
patron	= angel, backer, owner, sponsor
pattern	= client, design, form, motif, plan, style
pauper	= beggar, mendicant
pause	= break, comma, interval, lull, stop, wait
paving-stone	= flag
paw	= foot, grab, hand, handle, maul
pawn	= hock, pledge, puppet, stooge, tool, (p)
pawnbroker	= uncle
pay	= remit, reward, salary, screw, settle, wage
(promise(s) to) pay	= iou(s)
(unemployment) pay	= dole
pay for	= foot, stand, treat
paymaster	= bursar, cashier, purser
payment	= fee, hire, rent, reward, wage
pea	= pip, seed
peace	= calm, hush, quiet, repose, rest
peacemaker	= dove, (un)
peak	= acme, apex, ben, brow, bill, cap, crest, horn, pinnacle, mount, summit, tip, top, tor; name of mountain [see]
peal	= bell, chime, knell, ring, toll
(mother of) pearl	= nacre

peas (and beans)	=	pulse
peasant	=	churl, hind, lout, rustic, swain, yokel
(indian) peasant	=	ryot
pebble	=	lens, stone
pebbles	=	beach, shingle, shore
peculiar	=	bizarre, odd, queer, rum, strange, weird
peddle	=	barter, deal, hawk, push, trade, truck
pedlar	=	dealer, duffer, hawker, huckster, monger, pusher, tradesman
peek	=	glance, glimpse, look, peep
peel	=	flake, pare, rind, scale, skin
peep	=	chirp, glance, glimpse, look, peek
peer	=	equal, gaze, look, noble, peep, stare; name of [baron, count, duke, earl, lord, marquess, marquis, viscount]
peeve	=	anger, annoy, gall, grate, irritate, rile
peeved	=	angry, cross, irate, mad
peevishness	=	bile, gall, pet, sulk, temper
peg	=	die, dowel, fix, hob, nail, pin, stake, tee
pelt	=	beat, drub, fur, hide, pound, skin
pen	=	cage, coop, hutch, nib, prison, quill, sty, write
penalty	=	fine, forfeit, mulct, sanction
penchant	=	bent, bias, liking, taste
pencil	=	colour, draw, graphite, lead, write
(blue) pencil	=	censor
penitent	=	abject, contrite, sorry
penniless	=	broke, needy, poor, skint
(old) penny	=	copper, denarius, (d)
penury	=	dearth, lack, need, poverty, want
people	=	colonise, folk, inhabit, mankind, men, nation, public, race, settle, society, we
(lots of) people	=	army, crowd, host, legion, swarm
(those) people	=	them
per	=	by, each, via, (ea, p)
per annum	=	annually, (pa)
percentage	=	proportion, rate, ratio
perch	=	alight, bar, light, pole, rod, roost, settle
perfect	=	exact, entire, finish, flawless, ideal, model, precise, tense, whole
perform	=	act, do, enact, play, stage, work
performance	=	act, deed, feat, play, show, work; name of [matinee, recital, rehearsal]
(first) performance	=	premiere
performer	=	actor, artist(e), doer, player, turn
perfume	=	aroma, bouquet, incense, scent, smell
perhaps	=	ablin(g)s, maybe, perchance, possibly
peril	=	danger, hazard, menace, risk
period	=	day, dot, epoch, era, month, week, season, spell, stop, time, while, year;

		name of [autumn, easter, fall, lent, spring, summer, winter, xmas]
periodical	=	journal, magazine, organ, paper, review, serial, weekly, (mag)
perish	=	die, expire, fall, peg, rot, waste
permanence	=	fixity, good, survival
permanent	=	durable, fixed, lasting, stable
permanent way	=	railroad
permission	=	assent, consent, leave, licence, pass
permit	=	allow, grant, leave, let, pass, sanction
permitted	=	legal, let, ligit
persiflage	=	badinage, banter, raillery, repartee
person	=	being, human, one, soul, (ist)
(annoying) person	=	blighter, nuisance, pain, pest
(despicable) person	=	bounder, cad, cur, hound, rat, rotter, sneak
(destitute) person	=	beggar, mendicant, pauper
(important) person	=	bigwig, nabob, nob, pot, (vip)
(intellectual) person	=	academic, brahmin, don, professor
(irritating) person	=	blighter, nuisance, pain, pest
(little) person	=	dwarf, elf, fairy, goblin, leprechaun, pixie, sprite
(nasty) person	=	bounder, cad, cur, heel, rat, rotter
(old) person	=	codger, geezer, pa, pensioner, (oap)
(sly) person	=	fox
(superior) person	=	bigwig, nabob, nob, pot, toff
(top) person	=	name of [aga, ameer, amir, bey, emir, emperor, lord, king, president, ruler, shah, supremo, tsar]
(university) person	=	blue, freshman, graduate, sophomore, (ba, bed, ma)
(unpleasant) person	=	bounder, cad, cur, heel, rat, rotter
(wealthy) person	=	croesus
personal assistant	=	aide, batman, deputy, factotum, helper, secretary, (pa)
persuade	=	cajole, coax, con, induce, sway, urge
pert	=	bold, cheeky, forward, impudent, lively, saucy
pertain	=	apply, belong, concern, relate, vest
perverse	=	contrary, peevish, stubborn, wayward, wicked
pervert	=	abuse, debase, deprave, warp, twist
pest	=	bane, bother, bug, curse, pain, plague; name of insect [see]
pet	=	coddle, fondle, idol, pout, sulk, tiff
(domestic) pet	=	name of [cat, dog, hamster]
peter	=	dwindle, pan [Peter Pan], safe
petition	=	appeal, ask, beg, plea, prayer, suit
(church) petition	=	litany
petrol	=	gas, regular, super
petty	=	light, minor, small, trivial
pew	=	bench, form, seat
phase	=	aspect, chapter, period, stage, step, (ph)

philander	=	coquet, dally, flirt, trifle
philosophy	=	belief, doctrine, logic, reason, tenet, thinking, thought, wisdom, yoga
philosopher	=	name of [bacon, confucius, cynic, plato]
phobia	=	dislike, dread, fear, horror
phone	=	bell, blower, buzz, call, dial, ring
phoney	=	bogus, fake, false, pseudo, sham
photograph	=	image, print, sepia, shoot, snap
physic	=	cure, medicine, remedy
physician	=	doctor, healer, surgeon, (dr, md)
(old) physician	=	leech
piano	=	gentle, low, soft; name of [grand, joanna, upright], (p)
pick	=	best, choice, choose, elect, elite, harvest, opt, pluck, select
pick-me-up	=	bracer, tonic
pickle	=	bind, dilemma, fix, jam, mess, spot
picture	=	fresco, icon, image, mural, print, scape, scene, sketch, snap
pictures	=	art, cinema
pie	=	flan, pasty, tart; name of [apple, cottage, custard, mud, pork, shepherd's]
piece	=	bit, bite, cut, morsel, part, portion, scrap, slab, (pc)
(hair-)piece	=	toupee, wig
piece of meat	=	chop, cutlet
pier	=	dock, jetty, quay, wharf
pierce	=	bore, cut, gash, gore, slit, stab, wound
pig	=	boar, glutton, hog, porker, sow, swine
(young) pig	=	gilt, grice
pigeon	=	kind of [antwerp, archangel, barb, dove, drago(o)n, runt]
pigheaded	=	mulish, obstinate, stubborn
pigment	=	colour, dye, paint, stain, tint
pike	=	jack, pickaxe, spear, spike, toll
pile	=	heap, lot, mass, mint, mound, nap, store, wad
pillage	=	looting, plunder, ravage, sack, steal
pillar	=	atlantes, baluster, column, monolith, pier, pilaster
pillion	=	cushion, saddle, seat(ing)
pilot	=	airman, aviate, aviator, flier, fly, guide, lead(er), navigator
pimple	=	abscess, boil, pustule, spot
pin	=	(af)fix, brooch, clip, join, nail, peg, tack
pinch	=	filch, lift, nab, nick, nip, rob, steal, swipe, tweak
pine	=	ache, fir, fret, itch, long, mope, yen
pink	=	acme, best, blush, coral, puce, rose, rouge

pinnacle	=	acme, apex, crest, height, peak, top
pious	=	devout, godly, holy, pi
pip	=	blip, chirp, pea, peep, seed, spot
pipe	=	briar, duct, fife, hookah, horn, hose, tube
(melodic) pipe	=	chanter
(water) pipe	=	hose, hydrant
pique	=	grudge, huff, irk, miff, pet, rile, vex
pirate	=	buccaneer, corsair, copy, marauder, poach, raider, rover
pit	=	abyss, chasm, crater, dent, mine
pitch	=	bung, cast, chuck, hurl, tar, tone, toss
pitcher	=	ewer, jug
pith helmet	=	topee, topi
pittance	=	drop, mite, sou, trifle
pity	=	grief, pathos, rue, ruth, shame, sorrow
pivot	=	axis, axle, fulcrum, hinge, hub, swivel
placard	=	bill, display, poster
place	=	deposit, point, pop, put, set, site, stead, venue, (pl)
(change) place	=	flit, move
(familiar) place	=	hangout, haunt, resort
(first) place	=	head, lead, van
(last) place	=	crypt, end, grave, rear, tomb, vault
(leafy) place	=	arbour, bower
(meeting) place	=	forum, venue
(resting-)place	=	cemetery, grave(yard), tomb
(take) place	=	happen, occur
(that) place	=	there
(this) place	=	here
(wizard) place	=	oz
plagiarise	=	copy, crib, lift, pirate, steal
plagiarist	=	copycat
plague	=	annoy, bother, deuce, nuisance, pest; name of [bubonic, oriental]
plain	=	clear, dry, even, flat, neat, open, pampa(s), prairie, pure, simple, steppe
plain clothes	=	mufti
plain language	=	prose
plan	=	aim, chart, design, idea, map, organize, plot, project, scheme
(current) plan	=	circuit
plane	=	even, flat, jet, level, skim, smooth, surface; name of [boeing, comet, mig, mirage]
planet	=	name of [earth, jupiter, mars, mercury, neptune, pluto, saturn, uranus, venus]
planetary	=	erratic, mundane, solar, terrestrial, wandering
plant	=	annual, crop, factory, growth, hoax, machinery, pose, sow; kind of [aloe, bush, fern, flower [see], grain [see], grass [see], herb [see], hop,

		ivy, moss, reed, rush, shrub [see], tobacco, tree [see], vegetable [see], vine, yam, yarrow, yucca
(part of) plant	=	anther, calyx, leaf, petal, pistil, sepal, stalk, stamen, stem, style
(pot) plant	=	cannabis, hemp, poppy
(prickly) plant	=	name of [aloe, briar, bramble, brier, cactus, furze, gorse, whin]
(unwanted) plant	=	name of [clover, thistle, weed]
plaque	=	badge, medal, plate, shield, tablet
plasma	=	blood, lymph, milk, quartz, serum
plaster	=	cast, gypsum, mortar, smear, spread, stucco
platform	=	dais, pulpit, rostrum, stage, stand
plaudit	=	applause, praise
play	=	act, bat, caper, frolic, run, serve, strum; name of [comedy, drama, farce, thriller]
play on words	=	anagram, charade, pun
played first	=	led
player	=	actor, back, musician [see], striker, sweeper, wing
(poor) player	=	rabbit, rookie
(record) player	=	hi-fi, stereo, turntable
(rugby) player	=	flank, hooker, lock, prop; name of [lion, puma, springbok, wallaby]
(star) player	=	lead
(top) player	=	ace, seed
players	=	cast, side, team
playmate	=	chum, friend, pal
plaything	=	bauble, top, toy, trifle, trinket
plea	=	appeal, claim, entreaty, prayer, request, suit
plead	=	appeal, argue, ask, beg, crave, entreat, implore
pleasant	=	affable, amiable, fine, genial, nice
please	=	amuse, arride, charm, content, gratify, satisfy, suit, tickle
pleased	=	happy, glad
pleasure	=	bliss, delight, elation, joy, relish
pledge	=	hock, oath, pawn, swear, vow, word
plenty	=	ample, galore, heap, lot(s), much, pile, wealth
plinth	=	base
plot	=	bed, cabal, conspire, garden, plan, ploy, ruse, scheme
ploy	=	feint, manoeuvre, ruse, trick, wile
plug	=	ad(vert), bung, push, shoot, stop, (pr)
plugged	=	shot
plumb	=	delve, even, fathom, gauge, sound, vertical
plunder	=	loot, pillage, prey, raid, ransack, rifle, sack, spoil(s), swag
plunge	=	dip, dive, drop, fall, sink, thrust
(take the) plunge	=	bet, chance, dive, gamble, risk
plunger	=	gambler, piston

poacher's dog	=	lurcher
pod	=	case, cocoon, herd, husk, shell
poem, poetry	=	lines, rhyme, song, verse; name of [aubade, elegy, ode, lay, limerick, lyric, sonnet]
poet	=	bard, muse, rishi; name of [auden, blake, burns, chaucer, donne, eliot, gray, hardy, horace, keats, milton, ovid, pope, scott, shelley, spender, spenser, virgil, wordsworth, yeats], (pl)
(eastern) poet	=	omar
poignant	=	acute, bitter, intense, keen, sad, sharp, tangy
point	=	aim, dart, dot, end, gist, matter, ness, prong, reason, tang, thorn, tine, tip, top, train
(compass) point	=	rhumb, (e, n, s, w)
point of view	=	angle, opinion, slant
(jagged) point	=	barb, hook, spike
poise	=	aplomb, balance, cool, elegance, grace, hang
poised	=	calm, serene, suave, urbane
poison	=	bane, corrupt, pervert, toxin, venom; name of [arsenic, belladonna, hemlock, ptomaine, strychnine]
poisoner	=	name of [adder, asp, mamba, scorpion, viper]
poisonous creature	=	name of [adder, asp, mamba, scorpion, viper]
pole	=	anode, mast, perch, rod, spar, staff, (n, s)
polecat	=	fitch, foumart, skunk, weasel
police car	=	panda
policeman	=	bluebottle, bobby, cop(per), fuzz, peeler, rozzer, shamus
policemen	=	yard, (cid)
police officers	=	yard, (cid)
polish	=	buff, gloss, lustre, rub, sheen, shine
political group, faction	=	party
politician	=	democrat, labourite, liberal, republican, senator, tory, whig, (mep, mp)
politicians	=	party
poll	=	ballot, census, count, head, register, tally, vote
pomp	=	ceremony, fanfare, grandeur, parade, show, state
pony	=	crib, foal, horse, trot
pool	=	cartel, kitty, lake, lido, mere, pond, tarn
poor	=	bad, broke, indigent, mean, needy, skint, stony
poor actor	=	ham
poor player	=	rabbit, rookie
poorly	=	bad, ill, low, sick
pop	=	bang, bulge, burst, crack, da(d), father, music, snap, soda
pope	=	pontiff
(top of the) pops	=	hit

popular	=	famous, in, liked
porcelain	=	china [see]
porch	=	colonnade, portico, stoa
port	=	air, harbour, haven, left, mien, wine; name of [aden, antwerp, bergen, calais, delft, dieppe, dover, dunkirk, hull, kiel, malmo, naples, narvik, rio, rye, suez, tangier], (l)
porter	=	bearer, beer, carrier, stout
portend	=	augur, bode, herald, omen, presage, warn
portico	=	atrium, colonnade, porch, stoa
portion	=	bit, cut, lot, quota, part, piece, share, some
portmanteau	=	bag, blend, case, trunk
portrait	=	effigy, image, sketch
portray	=	depict, describe, paint, picture, show
Portugal and Spain	=	iberia
Portugese	=	dom
pose	=	air, attitude, feign, front, mien, model, sit
posed	=	sat
poser	=	enigma, model, mystery, problem, riddle, sitter, why
posit	=	affirm, assume, premise, presume
position	=	locus, place, rank, site, spot, status
(change) position	=	shift
positive	=	certain, downright, express, sure
possess	=	enjoy, have, hold, keep, obsess, own
possible	=	able, can, doable, may, on, viable
post	=	after, ante, bet, job, mail, send, stake, station
postage	=	mail
posted	=	bet, sent
poster	=	bill, notice, placard, sticker
pot	=	ante, bet, drugs [see], jar, pool, urn, shy
pot plant	=	cannabis, hemp, poppy
potent	=	cogent, influential, powerful, strong
(eastern) potentate	=	aga, ameer, amir, emir, shah, sultan
pothole	=	cave, grotto
potter	=	dabble, drinker, marksman, sniper, toper
pottery	=	china [see]
pouch	=	bag, bulge, poke, sac, sack, satchel, scrip
pound	=	beat, drub, lam, pen, quid, (l, lb)
pour	=	emit, flow, gush, spill, teem
poverty	=	distress, lack, need, penury, want
powder	=	ash, dust, talc
power	=	ability, amp, force, might, sway, watt, weight, volt
(friendly) power	=	ally
praise	=	bless, eulogy, extol, hail, kudos, laud
(over)praise	=	flatter
pram	=	wheeler
prate	=	babble, brag, chat, crow, gab, jaw, rabbit, talk, yak

prawn(s)	= scampi
pray	= appeal, ask, beg, beseech, entreat, implore, plead
prayer	= appeal, bead, collect, litany, orison, petition, plea
preach	= exhort, lecture, orate, rant, sermon
preacher	= apostle, clergy [see]
precede	= head, herald, lead, preface, usher
precious	= costly, dear, loved, prized, valued
precious stone	= gem, gemstone [see], jewel
precise	= correct, exact, formal, prim, proper
preclude	= avert, bar, deter, prevent
precursor	= forerunner, harbinger, herald
predator	= hunter
prefer	= adopt, choose, elect, pick, rather
preferred	= chosen, favourite, select, (pf)
prelate	= clergy [see]
preliminary race	= heat
prejudice	= bias, damage, harm, impair, mar, spoil
prejudiced	= partial, partisan
premier	= arch, chief, first, head, main, prime; name of [asquith, attlee, baldwin, balfour, churchill, disraeli, eden, gladstone, heath, home, major, peel, pitt, thatcher, walpole, wilson], (pm)
prepare	= adapt, fit, fix, groom, make, ready, set
preparation	= lotion, plan, study
prescribe	= decree, dictate, impose, ordain
present	= deliver, donate, gift, give, here, now, offer, tender, there, (ad)
(at) present	= now
present	= day, time anniversary, birthday, christmas, now, xmas, (ad)
preserve	= can, jam, keep, pickle, smoke, tin
preside	= chair, govern, head, lead, run
president	= abe [Lincoln], (p)
press	= coerse, crowd, crush, dragoon, force, iron, jam, shanghai, squeeze, urge, vat
press handout	= release
pressure	= force, push, strain, stress, weight
prestige	= fame, kudos, renown, stature, status
pretence	= deceit, facade, sham, show, veneer
pretend	= affect, fake, feign, purport, sham
pretty	= attractive, comely, fair, lovely
pretty girl	= belle
prevail	= exist, stand, succeed, triumph, win
prevaricate	= cavil, dodge, fib, hedge, lie
prevent	= avert, bar, deter, hinder, obviate, preclude, stop
(legally) prevent	= estop

previous	= ex, former, past, prior
prey	= game, kill, plunder, quarry, target, victim
(bird of) prey	= buzzard, eagle, falcon,, harrier, hawk, kestrel, kite, osprey, owl, raptor, vulture
price	= charge, cost, fee, ransom, rate, tariff, toll, value, (sp)
(starting) price	= odds, (sp)
prick	= goad, jab, pierce, puncture, spur, urge
pricker	= awl, barb, hook, jag, spur, thorn
prickly plant	= name of [aloe, briar, bramble, brier, cactus, furze, gorse, whin]
pride	= conceit, cream, ego, herd, vanity
priest	= abbe, clergy [see], lama, rabbi; name of [aaron, annas, eli], (fr, pr)
(Jewish) priest	= rabbi
prim	= formal, neat, proper, tidy, stiff
prima donna	= diva, star
primary	= first, initial, original, prime [see]
primate	= ape, baboon, monkey [see], man
prime	= best, charge, choice, cream, elite, first, top
prime minister	= premier; name of [see], (pm)
prince	= chief, greatest, ruler, sovereign
prince of the church	= cardinal
principal	= arch, chief, head, key, main, prime
principle	= axiom, canon, code, ethic, maxim, tenet
print	= edition, etch, issue, mark, stamp, type
printer	= compositor, litho; name of [caxton]
printer's measure	= em, en
printing type	= name of [aldine, bold, bourgeois, brevier, gothic, italic, minion, pearl, primer, roman, ruby, times]
prison	= cage, jail, jug, nick, pen, stir, ward
prison officer	= gaoler, jailer, screw, warden, warder
prison term	= life, sentence, stretch, time
prisoner	= con, convict, felon, jailbird, lag
prize	= award, esteem, reward, trophy, value
problem	= dilemma, enigma, hitch, knot, poser, riddle, rub, snag, teaser
proceed	= continue, flow, go, march, move, pass, wend
proceeds	= gain, money, profit, return
proclamation	= decree, edict, manifesto, notice
procure	= acquire, gain, get, obtain, win
produce	= breed, cause, create, grow, make, sire, stage, yield
production	= play, revue, show, yield
profess	= admit, aver, avow, own, vouch
profession	= calling, career, craft, metier, trade

professional	= adept, expert, paid, pro, slick
proficient	= adept, capable, expert, master, skilled
profile	= contour, outline, silhouette, sketch
profit	= avail, benefit, gain, promote, serve
profit(s)	= earnings, gain, return, surplus, yield
profound	= deep, heavy, sage, wise
progeny	= child, issue, offspring, scion, son
progress	= advance, career, gain, march, move
prohibit	= ban, (de)bar, forbid, stop, veto
prohibition	= ban, bar, stop, veto
project	= bulge, cast, jut, plan, scheme, screen, throw, transmit
projection	= brow, bulge, jut, ledge, nose, shelf
prolong	= delay, extend, lengthen, stretch
promenade	= front, parade, pier, stroll, walk
prominent	= bold, famous, noted, signal
promise	= augur, bode, pledge, plight, swear
promise(s) to pay	= iou(s)
promontory	= cape, head, ness, point
promote	= boost, foster, plug, push, raise
prompt	= aside, cue, egg, fast, prod, spur, urge
prone	= apt, bent, fain, flat, inclined, lying, subject
prong	= point, spike, tine, tip
proof	= evidence, ground, reason, witness
prop	= bolster, brace, shore, stay, support
propel	= drive, go, move, prod, push, spur, urge
propeller	= oar, prop, screw, scull
proper	= apt, correct, fit(ting), just, meet, prim, right, staid
prophet	= augur, oracle, seer; name of [eli, nahum]
prophetess	= sibyl
proportion	= bit, half, part, quarter, ratio
propose	= aim, mean, move, offer, plan, put, suggest
proposal	= bid, motion, offer, plan, tender
proposition	= deal, job, motion, plan, task, theorem
proprietor	= holder, owner, possessor
propriety	= courtesy, decency, decorum, etiquette, fitness
proscribe	= ban(ish), damn, doom, exile, outlaw
prosecute	= indict, sue, summon, try
prospect	= chance, dig, probe, sift, view, vista
prostrate	= flat, lying, prone
protect	= (de)fend, guard, screen, shield
protection	= armour, cap, cover, guard, hat, hood, mail, shield
protest	= aver, avow, demur, object, squawk
protrude	= bulge, jut, pop
protrusion	= bulge, chin, ledge, lip, nose
prove	= manifest, show, test, try

provide = bestow, cater, give, serve, yield
provide intelligence = advise, inform
provided = if
provider = donor, earner, giver, patron, source
provisions = eats, food, grub
provoke = annoy, inflame, irk, needle, rile, rouse, vex
prow = bow(s), fore, front, head, nose, stem
prowess = ability, bravery, skill, valour
prowl = forage, scour, search, stalk, steal
prudence = care, caution, sagacity, wisdom
prudent = careful, cautious, discreet, sage, wise
prune = clip, crop, cut, lop, pare, snip, trim
psyche = life, mind, moth, soul, spirit
psychic = medium, mental, mystic, occult, spiritual
pub = bar, inn, local, tavern
public = civic, civil, common, general, open, overt, people
public address = tannoy, (pa)
public school = name of [eton, harrow, radley, rugby]
public transport = bus, cab, coach, taxi, train, tram, tube, (br, ry)
publication = airing, book, issue, journal, mag
(yearly) publication = annual
publicize = air, broadcast, hype, plug, promote, push
publicity = ad, hype, plug, (pr)
publish = issue, leak, print, reveal, spread
pucker = contract, gather, purse
pudding = afters, dessert, sweet, trifle; name of [custard, jelly, rice, sago]
pull = drag, draw, haul, jerk, lug, reel, sway, tow, tug, yank
pulpit = ambo, dais, platform, rostrum, stage, stand
pulse = bean, beat, lentil, pea, rhythm, throb
pump = inflate, question, shake, siphon
punctilious = exact, formal, fussy, punctual
punctuation mark = colon, comma, dash, dot, period, stop
punish = abuse, amerce, beat, chasten, chastise, flog, lash, thrash, whip
punishment = abuse, fine, hiding penalty
(instrument of punishment) = cane, rack, rod, stocks, tawse
punt = back, bet, gamble, stake, wager
punter = backer, better, gambler
puny = feeble, frail, thin, tiny, weak
pupil = eye, learner [see], (l)
(former) pupil = alumnus, (ob)
puppet = doll, pawn, stooge, tool
puritan = moral, prig, prude, strict
pureed fruit = fool
purpose = aim, design, end, function, goal, idea, motive, object, point

purposeful	=	firm, fixed, positive, resolute
purse	=	contract, funds, money, pouch, pucker
pursue	=	chase, court, follow, haunt, trail, woo
push	=	barge, boost, elbow, heave, press, plug, prod, ram, shove
put	=	deposit, place, pose, posit, set
put aside	=	forget, ignore, keep, save
put off	=	adjourn, defer, deter, stall
put on	=	add, don, stage, wear
put on an edge	=	hone, sharpen, strop, whet
put right	=	emend, fix, mend, redeem, repair
put up with	=	abide, bear, endure, lump, wear
putrid	=	fetid, foul, rank, rotten, stale
puzzle	=	baffle, enigma, mystery, poser, problem, riddle, why
puzzled	=	beaten, clueless, lost, stuck
pygmy	=	dwarf, elfin, midget, tiny, wee

Q

quack	=	charlatan, fake, fraud, phoney, sham
quack medicine	=	placebo
quagmire	=	bog, fen, marsh, mire, morass, swamp
quail	=	cow(er), daunt, flinch, shake, wince
quaint	=	bizarre, droll, odd
quake	=	jar, quail, quiver, rock, shake, shiver, shock, tremble, tremor
quaker	=	friend
qualification	=	but, caveat, degree, proviso, skill, (ba, ma)
qualified	=	able, adept, expert, fit, skilful, (ba, ma)
qualify	=	entitle, mark, modify, pass
quality	=	class, grade, mark, trait, virtue
quantity	=	amount, lot, number, quota, sum, total
quantity of paper	=	quire, ream
quarrel	=	beef, bicker, brawl, fight, row, scrap, tiff
quarry	=	chase, game, mine, prey
quarter	=	area, billet, fourth, mercy, pity, region, side, zone, (e, n, s, w; q, qr)
(temporary) quarters	=	camp(er), tent
quartile	=	fourth, quarter
quartz	=	agate, chert, flint, onyx, opal
quash	=	annul, cancel, quell, revoke, void
quaver	=	breve, quake, shake, tremor, trill
queen	=	belle, empress, regina; name of [anne, bess, mab, mary], (er, hm, q, r)
question	=	ask, eh, how, pose(r), pump, query, quiz, what, when, why, (q, qu)
question master	=	catechist
queue	=	file, line, rank, row
queuing up	=	inline [in line], (li . . . ne)

quick	=	alive, core, deft, fast, fleet, hasty, prompt, rapid, smart
quickly	=	apace, fast, presto, pronto, soon
(go) quickly	=	haste, hurry, run, rush
quiet	=	pacific, peace, silence, silent, soft, still, (p, qt, sh)
quiff	=	curl, hair, lock, tress
quip	=	crack, epigram, gag, jest, joke, sally
quit	=	desert, exit, go, leave, resign, stop
quite	=	all, fully, rather, really, truly, utterly, very, wholly
(not) quite	=	barely, hardly
quits	=	equal, even
quiver	=	quake, shake, tremble, spasm, throb
quota	=	cut, part, ration, share, slice, whack
quotation	=	bid, motto, tag, tender, (quot)
quote	=	cite, name, recall, recite

R

rabbit	=	chat(ter), gab, gas, hare, prate, say, speak, spout, talk; name of [brer, bunny]
rabbit's tail	=	scut
rabble	=	crowd, dregs, herd, horde, mob, swarm
race	=	folk, hurry, nation, people, relay, run, rush, tribe; name of [derby, guineas, leger, national, oaks], (tt)
(preliminary) race	=	heat
race conditions	=	going
racecourse	=	name of [aintree, ascot, epsom]
racehorses	=	stable, string
rack	=	shake, stretcher, task, torture, wring
racket	=	bat, din, fuss, noise, ramp, row, sound, swindle
radiant	=	beaming, bright, lucent, shining
radical	=	basic, extreme, liberal, primary, ultra
radio	=	set, (cb)
radio-active rays	=	name of [alpha, beta, gamma, delta]
raffia	=	fibre, hemp
raffle	=	draw, lottery, sweep
rag	=	banter, chaff, fun, lark, paper, rate, rib, scold, scrap, wig
rage	=	anger, craze, fad, fume, fury, ire, madness, passion, storm, temper
ragged	=	rated, ribbed, torn, uneven, wigged
raid	=	attack, foray, onset, sally, sortie
rail	=	abuse, bar, fence, rant, rate, rod, scold, track, vituperate
railing(s)	=	balustrade, bannister, fence

railway	= line, metro, track, tube, (br, lms, ry)
raiment	= apparel, attire, clothes [see], dress, garb, habit
rain	= drizzle, fall, pour, shower, teem, torrent
raise	= boost, cock, breed, elevate, erect, grow, hoist, jack, lift, mount, produce, rear, uplift
raised	= bred, built, erect, hiked, up, upped
rake	= comb, lecher, libertine, rip, roue
rally	= assemble, assembly, banter, chaff, gather, improve, marshal, meet(ing), muster, recover, revive, unite
ram	= aries, butt, drive, drum, push, shove, strike, stuff, tamp
ramble	= hike, rave, roam, rove, stray, wander
rambler	= drifter, hiker, rover
ramp	= racket, rage, slope, storm, swindle
ran	= fled, flew, hied, kept, sped
rancid	= bad, fetid, foul, putrid, rank, stale
random	= aimless, casual, chance, spot, stray
range	= area, bounds, domain, extent, field, orbit, radius, scope, sphere
rank	= bad, class, degree, foul, grade, level, line, order, rancid, row, sheer, status, tier, utter; name of [admiral, brigadier, capt(ain), col(onel), commodore, maj(or), general]
(indication of) rank	= crown, pip, stripe
rankle	= anger, annoy, gall, irk, rile
ransack	= comb, loot, pillage, plunder, raid, rifle, sack, scour, search
ransom	= money, payment, payoff, price, redeem, release, rescue
rant	= bombast, declaim, preach, rail, rate, rave, scold, tirade
rap	= blow, hit, knock, talk, tap
rapid	= brisk, fast, fleet, quick, swift
rare	= few, raw, scarce, sparse, thin, unusual
rascal	= badmash, bezonian, heel, imp, knave, rake, rogue, scamp
rash	= brash, daring, hasty, madcap, reckless; name of [scurf, scurvy, shingles, spots]
rasher	= bacon, ham, slice
rasp	= file, grate, rub, scrape
rat	= apostate, cur, defect, desert(er), dog, inform, renegade, rodent, squeal, toad
rate	= charge, cost, count, earn, fee, judge, lecture, price, rail, rant, regard, scold, speed, tariff, tax, (kph, mph)
rating	= class, grade, rank, sailor, seaman
ratio	= degree, pi, rate, scale
ration	= allot, dole, limit, part, quota, share

rations	= diet, food, stores, supplies
rationale	= basis, grounds, logic, reason
rave	= drool, howl, rage, rail, rant, roar
raw	= crude, fresh, green, nude, rare, tender
raw metal	= mineral, ore
ray	= beam, light, radiate, radius, skate, (x)
(radio-active) rays	= name of [alpha, beta, gamma, delta]
reach	= arrive, attain, come, extend, gain, get, hand, pass, stretch
react	= behave, respond [see]
reactionary	= blimp, diehard
reactor	= pile
read	= browse, con, learned, scan, study
reading	= grasp, review, scrutiny, sermon, study, version
ready	= apt, fit, prompt, quick, ripe, set, willing
Reagan	= ron [Ronald Reagan]
real	= actual, genuine, right, true, very
(not) real	= bogus, fake, phony, pseudo, sham
realise	= clear, do, earn, fulfil, grasp, net, see, twig, understand
really	= indeed, quite, truly, very
realm	= kingdom, monarchy, nation, region, reign, state
reap	= gain, garner, gather, get, harvest, win
rear	= aft, back, breed, hind, last, raise, stern, tail, tower
reared	= bred
reason	= cause, excuse, grounds, logic, mind, motive, point, sense, think, wit, why
(without) reason	= crazy, daft, insane, mad, nuts, wild
reasonable	= cheap, fair, logical, modest, sound
rebel	= mutiny, revolt, riot, rise
rebound	= bounce, recoil, resound, ricochet
rebuke	= admonish, chide, rap, scold, wig
rebut	= argue, disprove, evert, refute
receive	= accept, collect, get, hear, obtain, take
received	= got, heard, taken
receiver	= ear, fence, radio
recent	= current, fresh, late, latter, modern, new, novel
receptacle	= cup, glass, holder, mug, vessel
reception	= applause, assembly, greeting, ovation, welcome
recess	= alcove, apse, bay, niche, nook, rise
recipe	= formula, (r)
recital	= concert, prom, story, tale
reckon	= add, cast, count, deem, guess, judge, tally, think, total
recluse	= anchorite, eremite, hermit
recognise	= admit, grant, identify, know, spot
recondite	= abstruse, arcane, esoteric, secret
record	= diary, disc, enter, entry, file, journal, ledger, list, log, tape, transcribe, (cd, ep, lp)

record player	= hi-fi, stereo, turntable
recorder	= judge, magistrate, video, (vcr)
recount	= recite, relate, report, tell
recover	= heal, mend, rally, recoup, regain, revive
recreation	= diversion, fun, pastime, play, sport
recruit	= convert, enlist, enrol, rookie, tyro
recruits	= draft, intake
rectify	= amend, emend, fix, mend, remedy, right
rector	= clergy [see]
recumbent	= flat, lying, prone
red	= ablush, angry, debt, florid, flushed, left, rosy, ruddy, soviet; shade of [cardinal, carmine, cerise, cherry, crimson, damask, henna, maroon, rose, ruby, scarlet]
(in the) red	= owing
(go) red	= blush, flush
redress	= amends, rectify, relief, remedy
reduce	= abate, contract, cut, diet, pare, slim, taper
reduced	= cut, less, minus
reduction	= cut, drop, fall
reed	= arrow, grass, rush, stalk
reef	= coral, knot, ridge, vein
reefer	= jacket, midshipman, pot
reel	= bobbin, dance, pull, rock, spin, swim, spool, stagger, whirl, wind
refine	= clarify, improve, perfect, polish
refined	= civil, delicate, genteel, urbane
refinement	= culture, nicety, nuance, polish, taste
reflect	= image, mirror, portray, rebound, think
reflection	= echo, idea, image, study, thought
reformatory	= name of [borstal]
refuge	= asylum, haven, port, retreat, shelter
refusal	= denial, no, option, rebuff
refuse	= decline, deny, litter, offal, resist, spurn, trash, waste
regal	= grand, majestic, noble, proud, royal
regard	= care, deem, esteem, heed, mark, note, observe, rate, respect, view
(with) regard, regarding	= about, anent, apropos, on, over, (re)
region	= area, district, domain, part, realm, sphere, tract, zone
register	= enrol, list, muster, poll, roll, roster, till
regret	= deplore, grieve, lament, rue, woe
regular	= petrol, private, soldier, uniform, usual
regulate	= adapt, adjust, control, fix
regulation	= canon, edict, law, order, rule
reign	= govern, kingdom, monarchy, nation, realm, rule, state
rein	= brake, bridle, check, curb, hold, limit

reinforcement	= brace, draft, increase, prop, support
reject	= deny, dump, jilt, refuse, scrap, spurn
rejoice	= delight, exult, gladden, glory, joy
relate	= apply, impart, refer, state, tell
relation	= bond, pi, ratio, relative [see], respect, (bro, sis)
relations	= clan, contact, family, kin(dred), liaison
relative	= aunt, brother, cousin, father, kin(sman), mother, niece, sister, uncle, (bro, sis)
(elderly) relative	= gran, nan, nanna
relax	= abate, ease, ebb, loose, repose, rest
relaxation	= ease, leisure, repose, rest
relay	= broadcast, race
release	= clear, emit, free, loose, issue, shed, untie, vent
reliable	= honest, safe, solid, sound, stable, sure, true
reliance	= confidence, faith, stock, trust
relief	= aid, break, cure, ease, help, solace
relieve	= aid, break, cure, ease, help
religion	= creed, cult, faith, sect; name of [amish, buddhist, druse, hindu, huguenot, islamic, jewish, judaist], (rc)
relish	= enjoy, fancy, flavour, like, sauce, savour, spice, tang, taste
reluctant	= loath, loth, shy, unwilling
rely	= bank, bet, count, depend, trust
remain	= abide, bide, last, stay, tarry, wait
remainder	= balance, dregs, heel, over, relic, residue, rest
remains	= ash(es), body, corpse, dregs, grounds, lees, residue, rest, sediment
remark	= comment, heed, note, notice
(cutting) remark	= barb, dig, gibe, insult
(witty) remark	= crack, quip, repartee, wisecrack
remedy	= cure, heal, nostrum, panacea, redress, repair, solution, specific, treat
remiss	= careless, lax, slack, sloppy, tardy
remit	= brief, defer, delay, pay, send
remnants	= balance, odds, residue, scraps
remote	= aloof, distant, far(away), obscure, slight, slim
remote station	= fort, outpost
remove	= doff, erase, evict, oust, purge
rend	= cleave, rip, split, tear
render	= give, make, pay, provide, show, yield
renegade	= apostate, rat, recreant, turncoat
renew	= refresh, restore, revive, update
renounce	= abandon, deny, disclaim, resign
renown	= eclat, fame, kudos, prestige, repute
rent	= charge, hire, lease, let, rift, rip, slash, split, tear, torn
rep	= agent, cloth, fabric, material, theatre, traveller
repair	= fix, go, mend, nail, patch, sew, stitch

repartee	= banter, exchange, retort, riposte
repay	= avenge, requite, revenge
repeat	= again, copy, ditto, echo, redo, renew
repent	= atone, lament, regret, rue
repine	= complain, fret
replica	= copy, duplicate, model
report	= bruit, bulletin, buzz, fame, news, relate, shot, story, tell
reporter	= editor, journalist, journo, (ed)
reporters	= press
represent	= depict, figure, portray, serve, show
representative	= agent, delegate, deputy, rep, (mp)
reprieve	= commute, pardon, redeem, relief, rescue, respite
reprimand	= chide, rap, rate, roast, scold, wig
reproach	= blame, chide, rap, rate, rebuke, scold, upbraid, wig
reproof	= blame, lecture, rap, rebuke, reproach
reprove	= censure, chide, criticise, rebuke, scold
reptile	= alligator, cayman, croc(odile), gavial, iguana, lizard, saurian, snake, tortoise, turtle; name of snake [see]
repudiate	= deny, disown, rat, reject, spurn, turn
reputable	= good, honest, proper, upright
request	= appeal, ask, plea, seek, solicit
require	= demand, lack, need, oblige, want, wish
requite	= avenge, repay, revenge
rescript	= decree, edict, decretal, mandate
research	= dig, explore, probe, quest, study
resent	= detest, dislike, hate
reserve	= book, spare, sub(stitute), (ta)
reserved	= aloof, cool, demure, modest, shy
reservoir	= basin, dam, pond, stock, tank, well
reside	= abide, dwell, lie, live, lodge, stay
resident	= citizen, denizen, inmate, occupier, settler, tenant
residue	= dregs, excess, extra, rest, surplus
resign	= cede, forgo, leave, quit, vacate
resigned	= left, passive, quit, stoic, submissive
resin	= amber, balm, balsam, benzoin, glue, gum, lac, sap
resist	= combat, counter, defy, fight, oppose, refuse, repel
resistance	= hindrance, opposition, refusal, (r)
resolute	= adamant, bold, firm, intent, set
resolution	= guts, heart, mettle, resolve, spirit
resolve	= determine, fix, settle
resort	= frequent, haunt, recourse, seaside, turn

(health) resort	= hydro, spa
(French) resort	= name of [cannes, nice, riviera]
respect	= admire, esteem, honour, regard
respite	= break, halt, hiatus, lull, pause, reprieve, rest, truce
respond	= answer, react, reply, retort
response	= answer, reply, retort, return
(nervous) response	= spasm, tic
responsibility	= duty, guilt, onus, power, trust
rest	= balance, base, break, ease, heel, lie, others, relax, repose, residue, respite, spell, support
rested	= lain, sat
restful	= calm, quiet, serene, soothing, tranquil
resting-place	= cemetery, grave(yard), tomb
restive	= edgy, tense, uneasy, uptight
restore	= fix, mend, paint, recover, renew, revive, update
restrain	= bridle, check, curb, muzzle, rein
restrict	= bound, bridle, confine, cramp, harness, rein, tie
restriction	= bit, bridle, cramp, harness, rein
result	= answer, arise, end, ensue, flow, fruit, issue, outcome, spring, stem, upshot
retain	= enjoy, grasp, hold, keep, own, save
retainer	= clip, fee, frame, servant
retaliation	= reprisal, revenge, vengeance
retinue	= entourage, following, suite, train
retire	= quit, recede, retreat, withdraw
retired	= abed, asleep
retiring habit	= neglige, nightcap, nightdress, pyjamas
retort	= answer, reply, response, riposte; name of instrument [alembic, convert]
retreat	= ashram, asylum, haven, hermitage, monastery, port, recede, refuge, retire, shelter, withdraw
return	= earn, gain, recur, remit, repay, yield
(sound) return	= echo
returned	= back, home
reveal	= betray, blab, disclose, divulge, expose, show, tell, uncover
revel	= bask, festivity, frolic, gambol, party, spree
revenge	= redress, repay, requite
revenue	= duty, income, tax, tithe, vat
revere	= adore, esteem, fear, respect, worship
reverence	= awe, esteem, fear, homage, respect
reverse	= annul, back, contrary, counter, invert, opposite, revoke, setback, tails, verso
review	= audit, check, inspect, notice, scan
reviewer	= arbiter, critic, judge
revise	= alter, amend, correct, edit, emend, redo, update
revive	= rally, recall, recover, renew, restore

revolt	=	mutiny, putsch, rebel, repel, riot, rise, rising, sicken
revolting	=	evil, foul, horrid, obscene, vile
revolution	=	circuit, coup, orbit, revolt, turn
revolutionary	=	che, novel, radical, rebel, red
revolve	=	circle, gyrate, orbit, spin, turn
revolver	=	gun, rotor, top, wheel
revue	=	play, review, show
reward	=	bonus, bounty, carrot, medal, pay, prize
rhyme	=	ode, logic, poem, suit, tally, verse
rhythm	=	beat, cadence, metre
rib	=	bone, chaff, kid, rag, tease
ribbon	=	band, strip, tape
rich	=	flush, opulent, wealthy
riches	=	fortune, wealth
rid	=	clear, dispose, free, lose, lost, purge
riddle	=	enigma, mystery, poser, problem, puzzle, sieve, why
ride	=	bait, canter, cycle, drive, travel, trot
rider	=	addendum, appendix, clause, codicil, condition, cossack, equestrian, horseman, hussar, jockey, (ps)
(bare back) rider	=	godiva [Lady Godiva]
ridge	=	crease, crest, fold, range, watershed
ridicule	=	banter, deride, gibe, guy, mock, taunt, twit
rifle	=	gun, gut, loot, ransack, rob, plunder, search, steal
rig	=	clothes [see], equip, fit, fix, tackle, tamper, trick
right	=	apt, correct, due, exact, fit, lien, just, meet, proper, tick, true, (r, rt)
(put) right	=	emend, fix, mend, redeem, repair
rights and wrongs	=	merits
right-hand page	=	recto
righteous	=	ethical, just, moral, virtuous
rigid	=	exact, fixed, harsh, set, stern, stiff
rigour	=	cruelty, difficulty, hardship, severity
rile	=	agitate, anger, annoy, irritate, upset
rill	=	brook, burn, rivulet, runnel, stream
rim	=	brink, border, edge, hem, lip, verge
rime	=	frost, ice
ring	=	arena, band, bell, call, circle, contact, disc, halo, hoop, loop, peal, round, toll, (o)
rink	=	ice
riot	=	anarchy, disorder, revel(ry), tumult
riotous gathering	=	mob
rip	=	cut, damage, libertine, rake, rend, rent, rive, roue, screw, split, tear
ripping	=	splendid, super, swell, terrific
riposte	=	answer, repartee, reply, retort, thrust

rise	= ascend, climb, grow, hill, lift, mount, recess, rouse, soar, swell, tor, up
rising	= ascent, up, revolt, upping
rishi	= ascetic, poet, sage, saint, seer
risk	= chance, danger, gamble, hazard, peril
risk money	= ante, bet, gamble, punt, stake, wager
rite	= ceremony, liturgy, ritual, service
rival	= compete, contend, contest, emulate, vie
rivalry	= conflict, contest, duel, needle, struggle, vying
rive	= cleave, rend, rip, split, tear
riven	= rent, split, torn
river	= banker, flower, runner, stream; name of [aire, avon, cam, dart, dee, exe, fal, isis, ouse, severn, shannon, tay, tees, test, thames, tyne, ure, usk, wash, wear, wye], (r)
(African) river	= name of [congo, gambia, limpopo, niger, nile, orange, vaal, zaire, zambesi]
(French) river	= name of [loire, rhone, saone, seine, somme]
(German) river	= name of [danube, elbe, lech, main, oder, rhine, ruhr]
(Indian) river	= name of [ganges, indus]
(Italian) river	= name of [arno, po, tiber]
(Oxford) river	= name of [isis]
(part of) river	= reach, stretch
(stretch of) river	= reach
rivet	= (af)fix, attach, bolt, enthral, fasten
road	= avenue, lane, motorway, route, street, way, (m, mi, rd, st)
(German) road	= autobahn
(mountain) road	= col, pass
road surface	= asphalt, tar
roadwork(s)	= stop
roam	= drift, prowl, range, rove, stray, wander
roast	= broil, cook, drub, flay, slam, swelter
rob	= burgle, loot, steal, swindle, thieve
robber	= bandit, brigand, burglar, gangster, outlaw, thief
(Irish) robber	= tory
(old) robber	= brigand, footpad, highwayman, pirate
robe	= gown, kimono, toga, vestment, wrapper
robust	= fit, healthy, potent, sound, strong
rock	= gem, reel, stone, shake, sway, swing, (gib)
rock music	= lullaby
rocks	= diamonds, ice, scree
rocket	= flare, maroon, missile, reprimand, retro, soar
rod	= bar, baton, cane, ingot, perch, pole, staff, stick, switch, whip
rodent	= name of [agouti, bandicoot, beaver, cavy, coypu, gerbil, guinea-pig, hare, jerboa, mouse, rabbit, rat, shrew, squirrel, vole]

rogue	= heel, knave, rascal, scamp, scoundrel, twister, villain
role	= duty, job, part, post, task
roll	= bap, bread, furl, list, rock, roster, run, toss, turn, wad
roller	= breaker, comber, wave
romance	= affair, amour, love, novel
romeo	= lover
rood	= arch, beam, cloth, cross, crucifix, loft, screen
roof	= apex, cover, crest, crown, peak, top
rook	= bleed, castle, crow, fleece, sharper, soak, sting
room	= den, lodge, margin, play, scope, space, stowage; name of [attic, ben, but, foyer, kitchen, loft, lounge, parlour, salon]
(brothers') room	= cell
(dining) room	= canteen, mess
(small) room	= cell, loo, toilet
root	= base, cause, grub, origin, plant, rad
rope	= bind, cord, hemp, lanyard, lasso, painter, string, tie, twine
rose	= brier, damask, flower, hip, up
rosette	= badge, cockade, favour, prize, ribbon(s)
roster	= duty, list, muster, roll, rota, scroll, table
rostrum	= dais, platform, pulpit, stage
rosy	= florid, flushed, hopeful, red, ruddy
rot	= bosh, bunk(um), decay, decline, spoil, tripe
rotten	= bad, corrupt, fetid, foul, rank, sour
rotter	= bounder, cad, cur, louse, rat, swine
rota	= list, roll, roster, register, table
roue	= letcher, libertine, playboy, rake
rough	= coarse, draft, harsh, hooligan, rowdy, thug, tough, uncut, uneven
roughly	= about, almost, around, circa, nearly, (c)
roughness	= asperity, severity
round	= about, almost, circle, lap, near, ring, rotund, (o)
round of tennis	= set
rouse	= call, incite, rise, stir, wake
rout	= defeat, mob, overrun, rabble, retreat, riot, trounce, tumult
route	= beat, course, path, road, steer, way
routine	= habit, regimen, regular, rote, usual
rove	= drift, range, roam, stray, wander
row	= brawl, din, hedge, line, noise, quarrel range, rank, tier, tiff
rowdy	= hooligan, rough, tough, thug
royal	= kingly, queenly, regal, sovereign
royal cipher	= muster
royal family	= name of [stuart, tudor, windsor, york]
rub	= buff, fray, grate, polish, shine, wipe

rub out	= destroy, dispatch, erase, kill, slay
rubber	= eraser, masseur, masseuse
rubbish	= bunk, chaff, debris, offal, refuse, rot, tat, trash, waste
ruche	= frill, gather, pleat, ruffle
ruddy	= florid, flushed, healthy, red, rosy
rude	= coarse, crass, impudent, insolent, low, raw, unbred, vulgar
rue	= deplore, pity, regret, sorrow
ruff	= collar, frill, trump; name of fish
ruffle	= disturb, flutter, frill, quarrel, toss
rug	= carpet, mat
rugby player	= flank, hooker, lock, prop; name of [lion, puma, springbok, wallaby]
ruin	= collapse, damage, downfall, havoc, rack, shatter, spoil, undoing, wreck
rule	= axiom, canon, control, decree, edict, govern, law, maxim, reign, run
ruler	= emperor, empress, king, monarch, prince, queen
(absolute) ruler	= autocrat, despot, dictator, tyrant
(eastern) ruler	= aga, ameer, amir, emir, shah, sultan
(Russian) ruler	= czar, tsar
rum	= odd, peculiar, queer, spirit
(more) rum	= odder
ruminate	= brood, muse, ponder, reflect, think
rumour	= bruit, buzz, canard, gossip, hearsay, noise
run	= bolt, bye, canter, control, double, flee, gallop, hie, hurry, jog, ladder, lope, manage, play, roll, rule, single, smuggle, speed, sprint, trot, (r)
runaway	= emigre, evacuee, fugitive, refugee
run away, off	= bolt, elope, flee, go, skedaddle
run after	= chase, pursue
run circles	= lap
run down	= disparage, ill, knock, pan, sick, slate
run naked	= streak
run out	= cease, end, finish, peter
rung	= bar, notch, rod, step, spoke, stave
runner	= athlete, bean, hare, harrier, horse, jogger, messenger, miler, river, ski, smuggler, sprinter, stolon, tendril, tout; name of river [see]
runway	= gangway, strip, track, trail
Rupert	= bear
ruse	= device, dodge, feint, ploy, trick, wile
rush	= charge, dart, dash, fly, reed, run, shoot, spate, tear
rushed	= flew, ran, shot, tore
Russian	= ivan, red, soviet; name of [lenin, stalin]

Russian boy, man = name of [boris, igor, ivan, serge]
Russian money = name of [rouble]
Russian ruler = czar, tsar
rust = corrode
rustic = arcadian, bucolic, country, pastoral, rural
rut = channel, furrow, grind, groove, heat, track,
ruth, grief, misery, pity, sorrow
ruthless = brutal, cruel, hard, harsh

S

sable = black, dark, fur, marten
sabotage = destroy, subvert, wreck
sack = axe, bag, boot, cashier, chop, fire, loot, pillage,
plunder, push, rifle, ruin, wine
sacking = hessian
sacred = blessed, divine, holy, solemn
sacrifice = forego, forfeit, lose, loss, surrender
sad = blue, dismal, doleful, down, glum, low, sombre,
sorry, triste, unhappy
(very) sad = awful, dire, tragic, wretched
saddle = burden, charge, col, encumber, lumber
sadness = blues, dolour, grief, misery, sorrow
safe = coffer, intact, ok(ay), peter, secure, vault
safety = asylum, cover, refuge, shelter
sag = droop, fall, flag, hang, sink
saga = epic, exploit, series, story
sage = green, guru, luminary, pundit, sapient, savant,
wise; name of [nestor, solomon, solon]
sail = canvas, cruise, embark, voyage
sailing boat, ship, vessel = name of (sailing) boat [see]
sailor = hand, jack, lascar, matelot, rating, salt, seaman,
tar, (ab, po)
saint = name of [andrew, david, george, patrick, peter],
(st)
salary = income, pay, stipend
sale = auction, bargain, bazaar, deal, market
sales talk = pitch
sallow = ashen, pale, pallid, wan
sally = foray, quip, raid, sortie, thrust
salt = corn, sailor [see], (ab)
salute = greet, hail, honour, kiss, tribute
salvage = glean, redeem, rescue, save
salve = balm, cream, ointment, salvage [see]
same = alike, ditto, equal, idem, twin, very, (do)
sample = model, pilot, taste, test, trial, try
sample of cloth = swatch
sanction = allow, back, ban, boycott, embargo, endorse,
justify, penalty, ratify, veto

sanctuary	=	altar, asylum, church, haven, refuge, shrine, shelter, temple
sand	=	desert, dune, grit, polish
sandbank	=	hurst, shoal; name of [dogger]
sane	=	lucid, sensible, sober, sound
sap	=	drip, fluid, fool, idiot, jerk, twit
Sarah	=	sal(ly)
sarcasm	=	contempt, irony, satire, scorn
sash	=	band, frame, obi, scarf
satan	=	devil, lucifer
satanic	=	devilish, diabolic, evil
satellite	=	moon, puppet, sputnik; name of [titan]
satisfaction	=	amends, justice, liking, redress
satisfactory	=	fair, ok(ay)
satisfied	=	content, happy, met
satisfy	=	fulfil, gratify, meet, pacify, please, sate, settle, square
saturate	=	douse, drench, soak, steep, water, wet
sauce	=	brass, cheek, lip, nerve, relish
saucy	=	cheeky, impudent, pert, smart, stylish
saurian	=	alligator, cayman, croc(odile), gavial
savage	=	brutal, cruel, feral, fierce, native, vicious, wild
save	=	also, but, collect, deliver, except, hoard, keep, redeem, rescue, store
savour	=	enjoy, like, relish, smack, taste
saw	=	adage, axiom, cut, gnome, maxim, proverb, saying; name of [fret, hack, panel, tenon]
say	=	declare, speak, state, tell, utter, voice, (eg)
saying	=	adage, axiom, gnome, maxim, proverb, saw
scale	=	balance, climb, extent, pitch, ratio
(musical) scale	=	do(h), ray, re, me, mi, fa(h), so(h), la(h), te, ti
scamp	=	imp, knave, rascal, rogue
scan	=	check, con, read, scour, skim, view
Scandinavian	=	dane, nordic, norse, swede, viking
Scandinavian money	=	name of [krone, ore]
scant(y)	=	bare, meagre, poor, sparse, thin
scar	=	blemish, cicatrice, cliff, hilum, mark, weal, wound
scarce	=	rare, scant, short, uncommon
scarcity	=	dearth, famine, poverty, rarity, want
scare	=	alarm, awe, daunt, fright, panic, shock, start
scarlet	=	immoral, red, sinful, vivid
scatter	=	diffuse, dispel, litter, sow, strew
scattered	=	sown, strewn
scene	=	arena, field, panorama, picture, set, site, view, vista
scene of fighting	=	front, theatre

scent	= aroma, odour, perfume, smell, spice, track, trail
scheme	= design, device, plan, plot, ploy, project, ruse
schism	= breach, chasm, rent, rift, split
scholar	= learner [see], (ba, l, ma)
scholarly	= erudite, learned
school	= academy, coach, college, drill, train
(public) school	= name of [eton, harrow, radley, rugby]
scientist	= boffin; name of [bell, darwin, edison, newton]
scoff	= consume, deride, despise, eat, gibe, jeer, mock, scorn
scoffed	= ate
scold	= berate, chid(e), jaw, nag, rag, rail, rate, shrew, termagant, wig
scoop	= exclusive, haul, ladle, scuttle, shovel
scope	= orbit, play, radius, range, reach, room
scorch	= bake, burn, flay, roast, singe, swelter
score	= chip, deuce, goal, mark(s), notch, scratch, tab, try, tally, twenty, win
scot	= levy, tax
Scot(sman)	= mac, mon; name of [an(gus), ian, jock, rab(bie), sandy]
Scots know	= ken
Scottish one	= yin
Scottish county	= name of [argyll, ayr, bute, elgin, fife, forfar, moray, nairn, perth, ross]
scoundrel	= cad, cheat, cur, heel, knave, rat, rogue
scour	= buff, comb, hunt, rub, scrub, search
scourge	= cat, curse, flay, flog, knout, plague, switch, whip
scowl	= frown, glower, lower
scramble	= eggs, hash, melee, rush, tussle
scrap	= bit, brawl, crumb, ditch, dump, fight, jot, piece, rag
scraps	= crumbs, odds, remnants
scrape	= abrade, brush, fix, graze, hole, jam, scratch, scrimp, shave, spot
scratch	= claw, erase, itch, mark, score, scrape, scribble, strike, withdraw
screen	= conceal, cover, film, hide, monitor, project, protect, rood, show, sieve, sift, vet
screw	= exact, extort, gaoler, jailer, pay, rip, salary, wage(s), wrinkle
scribe	= clerk, notary, pen(man), write(r)
scrip	= bag, pouch, satchel
script	= dialogue, hand, lines, text, words
scripture	= bible, granth, koran, talmud, tantra, torah, (nt, ot, re, ri)
scrounge	= beg, cadge, sponge, wheedle

scrub	= bath, cancel, clean, drop, drudge, forget, scour
scull	= boat, oar
sculptor	= name of [bernini, cellini, michelangelo, rodin]
sculpture	= atlantes, carve, chisel, model, statue
scuttle	= dash, hare, run, scoot, sink
scythe	= crop, cut, mow, shear, trim
sea	= billow, brine, deep, main, ocean, surf, tide, wave; name of [aegean, baltic, black, china, coral, dead, irish, med, north, red, tasman]
(stay at) sea	= avast
sea-animal	= name of [dolphin, dugong, morse, orc(a), porpoise, seal, sealion, walrus, whale]
seabird	= name of [albatross, auk, cormorant, gannet, gull, pelican, tern, skua]
sea-creature	= fish, fish [see], sea-animal [see]
sea-food	= scampi; name of fish [see]
sea mammal	= sea-animal [see]
seaman	= sailor [see]
seaside	= beach, coast, resort, sands, shore, strand
sea song	= shanty
seaweed	= alga(e), dulse, kelp, tang, wrack
seal	= cachet, clinch, close, cork, plug, secure, stamp, stop
seam	= fissure, join(t), junction, scar, union
sear	= arid, blast, burn, dried, dry, scorch, wither(ed)
search	= comb, ferret, hunt, quest, rake, rifle, scour
season	= pepper, salt, spice, term, time; name of [autumn, fall, spring, summer, winter]
seasoning	= mint, relish, sage, sauce, thyme
seat	= base, beam, hub, rear; name of [bench, chair, divan, ottoman, pillion, saddle, sedan, settee, settle, sofa, stall, stool]
second	= back, instant, moment, sponsor, support, transfer, (mo, s, sec)
second-hand	= old, used
secrecy	= hush, silence, stealth
secret	= closet, covert, deep, hidden, privy
secret agent	= bond [James], spook, spy
secret society	= tong
secrete	= bury, cache, hide, stash
section	= cut, part, piece, sector, slice, zone
secure	= close, confine, fortify, lock, reliable, safe
security	= bond, collateral, custody, guard, safety
security card	= pass, permit
sedate	= calm, composed, equable, placid, serene, sober, staid, tranquil
sedentary	= sitting, stationary
sediment	= dregs, grounds, lees

see	= espy, eye, lo, look, note, notice, observe, spot, twig, understand, vide, view, witness
seed	= egg, embryo, germ, grain, pea, pip
seedy bar	= dive
seem	= appear, look, sound
seep	= dribble, drip, emit, exude, leak, ooze
seepage	= dribble, drip, leak, trickle
seer	= augur, oracle, prophet, rishi
seethe	= boil, fume, rage, simmer, soak, stew
seize	= annex, arrest, capture, grab, snatch, take
seizure	= arrest, capture, fit, spasm, stroke
select	= choice, choose, chosen, elect, pick
self	= ego, me, same
self-satisfied	= smug
sell	= flog, hawk, market, retail, trade, vend
(try to) sell	= tout
seller	= bear, hawker, merchant, trader, vendor
(ticket) seller	= tout
semi	= demi, half, house, (bi)
send	= charm, dispatch, post, remit, thrill
senile	= aged, doting, feeble, old
senility	= anility, dotage
senior	= elder, higher, older
senior academic	= don, prof
sense	= crux, deem, feel, gist, grasp, gumption, nous, nub, wit; name of [hearing, sight, smell, taste, touch]
sensation	= feeling, hit, marvel, scandal, thrill, tingle, wonder, wow
(gaol, jail) sentence	= life, stretch, time
sentinel, sentry	= guard, lookout, picket, watch
separate	= divorce, part, sever, single, split
separated	= apart, asunder, split
sequin	= glitter, spangle
sere	= sear [see]
serene	= calm, placid, sedate, tranquil
serf	= bondsman, helot, slave, vassal
series	= chain, cycle, order, row, string, train
series of operations	= campaign
serious	= acute, deep, earnest, grave, grim, major, severe, sober, staid, stern
(not) serious	= carefree, frivolous, light
seriousness	= gravitas, gravity, severity
serum	= blood, plasma
servant	= butler, buttons, friday, help, lackey, retainer, serf, slave
(college) servant	= scout, skip
(hotel) servant	= bellboy, boots, concierge, housekeeper, maid, page, porter, valet

serve	=	act, avail, do, foster, treat, wait
service	=	ace, duty, fault, force, let, ministry, rite, teaset, use; name of [army, marines, navy], (raf, rm, rn)
(church) service	=	worship; name of [mass, matin, vespers]
(memorial) service	=	obit
servicemen	=	army, marines, militia, navy
servicewoman	=	wren, (ats)
servile	=	abject, base, low, menial, slavish
set	=	cast, firm, fix, circle, clique, coterie, gel, group, lay, plant, prepare, put, radio, ready, scene, sect, suite
(film) set	=	location
set aside	=	quash
set off	=	atone, balance, leave, mount, trigger
set down	=	alight, land, light, list
set forth	=	deliver, depart, go, leave, present
setback	=	check, relapse, reversal, reverse
setter	=	i, me [compiler of crossword]; name of [gelatin, glue, gum, jelly, paste]
setter's	=	mine, my [compiler's]
settle	=	agree, allay, bench, calm, determine, pay, people, resolve, seat, sink
settle down	=	compose, relax
(marriage) settlement	=	dowry, portion
settler	=	colonist, migrant, pioneer, planter
sever	=	cut, part, rend, split, sunder
severe	=	acute, bleak, grim, hard, harsh, stern, strict, violent
sew	=	attach, close, fasten, join, mend, stitch
sex appeal	=	it, oomph, (sa)
shabby	=	dingy, faded, mean, seedy, tatty
shabby goods	=	tat
shade	=	colour [see], ghost, hint, hue, spectre, spirit [see], tinge, tint
shadow	=	dog, dusk, gloom, shade, trace, umbra
shaft	=	arrow, axle, bar, barb, beam, dart, handle, ray, stalk, stem
shake	=	jar, quake, rock, shock, tremble, tremor, wink
shakes	=	ague, fever
Shakespearean forest	=	arden
shallow	=	idle, shoal, shelf, surface, trivial
shallow vessel	=	charger, platter, salver, tray
sham	=	bogus, fake, false, feign, fraud, hoax, humbug, pretend, pseudo
shambles	=	chaos, havoc, mess
shame	=	blot, infamy, odium, scandal, smear
shamus	=	detective, policeman, (pi)
shanghai	=	coerse, dragoon, force, press

shanty	= cabin, cot, hovel, hut, shack, song
shape	= build, cast, figure, form, mould, trim
share	= cut, divide, lot, part, portion, quota, ration, split, stock
shared	= joint, split
shares	= scrip, stock
(buy) shares	= invest, speculate
sharp	= acrid, acute, alert, argute, clever, intelligent, keen, smart, quick, wily
sharpen	= edge, grind, hone, strop, whet
sharpener	= grinder, grindstone, strop
sharpness	= acumen, edge
shatter	= break, dash, rive, ruin, smash, wreck
shave	= glance, kiss, pare, prune, scrape, skim, trim
shave(n) head	= tonsure
shear	= clip, crop, cut, lop, pare, prune, trim
shed	= barn, discard, ditch, drop, hut, moult, shack
sheen	= glaze, gloss, lustre, polish, shine
sheep	= ewe, flock, lamb, ram, teg, tup; name of [merino, leicester]
sheepish	= coy, shy, silly
sheer	= plumb, pure, steep, utter, vertical
sheet	= coat, film, leaf, linen, page, paper
shelf	= ledge, mantel, plank, rack, shoal, sill
shell	= blitz, bomb, case, conch, hull, husk, nut, pod, skin
shellfish	= mollusc; name of [abalone, clam, cockle, crab, lobster, mussel, oyster, prawn, scallop, shrimp, winkle]
shelter	= cover, lee, hangar, harbour, haven, port, refuge, shield, tent
shelve	= defer, delay, stay, store, table, waive
shield	= aegis, armour, defence, protect, screen; name of [blazon, buckler, targe(t)]
shift	= chemise, move, rota, ship, spell, stint, turn
ship	= boat [see], remit, route, send, (ss)
(Jason's) ship	= argo
(sailing) ship	= name of (sailing) boat [see]
(war)ship	= corvette, cruiser, destroyer, frigate, (sub)
shipping company	= line; name of [cunard]
ships	= armada, escadrille, fleet, flotilla
ship's back	= aft, counter, stern
ship's deck	= name of [focsle, orlop, poop]
ship's front	= bow, prow, stem
ship's kitchen	= caboose, galley
ship's stern	= aft, counter
shirk	= avoid, dodge, duck, evade
shiver	= shake, tremor, quake, quiver, smash

shivers	=	ague, fever, shakes
shock	=	appal, blast, heap, jar, jolt, pile, stun, trauma
shocking	=	atrocious, awful, dire, foul, odious
shoe	=	footwear [see]
(dancing) shoe	=	pump
shoemaker	=	cobbler, snob
shoot	=	bag, bud, fire, kill, scion, snipe, sprout, tendril, twig
shop	=	outlet, store, trade
shopping centre	=	arcade, mall, market, mart, plaza
short	=	blunt, brief, brusque, curt, deficient, little, scant, terse, under
(cut) short	=	abort, abridge, dock, lop
short break	=	hol[iday], vac[ation]
short dress	=	mini
short flight	=	hop
short walk	=	prom
shortage	=	dearth, deficit, lack, want
shortcoming	=	defect, fault, flaw, sin
shorten	=	abridge, cut, prune, trim
shortening	=	fat, lard
shot	=	attempt, bullet, fling, go, guess, hit, injection, jab, lob, nip, pellet, slug, snap, spell, stab, tot, try, turn
(bad golf) shot	=	hook, shank, slice
shots	=	barrage, enfilade, fusillade, volley
should	=	ought, must
shout	=	cry, roar, treat, well, whoop, yell
shove	=	drive, jostle, propel, push, thrust
shovel	=	dig(ger), scoop, spade
show	=	cabaret, comedy, depict, drama, expose, farce, flaunt, film, play, pomp, portray, represent, reveal, revue, screen
(passing) show	=	pageant, parade
show film	=	project
show off	=	air, boast, brag, flaunt, swagger
shower	=	fall, pelt, rain, stream
shred	=	cut, grain, scrap, speck, strip, tear
shrew	=	hag, harridan, mouse, scold, termagant, virago, vixen
shrewd	=	arch, argute, astute, clever, cunning, sharp
shrill	=	argute, high, screech, sharp, shriek
shrine	=	tabernacle, tomb
shrink	=	contract, cower, recoil, quail, wince
shrivel	=	dry, parch, sear, sere, wither, wilt
shrub	=	bush; name of [azalea, banksia, box, bramble, broom, buddleia, fuchsia, magnolia, myrtle, privet, rose, rue]

shuffle	= amble, drag, jumble, limp, mix
shun	= avoid, duck, eschew, evade
shut	= bar, close, fasten, seal, slam
shut up	= gaol, imprison, jail
shy	= cast, coy, demure, modest, throw, timid, toss, wary
sic	= so, thus
sick	= ailing, feeble, green, ill, infirm
sicken	= ail, disgust, nauseate, repel, revolt
sickening	= emetic, nauseous
sickness	= ailment, complaint, disease, disorder, illness, infirmity, malady, nausea
side	= bias, edge, eleven, flank, lateral, team, wing, (l, r)
(cricket) side	= leg, off, on
(soccer) side	= city, rovers, united; name of [arsenal, celtic, everton, rangers, spurs, villa, wolves]
sideways	= askew, aslant, oblique
(move, walk) sideways	= crab, edge, sidle
sidle	= crab, edge
siesta	= doze, nap, rest, sleep, snooze
sieve	= riddle, sift [see]
sift	= comb, filter, screen, sieve, sort
sight	= eye, mess, scene, see, view, vision
sighted	= saw, seen
sightseer	= eye, pupil, tourist
sign	= clue, hint, logo, mark, neon, omen, plus, symptom, token, trace, wave, zodiac [see]
(indian) sign	= totem
sign of approval	= nod, tick
sign of omission	= caret
sign on	= employ, enlist, enrol(l), hire
sign up	= enlist, enrol, join
signal	= beacon, cue, flag, flare, gesture, hint, light, marked, morse, very, wave
signet	= ring, seal
significance	= import, meaning, moment, sense, weight
signpost	= landmark, milestone
silage	= alfalfa, forage, lucerne
silence	= calm, hush, peace, quiet, stifle, still, (sh)
silent	= dumb, mum, mute(d), quiet, still, tacit
sill	= ledge, shelf
silly	= absurd, banal, clot, crazy, cuckoo, inane, mad, simple, twit
silk	= counsel, fabric, fibre, material, thread
similar	= akin, like, such, uniform
simmer	= boil, churn, fume, seethe, stew
simple	= artless, easy, herb, naive, plain, pure, silly

simpleton	= cretin, dope, dunce, fool, idiot, moron, muff, mug(gins), mutt, noodle
sin	= crime, err, evil, tort, vice, wrong
since	= after, as, now
sincere	= artless, candid, frank, open, true
sinful	= bad, evil, wicked, wrong
sing	= chant, croon, inform, squeal, yodel
singer	= bard, diva, kettle, minstrel, poet; name of voice [see]; name of songbird [see]
(old) singer	= bing [Crosby]
singers	= choir, chorale, chorus, glee
singe	= burn, char, scorch, sear
single	= one, lone, mono, run, unit, (i)
singlet	= vest
sink	= decline, droop, ebb, fall, founder, lower, sag, scuttle, settle
sinus	= cavity, hollow
sister	= nun, nurse
sit	= model, perch, pose, seat, settle
site	= locus, place, plot, point, position, scene, spot
(archaeological) site	= dig; name of [olduvai, thebes, ur]
sitter	= model, poser
(were) sitting	= sat
situation	= locus, job, place, post, site, spot
size	= bulk, extent, height, volume, width, (l, m, s)
(paper) size	= name of [atlas, crown, demy, elephant, foolscap, imperial, medium, quarto, royal]
skate	= glide, ski
sketch	= diagram, draft, draw, outline, paint
skid	= slide, slip, slew
skill	= art, craft, finesse, flair, knack, talent
skilful, skilled	= able, adept, deft, expert, hot
skilled man	= artisan
skim	= brush, cream, glide, scan
skimp	= pinch, scamp, scant, stint
skin	= buff, cover, cutis, fleece, fur, hide, husk, peel, pelt, rind, uncover
skin complaint	= name of [acne, eczema, fungus, impetigo]
skinflint	= miser, scrooge
skip	= bob, bolt, bucket, cage, caper, captain, flee, frisk, gambol, hop, jump, lope, miss, omit, pass, run
skipper	= captain
sky	= azure, blue, heaven
slab	= bar, block, chunk, piece, slice, wedge
slack	= idle, lax, limp, loose, remiss, slow
(not) slack	= tight, taut

slacken	= abate, ease, ebb, fall, reduce, wane
slag	= clinkers, dross, scoria
slam	= bang, beat, censure, criticise, hit, pan, whip; name of [grand, little]
slander	= calumny, defamation, defame
slang	= argot, cant, jargon, lingo, patois
slant	= aim, angle, bias, skew, slope, tilt
slap	= box, clout, cuff, hit, smack, whack
slap-up	= fancy, lavish
slash	= cut, gash, hack, reduce, rent, tear
slat	= blind, louvre, strip
slate	= malign, pan, rail, roast, tablet
slaughter	= butcher(y), carnage, kill, murder, slay
slaughter-house	= abattoir, butchery, shambles
slave	= helot, peon, serf, toil, vassal
slavish	= abject, base, low, menial, servile
sleazy bar	= dive
sled	= sledge, sleigh, toboggan
sledge	= hammer, sled, sleigh, toboggan
sleek	= glossy, lustrous, slick, smooth
sleep	= coma, doze, nap, nod, siesta, snooze
sleep soundly	= snore, (z, zz)
sleeping	= dormant
sleight	= dexterity, feint, ploy, ruse, skill trick(ery), wile
slender	= fine, lean, scant, slight, slim, thin
slew	= skid, slide, slip, twist
slice	= cut, carve, piece, sever, slit, wedge
slice of bread	= doorstep
slick	= oily, glide, sharp, sleek, slide, smooth, suave
slide	= chute, creep, drift, sag, slip, ski
slight	= flimsy, frail, insult, minor, slim, slur, snub, spurn, thin
slim	= little, narrow, remote, slender, slight, small, tenuous, thin
slime	= mire, mud, sludge
sling	= cast, cat(apult), chuck, hurl, support, throw, toss
slip	= bloomer, err(or), fall, glide, lapse, lose, sag, shake, slide, skid, slump, steal, trip
slipper	= mule
slippery fellow	= eel
slipway	= jetty, slip
slogan	= catchword, jingle, motto, watchword
slope	= angle, cant, lean, list, slant, tilt
slot	= fit, hole, niche, notch, slit
slow	= dim, dull, easy, lax, slack
slow(ly)	= adagio, largo, lento
(move) slowly	= crawl, ease, edge
slug	= belt, bullet, draught, hit, larva, shot, wallop

sluggishness	=	apathy, inertia, langour, torpor
slump	=	drop, droop, fall, loll, plunge, sag
slung	=	cast, flung, threw, thrown
slur	=	besmirch, slight, smear, stain
sly	=	adroit, canny, clever, crafty, cunning, deep, foxy
sly person	=	fox
smack	=	box, cuff, dash, hint, hit, slap, spank, smell, taste, touch, trace
small	=	dwarf, little, midget, minor, petty, tad, tiny, wee, (s)
small chapel	=	chantry, oratory
small boy	=	abbrev. name of boy [see]
small gambling	=	spec[ulation]
small island	=	ait, inch, isle
small number	=	few, (no)
small outlay	=	song
small room	=	cell, loo, toilet
small speculation	=	spec
smaller	=	less
smaller number	=	fewer
smallest	=	least
smalls	=	ads
smart	=	ache, bright, burn, chic, cute, fly, sharp, spruce, sting, suffer, throb, trim, wise
smash	=	break, burst, crash, prang, shatter, slam, wreck
smear	=	daub, mark, smudge, soil, taint
smell	=	aroma, nose, odour, reek, scent, stench stink, tang, (bo)
smelling	=	fetid, foul, high, putrid, rotten
smile	=	beam, blessing, grin, favour
smite	=	clout, hit, strike, swat, whack
smithy	=	forge
smoke	=	cigar, cure, fag, fume, puff
smoked fish	=	name of [bloater, finnan, kipper]
smooth	=	even, flat, iron, level, sleek, slick
smuggle(r)	=	run(ner)
snack	=	bite, morsel, snap
snag	=	catch, hitch, jag, rub, tear
snake	=	creep, cur, dog, louse, rat, reptile, serpent, toad; name of [adder, anaconda, asp, boa, cobra, mamba, python, rattler, viper]
snake-like	=	anguine
snap	=	bark, bite, break, crack, nip, pop
snare	=	bait, gin, lure, net, trap, wire
sneak	=	creep, secret, skulk, slink, steal
sneer	=	gibe, jeer, jest, leer, scoff, scorn
snide	=	bogus, coin(s), fake, false, sham
snigger	=	laugh, smirk, sneer, titter

snort	= drink, drop, grunt, slug
snorter	= gale, horse, pig
snout	= beak, nose, nozzle
snowman	= yeti
snub	= affront, cut, rebuff, spurn, slight
so	= sic, such, thus
so be it	= amen
soak	= bathe, douse, drench, lush, sot, souse, steep
soaked	= sodden, sopping, wet
sober (minded)	= dry, grave, sedate, staid, (aa, tt)
soccer side	= city, rovers, united; name of [arsenal, celtic, everton, rangers, spurs, villa, wolves]
social	= concert, party, public, soiree
social gathering	= concert, function, party, soiree
socialist	= labour, marx(ist), red
society	= body, club, gentry, guild, league, people, public, union, (s)
(secret) society	= tong
(whisky and) soda	= highball
sod	= divot, grass, turf
sodden	= soaked, sopping, wet
soft	= easy, gentle, lax, mild, piano, quiet, weak, simple, (p)
soft drink	= cola, mineral, pop
soil	= earth, dirt(y), grime, stain, taint
solace	= allay, comfort, console
soldier	= para, private, ranker, recruit, regular, rookie, trooper, (gi, nco, or, re)
(African) soldier	= askari
(German) soldier	= boche, hun, jerry
(new) soldier	= recruit, rookie
(old) soldier	= archer, dragoon, lancer, moth, redcoat, veteran
(young) soldier	= cadet
soldiers	= army, battalion, brigade, division, legion, men, platoon, troop(s), unit, (re)
sole	= (a)lone, one, only, single, unique
solemn	= august, glum, grave, sombre, staid
solicit	= ask, beg, canvass, crave, exact, tout
solicitor	= harlot, lawyer [see], tout
solid	= dense, firm, hard, reliable, sound, stable, valid
solution	= answer, liquid, remedy, result, solvent, (soln)
solve	= answer, crack, fix, unravel
solver	= thee, ye, you [solver of crossword]
solver's	= thine, thy, your(s)
solvent	= liquid, menstruum
sombre	= dark, dim, dun, gloomy, dismal, solemn
some	= about, any, few, number, part, portion
somebody, someone	= name, one, (vip)

some musicians	= brass, strings, wind
something	= being, entity, object
somewhat	= bit, rather, quite
son	= issue, (s)
song	= descant, melody, poem, poetry, rhyme, verse; name of [aria, anthem, aubade, ballad, carol, chant, chorus, ditty, hymn, lay, lyric, motet, psalm, rap, shanty]
(boatman's) song	= barcarole
(festive) song	= carol
(mournful) song	= dirge, elegy, lament, requiem
(part-)song	= madrigal
(sea) song	= shanty
songbird	= bulbul, canary, lark, nightingale, thrush
songster	= alto, bass, diva, songbird [see], tenor
sonnet	= ode, poem, verse
soon	= anon, early, fast, quick
soothe	= allay, balm, calm, ease, lull, salve
soothing	= quiet, restful, serene, tranquil
soothsayer	= augur, oracle, prophet, rishi, seer
sore	= bruise, burn, rash, red, stye, tender
sorrow	= dole, grief, misery, pain, regret, woe
sorrowful	= doleful, miserable, sad, unhappy
sorry	= abject, contrite, penitent, poor, sad, unhappy
sort	= brand, category, class, genus, group, ilk, kind, order, rank, type
soul	= being, body, life, mind, psyche, spirit
sound	= channel, firm, fit, gut, hale, inlet, healthy, noise, passage, plumb, robust, solid, strait, valid, well, whole
(drunken) sound	= hic
(speed of) sound	= mach(i) [Mach 1]
sound return	= echo
(sleep) soundly	= snore, (z, zz)
soup	= bisque, broth, fix, fog, jam, potage, trouble; name of [consomme, gazpacho, minestrone]
source	= author, fount, origin, root, well
South African	= cape, (sa)
south of France	= sud
southern	= austral, (s)
souvenir	= memento, relic, reminder, token
sovereign	= expound [ex pound], free, king, lofty, monarch, regal, royal, ruler, supreme, (l)
soviet	= red, russian
sow	= pig, plant, scatter, seed, strew
(young) sow	= gilt, grice
spa	= bath, resort, spring, well
space	= air, gap, leeway, margin, room, scope
spaceshot	= mission

Spain and Portugal	= iberia
span	= bridge, cross, life, reach, term, time
spangle	= glitter, sequin
Spaniard, Spanish man	= caballero, don, grandee, hidalgo, senor
Spanish drink	= name of [sangria, sherry]
Spanish friend	= amigo
Spanish money	= name of [peseta, pistole, real]
spank	= belt, box, cuff, hit, slap, smack
span(ner)	= bridge
spar	= argue, bicker, box, mast, pole, scrap
spare	= extra, lean, over, save, skimp, thin
spark	= court, flash, germ, suitor, swain, woo
sparkle	= fizz, gleam, glint, glow, shine
sparse	= bare, meagre, poor, scant(y), thin
spasm	= fit, hic, throe, tic, twitch
spat	= gaiter, shed, spawn
spate	= deluge, flood, flow, rush, torrent
spawn	= eggs, generate, hatch, issue, roe, spat
speak	= orate, say, spiel, talk, utter, voice
speaker	= lip, mouth, orator
spear	= assagai, blade, lance, pike, shoot, stalk, trident
specialist	= consultant, expert, master
specify	= cite, define, detail, name, set
specific	= drug, express, medicine, remedy, set
specimen	= copy, example, exhibit, sample, type
speck	= blemish, blot, dot, grain, iota, jot, mark, mote, spot
spectacle	= display, event, show, sight
spectator	= observer, viewer, watcher, witness
spectators	= crowd, gate
spectre	= ghost, shade, spirit [see], vision
speculate	= guess, hazard, muse, surmise, wonder
speculation	= conjecture, guess, theory, thought
(small) speculation	= spec
speculator	= stag
speech	= address, lecture, oration, spiel, talk
speed	= gait, haste, hurry, knot, pace, rate, run, tempo, ton, (kph, mph)
speed of sound	= mach(i), [Mach 1]
spell	= bout, charm, magic, mean, patch, period, term, time, trance
spelling test	= bee
sphere	= arena, ball, globe, orb, world
spice	= aroma, dash, flavour, hint, lick, relish, scent, smack, taste; name of [chilli, cloves, garlic, ginger, mace, mustard, nutmeg, pepper, salt]
spider	= arachnid; name of [tarantula]

spike	=	ear, head, impale, nail, point, spit, sprig
spill	=	fall, lose, shed, slop, upset
spin	=	drive, reel, swim, turn, twirl, twist, weave, whirl
spin out	=	delay, eke, extend, pad
spinner	=	rotor, top
spineless	=	feeble, wan, weak, yellow
spinster	=	maid, miss
spiral	=	coil, curl, twine, twist, wind
spire	=	cone, steeple, summit
spirit	=	alcohol, animus, courage, ethos, fuel, life, mind, mood, psyche, soul
(supernatural) spirit	=	name of [angel, banshee, brownie, elf, familiar, genie, ghost, ghoul, gnome, goblin, gremlin, hobbit, hob(goblin), imp, kobold, leprechaun, manes, nix, orc, peri, pixie, pixy, puck, shade, spectre, sprite, troll, wraith]
(alcoholic) spirit	=	name of [arak, bourbon, brandy, cognac, gin, grog, hooch, irish, liqueur, liquor, meths, rum, rye, scotch, schnap(p)s, vodka, whisk(e)y]
spirits	=	alcohol, humour, liquor, mood
spirited horse	=	arab
spiritual	=	divine, holy, pure, sacred, song
spiritual charge	=	cure [of souls]
spirituous liquor	=	name of spirit [see]
spite	=	grudge, malice, rancour, thwart, vex
spiteful woman	=	bitch, cat
spitfire	=	shrew, virago, vixen
splay	=	extend, open, spread
splendid	=	fine, good, grand, great, super, (ai)
splendour	=	glory, lustre, majesty, pomp
split	=	chasm, cleft, divide, rend, rent, rift, rip, rive(n), schism, share, tear, tell, told
spoil	=	harm, hurt, impair, loot, mar, pamper, plunder, rot, ruin, taint, upset
spoils	=	booty, haul, loot, pillage, plunder, prize, swag
spoilt child	=	bantling, brat
spoke	=	foil, radius, rod, rung, said, thwart
spoken	=	oral, verbal, vocal
sponge	=	clean, loofah, lush, soak, parasite, sot, toper, wash
sponsor	=	angel, back(er), donor, fund, patron
spool	=	bobbin, reel, wind
spoor	=	scent, track, trail
sport	=	exercise, fellow, game, toy, wear; name of [athletics, bowls, bowling, boxing, cricket, croquet, cycling, fives, football, gym(nastics), hockey, jogging, polo, rackets, riding, rugby, rugger, running, sailing, skiing,

		soccer, squash, surfing, swimming, tennis, wrestling], (ru)
sporting achievement	=	cap, colours
sports item	=	event, heat, race
sportsman	=	ace, athlete, blue, champion, player; name of [boxer, cyclist, diver, fencer, golfer, harrier, hunter, hurdler, jumper, rider, runner, sprinter, swimmer, wrestler]
spot	=	ace, blot, eye, light, mole, mote, nip, pimple, pip, see, sight, site, stain, tot
spots	=	acne, rash
spouse	=	consort, dutch, helpmate, helpmeet, husband, mate, partner, wife
(former) spouse	=	ex
spout	=	chute, gush, jet, rant, speak, spew, talk, tap
spray	=	bunch, hose, mist, posy, sluice, sprig, sprinkle, squirt, syringe, water
spread	=	extend, feast, laid, lay, open, plaster, ranch, set, smear, space, splay
spree	=	fling, frolic, orgy, revel
(drinking) spree	=	bender, binge, bout, toot
sprig	=	shoot, spray, twig, youth
sprightly	=	active, agile, alert, lively, nimble, pert, spry
spring	=	bound, coil, geyser, hop, issue, leap, lope, spa, stem, vault, well
spring(time)	=	may
sprinkle	=	dust, hose, powder, spray, water
sprint	=	dart, dash, hare, race, run, whiz
sprite	=	elf, fairy, fay, goblin, imp, pixie
sprout	=	bud, grow, shoot
spruce	=	dapper, neat, smart(en), trim
spume	=	foam, froth, spray, surf
spur	=	drive, egg, goad, urge, ridge, rowel, stimulus
spurn	=	disdain, rebuff, refuse, reject, scorn, slight, snub
spurt	=	gush, jet, spew, spate, spirt, squirt
squabble	=	argue, bicker, brawl, fight, row, tiff
squad	=	band, crew, gang, party, troop
square	=	buffer, equal, even, fair, fogy, level, plaza, quits, (sq, t)
squash	=	cram, crowd, crush, juice, mash, quell
squeal	=	rat, scream, shriek, sing, wail, yell
squeeze	=	crush, hug, jam, pinch, press, squash
squirm	=	crawl, toss, twist, wriggle, writhe
squirmer	=	eel, snake, worm
stab	=	go, guess, jab, pang, pierce, prick, try, wound
stable	=	even, fast, firm, solid, sound, stall, string, stud
stableman	=	groom, sice, syce
stack	=	heap, load, lot, mass, mound, pile

staff	= crook, mace, pole, rod, shaft, stick, support
stage	= apron, dais, drama, era, mount, phase, platform, produce, pulpit, rostrum, stand, step
(on) stage	= acting
stage girl	= name of [bluebell, tiller]
stagger	= amaze, lurch, reel, stun, sway, waver
stagnant	= immobile, static, still
staid	= demure, prim, proper, sober
stain	= blot, mark, smear, soil, spot, taint
stainer	= dye, ink, pigment
stair(s)	= flight, step(s)
stake	= ante, bet, peg, pole, post, risk, wager
stale	= fetid, musty, old, sour, tired, trite
stalemate	= deadlock, draw, impasse, tie
stalk	= follow, haunt, hunt, march, stem, stride, tail, track
(bean) stalk	= halm, haulm
stall	= booth, check, delay, halt, hedge, seat, stand
stallion	= stud
stamp	= brand, cachet, ilk, label, pound, print, seal
stampede	= charge, flight, rout, rush
stance	= attitude, position, posture, site
stand	= abide, base, bear, dais, easel, endure, platform, plot, prevail, pulpit, rise, rostrum, stall, stage, tee, tolerate, trestle, tripod
stand opposite	= face
stand up for	= champion, defend
stand up to	= confront, defy oppose, resist
standard	= example, flag [see], mark, norm, par, rule, set, (std)
standing	= credit, erect, rank, status, upright
staple	= fasten, leading, main, principal
star	= ace, actor, asterisk, chief, idol, main
(evening) star	= venus
star player	= lead
(group of) stars	= constellation, nebula; name of [bull, crab, orion, plough]
stare	= gape, gaze, leer, look, ogle, peer
stark	= bald, bare, grim, nude, rigid, stiff
starkers	= bare, naked, nude, unclad
start	= alpha, arise, begin, bolt, debut, open, onset, outset
started	= arose, began, begun
starter	= crank, novice, runner, soup, tiro, (l)
starting price	= odds, (sp)
starve	= deprive, fast, hunger
state	= air, aver, country, express, kingdom, mode, mood, nation, pomp, realm, say, tell, utter;

	name of [idaho, iowa, maine, ohio, utah], (ca, cal, ga, ma, va)
stated	= firm, said, set, told
stately	= august, grand, handsome, majestic
statement	= account, bill, report, tab
static	= fixed, immobile, inert, stagnant, still
station	= base, depot, place, post, rank, site, stop, (st)
(cattle) station	= ranch
(remote) station	= fort, outpost
station-wagon	= brake
statistics	= data, facts, info, (stat, stats)
statue	= bust, figure, nude, sculpture; name of [david, liberty, venus]
(large) statue	= colossus
status	= grade, place, position, rank, standing, stature
statute	= act, decree, edict, law, rule
staunch	= allay, fast, firm, loyal, stop, true
stay	= await, bide, cease, dwell, guy, halt, linger, peg, prop, remain, rope, stop, support(er)
stay at sea	= avast
stays	= corset
St Christopher	= kit
stead	= abet, aid, help, place
steady	= beau, even, fast, firm, sure, true
(go) steady	= court, date
steal	= bone, creep, kidnap, lift, loot, nick, pinch, rifle, rob, swipe, take, thieve, tiptoe
stealing	= larceny, robbery, theft
stealth	= cunning, secrecy
steam	= boil, gas, mist, poach, vapour
steed	= charger, horse
steep	= drench, sheer, soak, souse, stiff, wet
steer	= direct, guide, pilot, point, tip
steerage	= helm, rudder, tiller, wheel
stem	= axis, bole, curb, halt, prow, stalk, stop, trunk
stench	= pong, reek, smell, stink
step	= dance, pace, rung, stair, tread, walk
sterile	= barren, hybrid, impotent, infertile
stern	= back, grim, rear, rigid, severe, strict
(ship's) stern	= aft, counter
stew	= boil, braise, cook, fume, simmer, sweat, swot; name of [goulash, haricot, hash, olio, ragout, salmi]
steward	= manager, marshal, official, waiter
stick	= adhere, baton, cane, cleave, cohere, cue, fix, glue, gum, knife, maul, paste, rod, staff, switch, wand, whip
stick out	= beetle, bulge, jut, project, protrude

sticker	= barb, glue, gum, hook, knife, label, limpet, patch, prickle, stiletto, thorn
sticking	= adhesion, bond, cohesion
stiff	= body, corpse, hard, rigid, steep, tight
stifle	= choke, mute, smother, suffocate, throttle
still	= airless, allay, calm, even, quiet, shebeen, stagnant, static, yet
stimulate (interest)	= arouse, hold, whet
stimulus	= goad, fillip, impetus, impulse, push, spur, urge
sting	= bite, burn, do, hurt, nettle, rile, smart, swindle
stink	= niff, pong, reek, smell, stench
stint	= chore, cramp, duty, shift, skimp, task
stipend	= fee, income, pay, salary, wage
stir	= ado, ferment, fuss, gaol, jug, move, rise, tumult, uproar, wake
stitch	= crochet, knit, pain, sew
stoa	= colonnade, porch, portico
stock	= capital, carry, hoard, keep, normal, soup, stem, store, strain, supply, trunk
stock exchange	= bourse, (lse, se)
stock farm	= ranch
stocking	= hose, nylon
stockist	= dealer, supplier, trader
stodgy	= boring, dull, heavy, leaden, staid
stoic	= austere, indifferent, resigned
stone	= boulder, cobble, granite, marble, ore, pebble, rock, (st)
(precious) stone	= gem, gemstone [see], jewel
stoned	= drunk, high, tight
stooge	= pawn, puppet, tool
stool	= chair, seat, sill, throne
stop	= arrest, bar, bung, cease, check, desist, end, halt, pause, period, plug, quit, seal, station, staunch, stay, tarry, terminal, terminate
stop filming	= cut
store	= depot, fund, outlet, shop, stock, stow
(arms, weapons) store	= armoury, arsenal, magazine
storehouse	= barn, granary, mine, silo
storm	= attack, beset, rage, rail, rant, rave; name of [blizzard, cyclone, gale, hurricane, tempest, tornado, typhoon]
stormy	= dark, foul, rough, violent, wild
stor(e)y	= floor; name of floor [see]
story	= account, anecdote, fable, fib, lie, saga, tale, yarn
(heroic) story	= epic, saga
(news) story	= bulletin, report
stout	= ale, brave, drink, fat, porter, staunch
stow	= cease, pack, store

stowage	= room, warehouse
straight	= direct, erect, neat, plain, pure, right
straight flier	= crow
strain	= breed, gist, music [see], stock, stress strive, tension
strait	= channel, gut, narrow, passage, sound
strand	= beach, coast, fibre, shore, string
strange	= alien, odd, peculiar, queer, rare, rum, unco, weird
strap	= belt, bind, cord, leash, thong, tie
strapped	= bound, broke, needy, poor, tied
strategic move	= tack, tactic
straw bed	= pallet
strawberry	= arbutus
stray	= drift, err, roam, rove, wander
streak	= bar, flash, run, stripe, trace
stream	= beck, brook, burn, gush, lava, pour, rill, river, rivulet, runnel
streamer	= flag, ribbon, tape; kind of [banderol(e), pennant, pennon]
street	= avenue, crescent, road, way, (st)
(back) street	= alley
strength	= brawn, force, might, muscle, power
strengthen	= bolster, boost, brace, gird, steel
stress	= accent, brunt, emphasis(e), force, hassle, strain, tension
stretch	= exercise, prolong, pull, reach, spell, time, tract
stretch of river	= reach
stretcher	= elastic, litter, rack
strict	= firm, hard, harsh, rigid, severe, tense, total, true, utter
strident	= harsh, loud, rough, severe, shrill
strife	= battle, combat, conflict, fret, odds, row, trouble, war(fare)
strike	= attack, box, clout, delete, find, hit, lam, ram, smite, swat
(on) strike	= out
striker	= bat, club, match
string	= chain, cord, fibre, rope, row, series, stable, strand, twine, (g)
strip	= band, bare, denude, divest, loot, peel, rag, runway, sack, skin
stripped	= bare, naked, nude
stripe	= band, bar, blow, chevron, streak, weal
strive	= seek, strain, toil, try, vie, work
stroke	= blow, caress, fit, mark, pet, rub, swim; name of [back, breast, butterfly, crawl]
stroll	= amble, drift, mooch, mosey, walk
strong	= firm, forte, loud, potent, robust, staunch, tough

strong wind	=	cyclone, gale, hurricane, storm [see]
strong woman	=	amazon
strongbox	=	safe
stronghold	=	bastion, bulwark, castle, citadel, fastness, fort(ress), keep, refuge
structure	=	building, edifice, erection, fabric, form, framework, pile
struggle	=	battle, contest, effort, strain, trial, try, tussle, vie
strum	=	play, pluck, twang
strut	=	beam, brace, crossbar, prance, support, swagger
stub	=	butt, end, stump, tail
stubborn	=	adamant, obdurate, obstinate, rigid
stubborn creature	=	mule
stuck	=	clung, fast, firm, keen, set
stud	=	boss, dot, fleck, spot, stable, stallion, string
student	=	learner [see], (l)
(former) student	=	alumnus, (ob)
studious	=	anxious, diligent, studied, zealous
study	=	con, cram, den, learn, read, swot, take
stuff	=	cram, fill, jam, matter, pad, ram, wedge
stumble	=	fall, limp, lurch, reel, trip
stump	=	baffle, beat, foil, pose, stub
stun	=	bemuse, benumb, bewilder, daze, stupefy
stunt	=	check, cramp, dwarf, feat, trick
stupefy	=	bemuse, blunt, daze, dull, stun
stupid	=	daft, dense, dim, dull, dumb, inane, oafish, obtuse, silly, thick
sty	=	dump, pen
style	=	elegance, fashion, genre, manner, mode, name, pen(cil), ton, tone, trend, vein, vogue
(architectural) style	=	name of [baroque, classical, colonial, gothic, ionic, norman, regency, rococo, tudor]
(art) style	=	name of [baroque, cubism, dada, deco, noveau, op, pop, realism, rococo]
(hair) style	=	coiffure; name of [afro, bangs, beehive, bob, bun, chignon, pageboy, pigtail, plait, pouffe]
stylite	=	ascetic
sub	=	below, under
subject	=	citizen, issue, liable, matter, national, prone, theme, topic, treat
sublime	=	august, exalted, grand, high, lofty, proud
subscription	=	dues, fees, subs
subsidiary	=	branch, lesser, minor
substance	=	drift, matter, nature, purport, tenor
substandard	=	second, reject
substitute	=	ersatz, locum, proxy, reserve, swap, switch, temp

subtle	= acute, clever, crafty, cunning, deep
succeed	= ensue, follow, prosper, thrive, win
success	= fame, fortune, luck, triumph, star, win
(theatrical) success	= hit, run
successor	= heir, heiress, scion
such	= so, thus
sucker	= con, dupe, gyp, leech, straw, tick
sudden	= abrupt, hasty, headlong, hurried, rapid
sudden increase	= spurt, surge
suffer	= abide, ache, allow, bear, let, lump, smart
suffered	= bled, bore, let
suffering	= agony, anguish, ill, ordeal, pain, sick, torment, torture
sufficient	= ample, decent, enough, enow
suggest	= hint, imply, move, propose
suggestion	= clue, hint, proposal, tip, trace
suit	= action, adapt, case, fit, petition, plea, serve; name of [club, diamond, heart, spade]
suitable	= apt, due, fit(ting), proper, right
suite	= apartment, flat, retinue, set, train
suitor	= beau, lover, romeo, swain, tailor
sulk	= brood, huff, pet, pout
sultanate	= name of [muscat, oman]
sum	= add, amount, cast, count, score, tally, tot(al), whole
summarize	= abridge, condense, digest, shorten
summary	= brief, curt, digest, epitome, precis, resume, synopsis, terse
summer	= adder, totter
summit	= acme, apex, ben, crown, peak, top
summons	= call, citation, cite, invite, muster, order, writ
sun	= bask, sol, tan, (s)
sunburn	= brown, tan
sundry	= divers, legion, many, some, various
sup	= drink, sip, swallow
super	= extra, great, petrol, swell, top, (ai)
superior	= better, over, top, up, upper, (u)
superior officer	= sir
superior person	= bigwig, nabob, nob, pot, toff
supernatural spirit	= name of spirit [see]
supple	= flexible, lissom(e), lithe, pliant
supplement	= addendum, appendix, codicil, rider
supplicate	= beg, beseech, entreat, intreat, plead, pray
supplier	= dealer, merchant, stockist, trader
(fruit) supplier	= orchard
supply	= give, furnish, lithely, provide, stock, store
(water) supply	= fountain, source, spring, well
support	= alimony, arch, bolster, bra, guy, leg, pier, prop, second, shore, sling, staff, stay, strut, sustain

supporter	= bra, easel, guy, leg, patron, pier, stay, upright
(ardent) supporter	= admirer, aficionado, devotee, fan(atic)
sure	= certain, fast, firm, safe, secure
surf	= foam, froth, spray, spume
surface	= facade, face, plane, top, veneer
(road) surface	= asphalt, tar
surfeit	= cram, excess, fill, glut, gorge
surge	= billow, flood, gush, rush, swell
surgeon's knife	= name of [bistoury, scalpel]
surly	= dour, gloomy, morose, sour, sullen
surmise	= deduce, guess, infer, opine, think
surprise	= ah, amaze, astound, boo, oh, startle
surrender	= cede, resign, submit, waive, yield
surround	= border, circle, gird(le), hem, ring
survey	= audit, eye, scan, see, value, view
survive	= last, outlive, outwear
suspend	= adjourn, hang, debar, defer, shelve
sustain	= bear, bolster, prop, support, uphold
swag	= booty, loot, spoil
swain	= beau, lover, rustic, suitor, yokel
swallow	= accept, down, gulp, martin, sip, swift
swamp	= bog, drench, fen, flood, marsh, mire, morass, quagmire, soak, slough
swampy ground	= bog, fen, marsh, mire, morass, quagmire
swan	= cob, pen, poet
(young) swan	= cygnet, cygnus [L]
swat	= blow, hit, strike
swathe	= bandage, drape, wrap
sway	= bend, lurch, rock, roll, swing, wave(r)
swear	= attest, pledge, plight, promise, vow
sweep	= broom, brush, clean, lottery, range, reach, scope
sweeper	= besom, broom, brush
sweet	= bombe, confection, dessert, honey, jelly, pudding, sugar(y), trifle
sweet(meat)	= name of [bonbon, fudge, nougat, rock]
swell	= bulge, dandy, devine, dilate, super, toff
swelling	= bruise, mole, spot, stye, wart
swig	= drain, draught, drink, swill
swim	= bathe, crawl, dip, reel, snorkel, spin
swimmer	= diver, fish, snorkeller; name of fish [see], name of sea-animal [see], name of water creature [see]
swimmers	= fish, school, shoal
swindle	= cheat, con, defraud, do, fake, fraud, gyp, ramp, rook, sting, twist
swindled	= done, stung
swindler	= cheat, conman, crook, sharp, twister
swine	= boar, hog, pig, sow

swing	=	hang, knack, rock, sway, veer, whirl
swipe	=	hit, lift, pinch, slap, steal, swat
switch	=	baton, cane, change, rod, shunt, stick, swap, trade, whip
sword	=	bilbo, brand, epee, foil, rapier, sabre
swot	=	cram, study
sycophant	=	creep, fawner, toady
symbol	=	badge, emblem, mark, sign, token
sympathy	=	harmony, pity, rapport, warmth
symptom	=	mark, note, sign, token
syringe	=	dropper, sluice, spray, squirt
system	=	complex, entity, method, order, plan, scheme, setup

T

table	=	bench, board, chart, fare, food, graph, list, move, propose, rota, slab, spread
table mat	=	coaster
tablet	=	pad, pill, plaque, slab
tabloid	=	gazette, journal, (news)paper, rag
tacit	=	implicit, silent, unsaid
tack	=	food, gear, pin, nail, sew, staple
tackle	=	gear, grapple, grasp, pulley, rigging
(fishing) tackle	=	bait, float, fly, gaff, jig, line, lure, reel, rod, sinker, spinner, spoon
tag	=	dog, label, name, tab, tail
tail	=	dog, end, follow, queue, tag, track, trail, train
(rabbit's) tail	=	scut
tails	=	reverse, verso
tailless	=	anourous, manx
(of) tailor	=	sartorial
take	=	bear, brook, capture, get, nick, pinch, receive, seize, steal, study
take away	=	less, minus
take back	=	abjure, recant, unsay
take note	=	heed, listen, obey
take off	=	ape, copy, doff, mimic, peel, shed, strip, undo
take place	=	happen, occur
take the plunge	=	bet, chance, dive, gamble, risk
take to court	=	sue
tale	=	account, anecdote, fable, legend, novel, saga, story, yarn
talent	=	bent, flair, forte, genius, gift
talented	=	able, clever, gifted
talisman	=	amulet, charm, mascot
talk	=	chat, debate, discourse, gab, gas, prate, rabbit, say, speak, speech, spout
(sales) talk	=	pitch
talking bird	=	name of [budgie, cockatoo, macaw, parrot]

tall	= big, giant, high, lofty, long
tally	= add, agree, correspond, count, score, sum, tot(al)
talon	= claw, fang, ogee
tame	= docile, dull, flat, gentile, mild, pet
tamper	= alter, bribe, fiddle, meddle, rig, tinker
tan	= beat, belt, brown, colour, flog, hide
tang	= flavour, point, ring, tang, taste, twang
tangle	= coil, jam, knot, mess, mix(-up), ravel, snarl, twist
tank	= basin, cistern, reservoir; kind of [septic]
tanker	= oiler, ship
tap	= bug, cock, faucet, pat, rap, spout
tape	= band, record, ribbon, strip, tie
taper	= candle, fade, narrow, thin, wane
tapestry	= fabric, material; name of [arras, bayeux, russian]
taproom	= bar, pub, saloon
tar	= pitch, sailor [see]
tare	= darnel, vetch, weed, weight
target	= aim, bull, butt, end, goal, quarry
(easy) target	= sitter
tariff	= charge, duty, fee, levy, rate, price, tax, toll
tart	= acid, biting, cutting, flan, pie, sour
task	= chore, duty, job, mission, toil, work
taste	= bent, flavour, relish, sample, savour, smack, tang, touch
taunt	= deride, mock, ridicule, tall, tease, twit
taut	= neat, rigid, spruce, tense, tight, trim
tavern	= bar, inn, pub
tawdriness	= tat
tawdry	= cheap, gaudy, tacky, tatty, vulgar
tax	= duty, excise, rate, scot, tithe, vat
tax collector	= publican
taxi	= cab, limo
tea	= cha, char, (t)
teach	= coach, drill, instruct, school, train, tutor
teacher	= buddha, coach, don, head, master, mentor, pedagogue, sir, tutor
teaching	= precept, tuition
team	= eleven, group, side, (xi)
team of experts	= panel
tear	= dash, drop, rend, rent, rip, rive, run, rush, split
tearjerker	= onion
tease	= bait, card, chaff, mock, rag, rib, ridicule, taunt, try, twit, vex, worry
teaser	= enigma, problem, puzzle, riddle, stripper
teaset	= china, service
technique	= art, fashion, mode, method, way, wise

Teddy	=	bear
tedious	=	banal, boring, drab, dreary, dull, slow, tedious, vapid
tee	=	peg, stand
teeth	=	comb, force, power, rake
(false) teeth	=	bridge, crown, denture
(use) teeth	=	chew, comb
telegram	=	cable, telex, wire
telephone	=	blower, buzz, call, dial, handset, ring
television	=	box, set, tube
tell	=	count, describe, inform, order, recount relate, say, speak, state
telling	=	cogent, effective, sound, striking
temper	=	anger, fury, ire, mood, pad(dy), rage
temperature	=	heat, (c, f)
temple	=	church, edifice, pagoda, shrine
tempo	=	pace, rate, speed, time
temporary	=	acting, brief, interim, transient
temporary accommodation	=	camp(er), tent, tepee, wigwam
(use) temporarily	=	borrow, hire, lease, rent
temptress	=	charmer, siren; name of [circe, lorelei]
ten dollars	=	eagle
tend	=	care, incline, lean, nurse, serve
(one who) tends	=	nurse, sister
tendency	=	bent, bias, drift, leaning, trend, wave
tender	=	bid, delicate, gentle, kind, nurse, offer, present, proposal, sister
tenet	=	canon, doctrine, dogma, belief, opinion
(round of) tennis	=	set
tense	=	edgy, nervous, rigid, taut, tight; name of [aorist, future, historic, imperfect, past, perfect, pluperfect, present, primary]
tension	=	pressure, strain, stress, unease
(indian) tent	=	tepee, teepee, wigwam
term	=	call, lable, name, phrase, spell, time
(prison) term	=	life, sentence, stretch, time
terms	=	language, premise, proviso, standing
termagant	=	scold, shrew
terminal	=	depot, end, fatal, final, last, lethal
terrace	=	balcony, patio, row, stand, veranda(h)
terrain	=	field, ground, turf
terrible	=	awful, bad, dire, grim, lurid, serious
terrier	=	name of [bull, cairn, fox, irish], (ta)
terse	=	brief, crisp, curt, laconic, short
test	=	assay, check, examine, match, oral, prove, sample, trial, try, (mot)
(spelling) test	=	bee
testament	=	proof, tribute, will, witness, (nt, ot)

text	=	script, subject, theme, verse, words
texture	=	being, fabric, feel, fibre, nature, web
thank(s), thank you	=	ta
that place	=	there
the old	=	ye
the thing	=	it
theatre	=	rep[ertory], stage
(old) theatre	=	vic
theatrical	=	dramatic, scenic, stagy, stilted
theatrical success	=	hit, run
theft	=	larceny, robbery, stealing
theme	=	idea, matter, subject, text, topic
there	=	yonder
(be) there	=	attend, pitch, show
therefore	=	as, ergo, hence, so, then(ce), thus
these days, this day	=	now, present, (ad)
thick	=	deep, dense, fast, firm, solid, stupid
thicket	=	brake, copse
thief	=	burglar, crook, mugger, robber, rustler
thin	=	lank, lean, puny, rare, slender, slight slim, weak
thing	=	affair, article, being, event, it, item, matter, object
(in) thing	=	fad, fashion, graze, rage, trend, vogue
(good) thing	=	boon, godsend, windfall
think	=	brood, deem, fancy, imagine, mull, muse, ponder, reckon, ruminate
this place	=	here
this way	=	so, thus
thorn	=	barb, point, spike
thoroughfare	=	road, street, way, (rd, st)
those against	=	cons, noes
those for	=	ayes, pros
those people	=	them
though	=	albeit, still, while, yet
thought	=	belief, idea, notion, opinion, view
thoughtful	=	kind, musing, pensive, rapt, wary
thousand dollars	=	grand, (g)
thrash	=	batter, beat, do, lam, party, punish, whip
thread	=	cord, cotton, lisle, string, yarn
threaten	=	bully, cow, impend, menace, warn
threatening	=	grim, ominous, sinister
three(some)	=	ternary, thrice, treble, triple, (tri)
throttle	=	choke, gullet, strangle, throat
through	=	between, by, per, via
throughout	=	amid, around, over(all), within
throw	=	cast, fling, hurl, lob, project, shy, sling, toss, unseat
throw out	=	discard, ditch, dump, eject, evict, expel, oust, reject

thrush	=	name of [mistle, ousel, song]
thrust	=	butt, drive, force, impel, lunge, plunge, ram
thug	=	bully, lout, punk, rough, tough
thumb	=	hitch, poliex
(little) thumb	=	tom [Tom Thumb]
thus	=	ergo, hence, sic, so, then, therefore
tiara	=	coronet, crown, diadem, turban
tic	=	jerk, spasm, twitch
tick	=	correct, credit, instant, moment, right slate, trice
ticker	=	clock, heart, watch
ticket	=	coupon, docket, pass, slip, tag, token
ticket seller	=	tout
tide	=	current, ebb, flow, neap, stream, trend
tidy	=	clean, groom, neat, spruce, trim
tie	=	bind, bond, draw, fasten, knot, lace, match
tier	=	bank, file, layer, level, line, rank, row
tiff	=	drink, fight, pet, quarrel, row, sip
tight	=	close, drunk, fast, firm, mean, near, taut, tense, tipsy
(not) tight	=	lax, loose, sober
tighten up	=	screw, tense
tile	=	hat, slate
till	=	cultivate, drawer, register, until [see]
tiller	=	farmer, gardener, handle, helm, lever
tilt	=	cant, heel, incline, list, slant, slope
timber	=	forest, log, lumber, plank, wood [see]
timbered	=	wooden
time	=	age, date, epoch, era, period, spell, term; name of [day, eve(ning), hour, ides, month, morn(ing), night, noon, week, year], (t)
(long) time	=	aeon, age(s), eon
(lots of) time	=	ages, eons, moons
(modern) time(s)	=	now, present, (ad)
(not in) time	=	late, tardy
(present) time	=	anniversary, birthday, christmas, now, xmas, (ad)
time off	=	leave, hol(iday), vacation
timekeeper	=	clock, watch
timely	=	prompt, punctual
timer	=	clock, watch
tin	=	can, loaf, (sn)
tin fish	=	torpedo
tincture	=	colour, flavour, smack, spice, tinge
tinge, tint	=	colour, dash, hint, hue, tincture, tint
(hair) tint	=	dye, henna, ochre
tiny fellow	=	tim [Tiny Tim]
tiny insect	=	mite
tip	=	apex, cant, dump, end, gift, gratuity, list, point, spill, tilt

tip-off	=	clue, hint, wink
tip off	=	advise, caution, suggest, warn
tipsy	=	askew, drunk, tight
tiptoe	=	creep, glide, slink, sneak, steal
tiptop	=	super, (ai)
tirade	=	abuse, harangue, outburst
tire	=	annoy, bore, cloy, droop, fag, flag, irk, pall, weary
tiresome	=	annoying, boring, tedious
tiro	=	learner [see], (l)
titan	=	giant
titanic	=	colossal, giant, gigantic, great, huge, monstrous, vast
tithe	=	levy, tax
titian	=	red
title	=	caption, claim, handle, heading, label, name, right, term
to	=	at, onto, till, toward, until, upon
to-do	=	ado, fuss, quarrel
toady	=	fawn, flatter, grovel, sycophant, tadpole
toast	=	pledge; name of [cheers, prosit, salud, sko(a)l, slainte]
tobacco	=	arnica, plug, quid, smoke, weed
toboggan	=	sled, sledge, sleigh
toff	=	beau, dandy, nob, swell
together	=	calm, cool, jointly, stable, united
(join) together	=	cement, fuse, glue, unite, wed, weld
toil	=	drudge(ry), grind, labour, slog, travail, work
toilet	=	bog, head, john, latrine, lavatory, loo, privy
token	=	badge, mark, note, pledge, relic, sign, symbol
tolerate	=	abide, accept, bear, endure, stand, stomach
toll	=	charge, chime, gate, knell, peal, ring
Tom	=	cat, thos
(little) Tom	=	thumb [Tom Thumb]
tome	=	book, volume
ton	=	century, fashion, hundred, mode, style, (c)
tone	=	accent, air, pitch, stress, tenor, timbre, vein
tongue	=	argot, dialect, idiom, language [see], lingo, voice
too	=	also, besides, further, over, very
too much	=	overkill, troppo [musical]
tool	=	device, dupe, gadget, pawn, puppet, stooge, utensil; name of [adze, anvil, awl, axe, beetle, bevel, bit, bradawl, chisel, drill, file, fork, gimlet, hammer, hatchet, hoe, lathe, machete, mower, pick, saw, scythe, sickle, spade, spanner]
tooth	=	cog, denture, fang, prong, taste; name of [canine, eye, incisor, milk, molar, wisdom]

top	=	apex, best, brow, cap, ceiling, head, hat, lid, peak, spinner, (t)
top award, mark	=	alpha
top man, person	=	name of [aga, ameer, amir, bey, emir, emperor, lord, king, monarch, president, ruler, shah, supremo, tsar]
top of the pops	=	hit
top player	=	ace, seed
topic	=	issue, matter, point, subject, theme
tor	=	hill, peak, rise
torch	=	brand, fire, ignite, light
torn	=	cut, rent, riven, slit, split, unsure
torso	=	trunk
tort	=	crime, evil, injury, sin, wrong
torture	=	agony, anguish, pain, rack, torment
tory	=	blue, (con)servative, right
toss	=	cant, cast, fling, hurl, pitch, shy, throw
tosspot	=	drunk(ard), lush, soak, sot, toper, wino
tot	=	baby, child, dram, infant, mite, nip
tot(al)	=	add, amount, cast, count, mass, sum
total	=	complete, entire, full, utter, whole
totally	=	all, fully, quite, wholly
tote	=	bear, carry, convey, drag, lug
touch	=	abut, borrow, brush, feel, flair, pat, sense, stroke, trace
touchy	=	cross, peevish, surly, testy
tough	=	firm, fit, hard(y), rough, stiff
tour	=	jaunt, outing, trip, travel, visit
tourist	=	tripper, visitor
tow	=	drag, draw, haul, lug, pull, tug
tower	=	belfry, column, minaret, obelisk, pillar, steeple, turret
tower guardian	=	beefeater, yeoman
town	=	borough, burg, burgh
(big) town	=	city
town crier	=	bellman
townsman	=	burgher
toy	=	dally, hobby, plaything, sport, trifle
trace	=	copy, detect, draw, find, hint, little, tinge
tracer	=	bullet, detective, shell, spotter
track	=	course, follow, lane, line, orbit, path, rail, scent, spoor, tail, trail, way, (ry)
tract	=	belt, land, lot, parcel, plot, zone
trade	=	art, barter, commerce, craft, custom, deal, sell, swap, traffic, vend
trademark	=	brand, label, logo
trader	=	broker, buyer, dealer, merchant, vendor
tradesman	=	dealer, duffer, hawker, huckster, merchant, monger, pedlar, pusher, vendor

tragic	=	awful, deadly, dire, fatal, sad
trail	=	dog, drag, droop, follow, hunt, path, scent, spoor, stalk, tow, track, wake
train	=	coach, direct, drill, express, point, retinue, school, suite, teach, tutor, wake
trainee	=	learner [see], (l)
traitor	=	judas, quisling, rat, rebel, snake
tramp	=	hike, hobo, march, traipse, tread, trek trudge, vagrant, walk
trample	=	crush, flatten, squash, stamp, tread
trampled	=	trod(den)
trance	=	daze, dream, muse, spell, stupor
tranquil	=	calm, restful, sedate, serene
tranquillize	=	calm, compose, lull, sedate, soothe
transaction	=	affair, business, coup, deal, deed
transcribe	=	engross, note, record, render, tape
transept	=	arm, wing
transfer	=	cede, consign, (re)move, shift
transform	=	alter, change, convert, renew
transgression	=	fault, sin
transit	=	motion, passage, portage, route
transition	=	change, flux, shift
transitory	=	ephemeral, fleeting, passing, transient
translate	=	convey, impart, interpret, render
translation	=	change, gloss, move, version
transport	=	bear, carry, fetch, haul, move
(means of) transport	=	vehicle [see]
(public) transport	=	bus, cab, coach, taxi, train, tram, tube, (br, ry)
trap	=	ambush, catch, dupe, ensnare, gin, net, noose, pitfall, snare, trick
trash	=	junk, litter, refuse, rubbish, waste
travail	=	labour, slog, suffer, toil, work
travel	=	cross, fly, hike, go, ride, roam, rove, tour
traveller	=	gypsy, hiker, nomad, rep(resentative), rider, rover
trawl	=	drag, fish, line, net
tray	=	salver
tread	=	rung, step, stamp, trace, track, trample, walk
treasure	=	cache, cherish, hoard, prize, trove, wealth
treasurer	=	bursar, cashier, purser
treat	=	confer, consult, doctor, handle, host, joy, negotiate, shout, stand
treatment	=	cure, remedy, medicine, therapy
tree	=	kind of [conifer, deciduous, evergreen]; name of [abele, acacia, alder, ash, asp(en), bael, balsa, banyan, baobab, bay, beech, birch, deal, elder, elm, fir, maple, oak, pine, plane, teak, yew]
(family) tree	=	genealogy, lineage, pedigree

(Japanese) tree	=	bonsai
trees	=	coppice, copse, forest, orchard, silva, spinney, thicket, wood
(of) trees	=	arboreal
tremble	=	quake, quiver, shake, shiver
trench	=	border, ditch, furrow, verge
trenchant	=	biting, caustic, cutting, sharp
trend	=	craze, drift, fad, tendency, tenor, tide, vogue
tress	=	braid, curl, hair, lock, plait, ringlet
trial	=	assay, attempt, case, check, go, hearing, ordeal, proof, sample, shot, test
tribe	=	blood, caste, clan, people, race
tribute	=	eulogy, honour, praise, salvo, wreath
trick	=	antic, cheat, con, gyp, ruse, stunt
trickery	=	cunning, deceit, fraud, sleight
trickle	=	dribble, drip, seep(age)
tried to find	=	sought
trier	=	judge, magistrate
trifle	=	bagatelle, bauble, fiddle, flirt, nothing, sweet, toy, trinket
trim	=	clip, edge, fit, neat, pare, smart, tidy
trinket	=	bauble, bibelot, bijou, curio, jewel
trip	=	boob, err, fall, jaunt, outing, stumble, tour
tripe	=	bunk(um), drivel, hogwash, rot, trash
tripper	=	tourist, visitor
trite	=	banal, bland, corny, stale, vapid
triumph	=	crow, coup, exult, feat, joy, success, win
trivial	=	frivolous, minor, paltry, petty, small
troll	=	dwarf, fish, sing, spirit
trolley	=	bus, car, cart, pulley, truck
troop	=	band, body, crew, crowd, gang, squad
trooper	=	mountie, private, soldier
troops	=	men, scouts
trophy	=	award, booty, cup, memento, prize
tropic	=	name of [cancer, capricorn]
tropical disease	=	name of [cholera, malaria, typhoid]
trot	=	canter, crib, crone, hag, lope, pace, run
trouble	=	ail, bother, distress, grief, harm, pain, pester, row, strife, upset, vex, woe, worry
trounce	=	beat, defeat, drub, lick, rout, thrash, whip
trousers	=	jeans, pants, slacks, trews
truce	=	armistice, break, lull, peace, respite
truck	=	barter, cart, peddle, wagon
true	=	actual, correct, just, proper, real, right
(not) true	=	false, lies, wrong
trug	=	basket, (milk-)pan
truly	=	indeed, quite, really, very
trunk	=	body, bole, box, chest, stalk, stem, torso
trust	=	belief, care, duty, faith, hope, rely

try	=	aim, attempt, essay, go, hear, irk, stab, strive, taste, tax, tease, test
try to find	=	hunt, seek
try to sell	=	tout
try to win	=	court, woo
tub	=	barrel, bath, cask, vat
tube	=	duct, inner, metro, pipe
tuck	=	food, fold, gather, grub, nosh, pleat
tug	=	drag, haul, jerk, lug, pull, tow, yank
tumbler	=	acrobat, glass
tun	=	barrel, butt, cask, keg
tune	=	accord, concert, harmony, music [see]
tungsten	=	wolfram, (w)
turbulent	=	rough, rowdy, unruly, violent, wild
turf	=	clod, divot, grass, green, sod, sward
Turkish officer	=	bey
turmoil	=	bedlam, chaos, furore, row, uproar
turn	=	addle, alter, bend, curd, fit, go, pivot, plough, rev, rot, twist, veer; name of [about, left, right], (s, u)
turn away	=	avert
turn down	=	lower, mute, refuse, spurn
turn in	=	retire, sleep
turn out	=	evict, evolve, expel, oust, result
turn over	=	roll, tip, topple, upset, (to)
turner	=	lathe, key
turning lane	=	filter
turret	=	belvedere, minaret, tower
tussle	=	brawl, fight, scrap, struggle, vie
tutor	=	coach, crammer, guardian, teach(er), train(er)
tutorial	=	conference, meeting, seminar
TV	=	box, set, tube
twice	=	double, doubly, twofold, (di)
twine	=	coil, curl, string, twist, wind, yarn
twist	=	coil, contort, curl, spin, swindle, thread, turn, twine, warp, wind, wrest, writhe, yarn
twister	=	cheat, girder, rogue, swindler, tornado
twit	=	gibe, idiot, ridicule, taunt, tease
twitch	=	blink, flutter, jerk, spasm, tic
(nervous) twitch	=	spasm, tic
two	=	brace, couple, deuce, duo, duet, dyad, pair, twain
two kisses	=	double-cross, (xx)
two(some)	=	brace, couple, duet, duo, pair, (bi)
type	=	breed, class, form, group, ilk, kind, model, print, sort
(body of) type	=	form(e)
(printing) type	=	name of [aldine, bold, brevier, bourgeois,

		gothic, italic, minion, pearl, primer, roman, ruby, times]
tyrant	=	bully, despot, dictator, hitler
tyro	=	learner [see], (l)

U

ugly	=	dark, horrid, nasty, vile
ukase	=	decree, edict, law
ulcer	=	abscess, boil, fester, sore
ultimate	=	acme, end, epitome, final, last, (ult)
ultra	=	rabid, super, utmost
umbo	=	boss, knob
umbra	=	ghost, shade, shadow, spirit, wraith
umpire	=	arbiter, call, judge, ref(eree)
unassuming	=	humble, meek, modest, quiet
unbalanced	=	daft, insane, mad, mental, nuts, uneven
unbred	=	rude, uncouth, vulgar
uncertain	=	fickle, iffy, moot, unsure, vague
uncertainty	=	concern, doubt, query, suspense, wonder
uncle	=	name of [bob, remus, sam, tom]
(your) uncle	=	name of [bob]
unclean	=	dirty, evil, foul, impure, soiled
uncover	=	bare, expose, open, peel, reveal, skin
uncovered	=	bare, naked, nude
uncut	=	complete, rough
under	=	below, beneath, down, inferior, less, lower, sub
(knuckle) under	=	submit, yield
under(clothes), garment	=	underwear [see]
under the weather	=	ailing, ill, poorly, sick
undercooked, underdone	=	blue, rare, raw
underground	=	metro, tube
underhand	=	crafty, devious, furtive, secret, sly
underline	=	highlight, mark, stress
understand	=	catch, dig, gather, grasp, know, realise, see, twig
understanding	=	accord, deal, grasp, intellect, reason
understood	=	dug, known, roger, saw, tacit
undertaking	=	affair, contract, effort, pledge, task, vow, word
underwear	=	name of [bodice, bra, chemise, hose, shift, singlet, slip, vest]
underworld	=	dis, hades, hell
underwrite	=	back, cover, fund, insure, sanction
underwriter	=	backer, guarantor, insurer, sponsor, (uw)
undo	=	free, loose, open, untie, upset, wreck
undoing	=	bane, downfall, ruin
undress	=	disrobe, nudity, shed, strip
unearth	=	discover, find, exhume, expose, reveal
uneasy	=	edgy, nervous, restive, tense, uptight
unemployed	=	idle, jobless, redundant

unemployment pay	=	dole
unfermented beer	=	wort
unfold	=	evolve, open, reveal, show, spread
unfortunately	=	alack, alas, sadly
unfriendliness	=	animus, hatred, hostility, ice
unfriendly	=	aloof, dour, hostile, icy, sour
ungainly	=	awkward, clumsy, gawky
unhappy	=	blue, down, gauche, gloomy, inept, sad
uniform	=	even, level, like, same, tunic
uninspired	=	drab, dull, humdrum, prosaic, tame
uninspiring	=	drab, dull, humdrum, prosaic, tame
union	=	club, guild, joint, league, merger, (num, nur, tu)
(join) union	=	marry, wed
unique	=	alone, lone, one, only, single, sole
unit	=	cadre, entity, item, one, troop, whole, (u)
(army) unit	=	platoon, squad, troop
unite	=	band, blend, fuse, join, link, marry, merge, wed
United States	=	america, (us, usa)
unity	=	harmony, oneness, singleness
universal	=	cosmic, generic, global, (u)
universal language	=	name of [esperanto, ido]
university	=	name of [cambridge, harvard, oxford, yale], (u, univ)
(at) university	=	up
university location	=	campus
university person	=	blue, freshman, graduate, sophomore, (ba, bed, ma)
unknown	=	anon(ymous), (x, y)
unparalleled	=	alone, peerless, singular, unique
unpleasant person	=	bounder, cad, cur, heel, rat, rotter
unpretentious	=	honest, humble, modest, plain, simple
unpunctual	=	late, tardy
unqualified	=	outright, total, unfit, utter
unravel	=	free, loose, solve, undo, untie
unreal	=	bogus, fake, false, mock, sham
unrefined	=	coarse, crude, earthy, raw, rude
unruffled	=	calm, cool, even, flat, level, smooth
unsatisfactory	=	bad, mediocre, poor, weak
unseat	=	depose, oust, remove, throw
unselfishness	=	altruism
unsmiling	=	glum, grim, sad
unspecified	=	ambiguous, obscure, unclear, vague
untamed	=	feral, fierce, savage, wild
untamed hawk	=	haggard
untie	=	free, loose, release, undo, unravel
untrue	=	disloyal, false, lies
untruth	=	deceit, fib, lie, perjury, whopper
unusual	=	bizarre, odd, queer, rare, strange

unwanted plant	=	name of [clover, thistle, weed]
unwell	=	ailing, ill, poorly, sick(ly)
unwieldly	=	awkward, bulky, clumsy
up to	=	till, until
upbraid	=	berate, chide, rate, reproach, scold
update	=	refresh, renew
uphold	=	aid, back, defend, maintain, promote
uplift	=	edify, elevate, hoist, improve, raise
upright	=	erect, honest, just, post, true
uproar	=	bedlam, brawl, clamour, din, fuss, row
upset	=	bother, bug, capsize, spill, spoil, tip
upside down	=	chaotic, inverse, inverted
urban area	=	city, town
urge	=	egg, goad, impulse, itch, press, prod, spur
(of) us	=	our
usage	=	custom, form, habit, mode, use, wont
US coin	=	name of [cent, dime, eagle, nickle, quarter]
US currency, money	=	name of [cent, dime, dollar, nickle, quarter]
US girl	=	gal
use	=	application, apply, avail, custom, employ, habit, ply
use teeth	=	chew, comb
use temporarily	=	borrow, hire, lease, rent
used	=	old, wont, worn
used to	=	familiar, inured, wont
useless	=	abortive, futile, vain
usher	=	escort, guide, lead, pilot, steer
usual	=	general, norm, normal, par, stock
utensil	=	name of [basin, bowl, broom, cooker, cruet, cup, dish, drier, fork, grater, grill, hob, iron, jug, kettle, knife, ladle, mixer, oven, pan, plate, pot, saucer, scoop, sieve, sink, skillet, spoon, stove, tongs, tray, whisk, wok]
utilize	=	employ, exploit, use
utmost	=	best, chief, final, last, top, ultra
utter	=	complete, emit, say, sheer, speak, total, voice

V

vacancy	=	gap, job, post, room, space, void, (o)
vacant	=	bare, blank, empty, void
vacation	=	holiday, leave, (vac)
vacillate	=	dither, falter, sway, waver
vacuum	=	gap, space, void
vague	=	dim, elusive, faint, hazy, obscure
valiant	=	bold, brave, fearless, gallant, stout
valid	=	cogent, genuine, legal, solid, sound
valley	=	dale, dell, glen, strath, vale
(deep, narrow) valley	=	defile, gorge, gulch, gully, ravine
value	=	carat, esteem, merit, prize, worth

van	= front, lead
vanish	= clear, disappear, dissolve, evanesce, fade, melt
vanity	= case, conceit, ego(tism), pride
vapour	= breath, fog, haze, mist, steam
variance	= discord, dispute, odds, strife
varied	= diverse, mixed, motley, sundry
variety	= choice, genre, range, sort, type
various	= divers, many, several, varied [see], (var)
vary	= alter, change, differ
vase	= ming, urn
vat	= barrel, tub
Vatican ambassador	= nuncio
vault	= bound, crypt, jump, leap, spring, tomb
vegetable	= green, legume; name of [artichoke, asparagus, bean, beet, broccoli, carrot, celery, corn, cos, kale, leek, lettuce, onion, parsnip, pea, potato, radish, skirret, swede, tomato, turnip]
vehicle	= carriage, transport [see]; name of [bike, car [see], cart, cycle, lorry, moped, sled, truck, van, wagon]
(horse-drawn) vehicle	= name of [barouche, berlin, brougham, buggy, cart, chaise, chariot, dray, fiacre, fly, gig, hackney, hansom, landau, phaeton, sulky, surrey, trap, troika, wagon]
(wartime) vehicle	= name of [jeep, tank]
veil	= cloak, cover, disguise, mask, shroud
(Indian) veil	= name of [purdah, yashmak]
venal	= corrupt, mercenary
venom	= bane, poison, spite
vent	= air, duct, emit, express, gap, hole, outlet, issue, utter, voice
venture	= chance, dare, hazard, risk
venue	= arena, place, site
veranda	= loggia, patio, porch, stoep, stoop
verbal	= literal, oral, spoken
verdict	= finding, guilty, judg(e)ment, opinion
verge	= abut, border, bound, edge, hem, rim
vermin	= bug, parasite, rodent; name of [flea, leech, louse, mole, mouse, rat, squirrel, tick, vole, weasel]
vernacular	= dialect, indigenous, native, slang
verse	= poem, rhyme, stanza, (v)
version	= account, design, form, kind, reading, style, type, variant
versus	= against, (v, vs)
vert	= green
vertical	= apeak, erect, plumb, sheer, upright
very	= actual, exact, light, real, same, true

very bad	=	abysmal, rank
very big	=	colossal, gigantic, huge, jumbo, titanic, (os)
very best	=	cream, elite, pick, prime, top
very good	=	capital, pi, pious
very large	=	colossal, gigantic, huge, jumbo, titanic, (os)
very long	=	age(s), eons, moons
very old	=	aged, ancient, antique, elderly, (vo)
very much	=	ultra
very sad	=	awful, dire, tragic, wretched
vessel	=	boat, container, craft, receptacle, ship, vein; name of boat [see]; name of container [see], (ss)
(old) vessel	=	ark; name of [argo, mayflower, victory]
(sailing) vessel	=	name of (sailing) boat [see]
(shallow) vessel	=	charger, platter, salver, tray
(widow's) vessel	=	cruse
vest	=	belong, confer, endow, lodge, singlet
vestige	=	hint, relic, residue, scrap, sign, trace
vestment	=	alb, amice, chasuble, dress, habit, robe, surplice
vet	=	check, examine, review, scan, screen
vetch	=	forage, herb, pea, tare, weed
veteran	=	adept, expert, old, pro, senior
veto	=	ban, embargo, forbid, kill, prohibit
vex	=	annoy, fret, gall, irk, rankle, tease
via	=	per, through, way
vibes	=	air, aura, feel, mood, tone
vicar	=	clergy [see]
vice	=	clamp, deputy, evil, sin, wrong
vicious	=	cruel, evil, fierce, nasty, savage, vile, wild
victim	=	butt, dupe, gull, martyr, prey, puppet, stooge, sucker
(murder) victim	=	abel [Biblical]
victor	=	champ, first, winner
victory	=	conquest, triumph, win, (v, ve)
vie	=	compete, contend, contest, rival, strive
view	=	con, deem, espy, eye, look, prospect, regard, scan, scene, see, sight, study
(point of) view	=	angle, opinion, slant
viewer	=	eye, onlooker, watcher
viewpoint	=	angle, ringside, slant, stance
vigil	=	eve, watch
vigilant	=	alert, cautious, wary, watchful
vigour	=	brio, dash, elan, go, gusto, oomph, pep
vile	=	base, evil, foul, horrid, low, ugly
villa	=	chateau, house, manor, mansion
village	=	hamlet
villain	=	heel, knave, rascal, rogue, scamp
vindicate	=	absolve, acquit, clear, uphold
vinyl	=	disc, record

violent	=	berserk, brutal, cruel, savage, wild
violin	=	fiddle;
		name of [amati, strad]
violinist	=	bower
virago	=	scold, shrew, termagant
virile	=	lusty, macho, male, manly, potent, robust, strong
virtue	=	attribute, merit, trait, value, worth
virtuous	=	chaste, ethical, just, moral, righteous
virus	=	bug, germ
vision	=	dream, ghost, image, mirage, sight, spectre, view, wraith
visa	=	pass
visit	=	call, frequent, sojourn, stay, stop
visitor	=	caller, guest, tourist, tripper
(frequent) visitor	=	habitue
vital	=	alive, basic, crucial, essential, key, vibrant
vitality	=	brio, elan, energy, go, life, pep, vim
vituperate	=	baste, berate, lash, rail, rant, scold
vivacity	=	brio, dash, elan, energy, go, life, pep, vigour, vim
vivid	=	bright, clear, gay, red, scarlet
vocabulary	=	argot, cant, glossary, jargon, language
vocation	=	calling, career, job, metier, trade
voice	=	air, express, say, tone, utter; kind of [active, middle, passive];
		name of [alto, baritone, bass, contralto, soprano, tenor, treble]
void	=	bare, empty, free, null, space, vacant
volcano	=	name of [etna]
volume	=	amount, book, bulk, mass, tome;
		name of [gallon, litre, pint, quart], (v, vol)
volunteer	=	offer, propose, suggest, undertake
vote	=	ballot, elect, opt, poll, suffrage
vow	=	affirm, oath, pledge, plight, promise, swear, troth
voyage	=	crossing, cruise, passage, sail, trip
vulgar	=	coarse, crude, gross, low, ribald, rude
vulnerable	=	exposed, weak

W

wad	=	ball, chunk, lump, plug, roll
waffle	=	blather, jabber, prate, prattle
wag	=	card, clown, comic, joker, wave, wit
wage	=	conduct, pledge, pursue, wages [see]
wages	=	earnings, pay, salary, screw, stipend
wager	=	ante, back, bet, flutter, gamble, pot, risk, stake
wagon	=	cart, truck
wait	=	bide, delay, pause, serve, stay, tarry

waiter	=	boot, server, steward(ess)
wake	=	arise, funeral, rouse, stir, train, vigil
walk	=	gait, hike, mall, pad, promenade, step, stroll, tramp, tread
(short) walk	=	prom
walk out	=	court
walk obliquely, sideways	=	crab, edge, sidle
walker	=	foot, hiker, rambler, wayfarer
wall	=	barrier, fence, hedge, rampart
wall decoration	=	arras, cornice, frieze
wall game	=	name of [fives, pelota, racquet, squash]
wallow	=	blunder, flounder, lurch, stumble
waltz	=	dance, valse
wan	=	ashen, pale, pallid, waxen, white
wand	=	baton, rod, stick
wander	=	drift, roam, rove, stray, veer
wanderer	=	drifter, gypsy, migrant, nomad, rover
wandering	=	migrant, nomadic
wane	=	abate, decline, fade, ease, ebb, weaken
want	=	covet, crave, lack, need, shortage, thirst, yearn, yen
war	=	battle, combat, fighting, strife
(old) war	=	name of [boer, crimea(n), roses]
(one against) war	=	dove
(one for) war	=	hawk, jingoist
ward	=	area, charge, district, guard(ian), minor, prison
war-horse	=	charger, steed, trooper
warehouse	=	depot, store
warm	=	cosy, heat(ed), hot, snug, tepid
warmonger	=	hawk
warn	=	admonish, caution, notify, threaten
warner	=	alarm, horn, siren
warning	=	alarm, amber, fore, horn, portend, siren
warp	=	bias, deform, pervert, twist
warrant	=	deserve, earn, merit, pledge, vouch(er)
warrior	=	brave, fighter, soldier
warship	=	name of [corvette, cruiser, destroyer, frigate, sub(marine)]
(ancient) warship	=	bireme, galley, trireme
wartime vehicle	=	name of [jeep, tank]
wary	=	alert, cagey, canny, chary, leery
wash	=	bath(e), clean, launder, rinse, scrub, sponge
washing	=	dhobi, laundry
waste	=	barren, debris, desolate, junk, refuse, scrap
(coal) waste	=	slag, soot
wasteland	=	desert
watch	=	clock, eye, gaze, guard, look, mind, monitor, regard, see, ticker, vigil; name of [albert, fob, hunter, stop]

watch out	=	cave, fore
watcher	=	bystander, spectator, viewer, witness
watchman	=	guard, lookout, picket, sentinel, sentry
water	=	aqua, brine, fountain, lake, ocean, rain, river, sea, spring, well; name of river [see]
(frozen) water	=	ice
water-bird	=	name of [avocet, coot, duck, eider, gannet, godwit, goose, gull, heron, mallard, pelican, pen, scooper, smew, stilt, swan, teal]
water creature	=	name of [beaver, eft, frog, newt, otter, seal, sealion, terrapin, toad, turtle, walrus]
water diviner	=	dowser
waterfall	=	cascade, cataract, falls [see], force
water-lily	=	lotus
water pipe	=	hose, hydrant
water supply	=	fountain, source, spring, well
waterway	=	canal, river
wave	=	beckon, curl, crimp, flap, greet, wag; name of [billow, bore, breaker, comber, roller]
waves	=	sea, surf, tide
waver	=	dither, falter, hesitate, seesaw, shake, sway, vacillate
wax	=	grow, increase, polish
way	=	avenue, how, lane, method, mode, path, road, route, street, track, (ave, mo, rd, st; e, n, s, w)
(by) way of	=	via
(old) way	=	via
(permanent) way	=	railroad
(this) way	=	so, thus
way to go by	=	via
way out	=	egress, exit
we object	=	us
wealth	=	capital, assets, fortune, lucre, means, money, riches, treasure, welfare, worth
wealthy	=	flush, loaded, opulent, rich
wealthy person	=	croesus
weak	=	feeble, frail, infirm, puny
weaken	=	enervate, fade, flag, sap, wane
weapon	=	arm; name of [arrow, bazooka, bomb, bow, cannon, claw, gun, horn, missile, pistol, rifle, spear, sword]
weapons	=	artillery, ordnance
weapons store	=	armoury, arsenal, magazine
wear	=	abrade, bear, chafe, don, dress, erode, gear, garb, sport
(under)wear	=	bra, hose, vest, singlet, slip
(grow) weary	=	cloy, fade, jade, pall, tire

weather	= brave, climate, clime, season, stand; type of [fog, mist, rain, sleet, snow, storm, sun, wind]
(under the) weather	= ailing, ill, poorly, sick
(wet) weather	= dew, rain
weave	= plait, stagger, sway, twist, wobble
weaver	= loom
web	= lattice, mesh, net, screen
webster	= spider
wed	= hitch, join, marry, mate, unite(d)
wedding	= bridal, marriage, union
wee	= midget, small, tiny
weed	= cigarette, grass, hoe, pot, tobacco, rid, uproot; name of [clover, darnel, dock, herb, nettle, thistle, vetch]
weep	= cry, greet, keen, sob, wail
weigh	= count, ponder, study, tell, think
weight	= mass, power, tare, ton, troy, (wt)
weird	= eccentric, eerie, odd, queer, rum, strange
(measure of) weight	= drachm, dram, grain, gram, ounce, pound quarter, quintal, scruple, stone, ton, tonne, (cwt, g, lb, oz, t)
welcome	= ave, greet, hail, hello, hi, nice
weld	= fuse, join, solder
well	= artesian, fit, fount, hale, rig, sound, spa, spring
(as) well	= also, and, besides, too
(do) well	= prosper, succeed, thrive
(not) well	= ailing, ill, sick
well away	= far
well-known	= famous, notable, noted
well-liked	= in, popular
welsh	= renege
Welsh county	= name of [brecon, flint, gwent, radnor]
Welshman	= name of [dai, emlyn, evan, owen, taffy]
went	= left, quit, ran
went ahead	= led, nosed
were ahead	= led
were sitting	= sat
west(ern)	= occident(al), (w)
wet	= damp, dank, douse, drench, humid, moist, soak, soaked, sodden, steep
(was) wet	= rained
wet weather	= dew, rain
wetland	= bog, fen, marsh, morass, quagmire, swamp
whale	= name of [beluga, blue, cachalot, baleen, finback, grampus, killer, minke, narwhal, orc(a), rorqual, sperm]
whales	= gam, herd, pod, school
wharf	= dock, jetty, pier, quay
wheat	= emmer, grain

wheel	= circle, deal, disc, helm, pivot, roll, spin, tiller, trade, turn, (o)
wheeze	= anecdote, joke, plan, scheme, trick
whelp	= cub, cry, pup, young, youth
when	= as
whiff	= aroma, dash, hint, smell, taste
whim	= caprice, conceit, fancy, freak, vagary
whip	= beat, cat, cane, chastise, flog, knout, lash, punish, rod, scourge, stick, switch, whisk
whirl	= eddy, gyrate, spin, swirl, twirl
whisk	= beat, dash, flick, fly, whip
whisky	= name of [malt, scotch]
whiskey	= name of [bourbon, irish, rye]
(illicit) whiskey	= moonshine
whisky and soda	= highball
whisper	= breathe, gossip, hint, hiss, murmur, sigh, trace
whistler	= kettle
whit	= crumb, iota, jot, little, mite, speck
white	= ashen, pale, pallid, ivory, wan
whiten	= blanch, bleach, pale
whole	= all, complete, entire, fit, intact, integral, lot, sum, total, well, unit(y)
whoop	= cough, cry, shout, yell
wicked	= arch, bad, evil, foul, vile, wrong
wide	= ample, broad, vast, (w)
widen	= dilate, expand, extend, stretch
widespread	= broad, common, epidemic, rife
widow	= relict
widow's vessel	= cruse
wife	= bride, dutch, helpmate, helpmeet, mate, partner, spouse
wig	= chide, rail, rap, rate, rebuke, scold; name of [brutus, toupee]
wild	= berserk, feral, frantic, hectic, mad, savage
wild fancy	= bog(e)y, chimera
wild horse	= bronco, mustang
wildebeest	= gnu
wile	= art, craft, guile, ploy, ruse
will	= aim, choice, decree, desire, resolve, testament, wish
(ill) will	= acrimony, animosity, animus, grudge, hostility, rancour, spite, strife
willing	= able, eager, game, ready
willow	= bat, osier, pussy, withe, withy
win	= earn, gain, land, prevail, succeed, success, victory, (v)
(try to) win	= court, woo
winning	= charming, endearing, engaging, winsome
winner, winning position	= first, (ist)

wince	= cower, flinch, quail, shrink
wind	= air, blow, breeze, coil, draught, reel, turn; name of [austral, berg, bise, bora, boreal, chinook, fo(e)hn, helm, khamsin, levanter, mistral, simoom, sirocco, trade, zonda]
(strong) wind	= cyclone, gale, hurricane, storm [see]
winding	= bend, curve, spiral, turn, twist
window	= type of [bay, bow, casement, dormer, french, lattice, louvre, oriel, sash]
wine	= type of [chateau, madeira, port, ruby, sack, sherry, tokay]
(French) wine	= vin; name of [beaune, burgundy, chablis, champagne, claret, graves, macon, medoc, muscat(el), sauternes]
(German) wine	= name of [hock, mosel, rhine, riesling]
(Italian) wine	= name of [asti, chianti, frascati]
wing	= arm, flap, fly, pennon, pinion, side, transept, wound
(forty) winks	= kip, nap, sleep
winsome	= charming, endearing, engaging, winning
wipe out	= destroy, efface, erase, expunge
wire	= cable, flex, message, telegram, thread
wise	= astute, clever, erudite, learned, mode, sage, smart, way
wise bird	= owl
wise man	= guru, elder, magus, oracle, pundit, sage, savant; name of [nestor, solomon, solon]
wise men	= magi
wish	= aspire, covet, crave, desire, hope, long, want, will
wishbone	= merrythought
wit	= attica, brain, comic, humour, mind, sense, wag
(to) wit	= namely, viz
witch	= crone, hag, sorceress
with	= among, and, by, for, per, pro, via, (w)
withdraw	= go, leave, recant, remove, retreat, secede, quit
withdrawn	= aloof, distant, quiet, shy, unsocial
wither	= blight, decay, droop, fade, sear, sere, wane, wilt
withered	= arid, dry, sear, sere
without	= beyond, ex, lacking, less, minus, outside, past, sine, (wo)
without issue	= childless, (sp)
without reason	= crazy, daft, insane, mad, nuts, wild
witness	= attest, see, sign, testify, vouch
(false) witness	= liar, perjurer
witty	= bright, clever, droll, funny
witty remark	= crack, quip, repartee, wisecrack
wizard	= ace, mage, magus, merlin, warlock, whiz

wizard place	=	oz
wolfram	=	tungsten, (w)
woman	=	bird, chick, dame, female, her, lady, madam, maid(en), she
(brawling) woman	=	scold, shrew, termagant, virago
(German) woman	=	frau
(ill-tempered) woman	=	scold, shrew, termagant, virago
(indian) woman	=	squaw
(married) woman	=	bride
(old) woman	=	beldam(e), crone, dutch, hag, ma, mother virago, wife, witch
(old-)womanish	=	anile
(spiteful) woman	=	bitch, cat
(strong) woman	=	amazon
wonder	=	amaze, awe, doubt, marvel, query, think
wont	=	custom, given, habit, rule, used, way
wood	=	coppice, copse, forest, grove, hurst, log, lumber, plank, spinney, thicket, timber, trees; name of tree [see]
(old) wood	=	hurst
wooden	=	awkward, clumsy, dull, ligneous, oaken, slow, timber
woodcutter	=	adze, axe, chisel, hatchet, saw
woodworker	=	carpenter, joiner
wool	=	fleece, hair, yarn
wool producer	=	alpaca, angora, ewe, goat, lamb, llama, ram, sheep
word	=	advice, couch, news, pledge, talk, term
(last) word	=	amen, finis
words	=	lyrics, prose, quarrel, row, text
(play on) words	=	anagram, charade, pun
work	=	go, job, operate, opus, ply, task; name of [book, ode, poem, writing], (op)
(hard) work	=	grind, labour, slog, sweat, toil, travail
(musical) work	=	opus, (op)
work hard	=	grind, labour, slog, sweat, toil, travail
works	=	factory, foundry, mill, plant
(collected) works	=	omnibus, volume
worker	=	ant, artisan, hand, labourer, man
(militant) worker	=	striker
workers	=	labour, men, staff, union, (tu)
working	=	on
(not) working	=	off
world	=	cosmos, earth, globe, orb, planet
worldly	=	blase, carnal, lay, secular, urbane
worm	=	name of [cut, flat, earth, glow, hook, round, silk, tape, wire]
worn	=	jaded, spent, tatty, tired, trite
worry	=	care, fear, fret, nag, tease, vex

worship	= adore, kneel, love, pray, revere, service
(hero) worshipper	= leander
worth	= cost, merit, price, rate, value, virtue
wound	= cut, gash, harm, hurt, scratch, shoot, stab, wing
wounded	= bled, cut, hit, hurt, shot, stung
wow	= blimey, cor, my
wrack	= collapse, ruin, seaweed
wrangle	= argue, bicker, quarrel, row, tiff
wrap	= bind, cloak, cover, lag, muffle, package, shawl
wrapper	= case, cover, jacket, sheath, sleeve
wrapping	= foil, paper
wreak	= avenge, execute, inflict, punish
wreath	= chaplet, garland, memorial
wreck	= break, mar, ruin, smash, spoil
wreckage	= flotsam, fragments, jetsam, remnants
wrench	= force, jerk, sprain, wrest, yank
wrest	= pull, seize, twist
wriggler	= eel, snake, worm
wrinkle	= crease, fold, furrow, hint, line, screw
writ	= citation, decree, order, summons
write	= draft, pen, print, scribble
write music	= compose
writer	= author, biro, nib, pen, pencil, scribe; name of [bacon, belloc, bronte, bunyan, camus, defoe, dumas, goethe, hugo, ibsen, lamb, more, swift, twain, vidal, wilde]
writer's name	= byline
(old) writer	= name of [aesop, cicero, dante, homer, ovid, plato, virgil]
writing	= hand, print, prose, scrawl, script, (ms)
(used for) writing	= pad, pen, pencil
writhe	= squirm, toss, twist, w(r)iggle
wrong	= amiss, bad, crime, cross, evil, sin, tort, (x)
(do) wrong	= cheat, harm, hurt, sin
(go) wrong	= boob, err, fail
(rights and) wrongs	= merits
wry	= (a)skew, aslant, crooked

X

x	= cross, kiss, ten, wrong
xerox	= copy
xmas	= noel, yule
x-ray	= rontgen, scan
xx	= double-cross, score, twenty

Y

yacht	= ketch, sail, sloop
yank	= hitch, jerk, pull, snatch, tug

yap	=	bark, chatter, jabber, talk, yelp
yardstick	=	guage, measure, ruler
yarn	=	anecdote, fable, fibre, lisle, story, tale, thread, twist; name of [denim, mohair, nylon, rayon, serge, tweed, twill, velvet, wool]
(every) year, yearly	=	annual, (pa)
yearly publication	=	annual
years	=	age
yearn	=	covet, crave, long, pine, wish, yen
yell	=	bawl, cry, hoot, howl, shout, whoop
yellow	=	chicken, coward, craven, lemon, yolk
yelp	=	bark, cry, howl, yap
yen	=	ache, crave, long(ing), pine, yearn
yes	=	ay, yea
yet	=	besides, but, even, further, still
yield	=	bend, bow, cede, crop, give, harvest, produce, sag
yielded	=	bent, gave, given
yielding	=	docile, easy, elastic, pliable, soft
yonder	=	that, there
you and I	=	we
you and me	=	us
you old	=	thee, thou, ye
young	=	brood, callow, fresh, fry, green, raw, whelp
young animal	=	calf, cub, foal, kid, kitten, lamb, pup
young animals	=	litter
young brave, indian	=	papoose
young child	=	bantling, infant, tot
young dog	=	pup
young fish	=	name of [elver, parr, sprat, tiddler]
young lady	=	deb, girl, miss
young pig, sow	=	gilt, grice
young soldier	=	cadet
young swan	=	cygnet, cygnus [L]
younger	=	junior
youngest	=	kid
youngster	=	boy, calf, cub, girl, juvenile, kid, lad, lass, pup, youth
your old	=	thine, thy
your uncle	=	name of [bob]
yours truly	=	me
youth	=	lad, sprig, teenager, urchin
youthful	=	fresh, juvenile, spry, vernal, young

Z

zeal	=	ardour, fervour, fire, passion, verve
zealot	=	bigot, fanatic, fiend, maniac
zealous	=	afire, ardent, eager, earnest, fervent, keen, rabid

zenith	=	acme, apex, climax, summit, top
zero	=	cipher, duck, love, nil, nought, (o)
zest	=	elan, gusto, heart, relish, taste
zodiac	=	sign(s), star(s);
		name of [Aquarius, Aries, Capricorn, Cancer, Gemini, Leo, Libra, Pisces, Sagittarius, Scorpio, Taurus, Virgo]
zone	=	area, belt, district, region, section, sector, sphere
zoo	=	menagerie
(floating) zoo	=	ark
zoo attendant	=	keeper